THE SOULS

THE SOULS

✿ Jane Abdy and Charlotte Gere

SIDGWICK & JACKSON
LONDON

First published in Great Britain in 1984
by Sidgwick and Jackson Limited
Copyright © 1984 Jane Abdy and Charlotte Gere

Designed by James Campus

ISBN 0-283-98920-3 (hardcover)
ISBN 0-283-99062-7 (softcover)

Photoset in Great Britain by
C. Leggett & Son Limited
Mill Green Road, Mitcham, Surrey
Printed in Great Britain by
R.J. Acford, Chichester, Sussex
for Sidgwick and Jackson Limited
1 Tavistock Chambers, Bloomsbury Way
London WC1A 2SG

Frontispiece. Margot Tennant in 1888,
at the time when she was 'the electric charge'
of the Souls

❀ CONTENTS

✣ ACKNOWLEDGEMENTS

No one could have been more generous in their help with this book than the families of the Souls, their sisters, daughters, and their descendants; they have talked to us of their memories, shown us their houses, and have lent archives, letters and photographs which they have allowed us to reproduce. Especial thanks are due to Irene, Countess of Plymouth, and to Lady Diana Cooper. We would also very much like to thank Lady Mary Lyon, Lord Neidpath, the Earl and Countess of Plymouth, Lord and Lady Charteris, and the Hon. Mrs Pearson. The late Viscount Gage, the Dowager Viscountess Gage and the Hon. Mrs Cazalet helped with research on Lady Desborough, and Plessey Automation, the present occupants, showed us Taplow Court and gave us marvellous photographs. Mrs Marcella Rice talked to us of her step-father, Lord Curzon, and Viscount Scarsdale very kindly allowed us to use his archives and photographs. Mrs Christopher Cust lent rare books and papers, and Viscountess Templetown has given us the benefit of her childhood memories. Baroness Elliot of Harwood, Lord Crathorne, the Hon. Sir Hugh Fraser and Mr Peter Lubbock have much assisted with the Tennant family. The staff in the archive at the National Portrait Gallery, and in particular Mr Terence Pepper, have drawn to our attention much relevant material, notably the album of photographs showing guests at Aston Clinton. We are also grateful to Mrs Catherine Bell, the Hon. Mrs Marten, the Hon. Lady Lindsay, Miss Kay Hubble, Mr Innes-Smith, Mr John Cornforth, Lord Egremont, Mr Richard Dorment, Mr Geoffrey Houghton-Brown, Mr Russell Lewis and Mr James Miller. Many valuable suggestions have been made at the editorial stage by the staff of Sidgwick and Jackson and by Mr Ralph Hancock. We are grateful for their patient assistance.

In addition Jane Abdy is indebted to the Dowager Viscountess Hambleden, Anne, Countess of Rosse, the Hon. Lady Mosley, the Rev. Charles-Roux and Mr Hugo Vickers who have all given help and advice, and to Mr Philip Howard for helping with the translation of the latin dedication of the Curzon album; and Charlotte Gere would like to thank Mr Stanley Olson and her husband, Mr John Gere, for their help.

Many of the illustrations are taken from private and family collections and the Authors and Publishers are very grateful to the following for making them available: Irene, Countess of Plymouth, Lady Diana Cooper, the Hon. Mrs Cazalet, Lady Helen Asquith, the Earl and Countess of Plymouth, the late Viscount and the Dowager Viscountess Gage, Lord Neidpath, Viscount Scarsdale, the Duke of Westminster, Lord Brownlow, Mr Geoffrey Houghton-Brown and the Minneapolis Institute of Art.

We would also like to thank all those mentioned below who have given permission for photographs in their possession, or in which they own the copyright, to be reproduced: BBC Hulton Picture Library, 48, 58; Belton House, Lancashire (photographs by Gerald Wright), 70, 80; The British Library, 24, 55, 92, 110 (right), 116, 139, 144, 168, 178; The Corcoran Gallery of Art, Washington D.C. (gift of John Campbell White), 161; Country Life, 89 (above), 103 (right), 119, 166 (above and below); The Courtauld Institute of Art, 94; The Fine Art Society Ltd, 40; Gallery B2, London, 83; Julian Hartnoll, 130; The Heim Gallery, London, 78; The Mansell Collection, 2, 31 (left), 37; The Metropolitan Museum of Art, New York (Catherine Lorillard Wolfe Collection, Purchase, 1927, Wolfe Fund (27.67)), 100; National Monuments Record, 51, 120; The National Museum of Wales, Cardiff, 122; National Portrait Gallery, London, 43, 49 (right), 53, 72, 76, 142, 147, 152, 163, 172, 180; The Piccadilly Gallery, London, 44; Plessey Automation, Taplow, Berks, 60 (three photographs), 66; The Scottish National Portrait Gallery, Edinburgh (photograph by Antonia Reeve Photography), 31 (right); Sotheby's Belgravia, 85 (right), 128, 171; The Tate Gallery, London, 50, 138; Christopher Wood Gallery, 85 (left); and York City Art Gallery, 176

✿ INTRODUCTION

The Souls often voiced their dislike of the name which had been attached to them by their more jocular acquaintances; yet the insubstantial label suits this group of high minded, high spirited friends far more than the earlier self-adopted sobriquet, 'The Gang'. Consuelo Marlborough described them as 'A brilliant company, a select group in which a high degree of intelligence was to be found happily allied to aristocratic birth . . . I think there is some justification for the name of "Souls", since many have become immortal.' Perhaps the 'Constellation' might have been more apt, for all the members of this group were stars. The two most famous men in the circle were A. J. Balfour, leader of the Tory party and later Prime Minister, and George Curzon, his Viceroy of India. Harry Cust and George Wyndham were to prove to be two shooting stars. H. H. Asquith, Liberal Prime Minister for eight years, was married to the most ebullient young Soul, Margot Tennant. The women of the coterie were admired for their social gifts, their loveliness, their sense of fantasy and fun. Christabel Aberconway, who could be described as a latter day Soul, as she was related by marriage to Lady Horner and was a good friend of Lady Desborough's, said that the attributes of a female Soul were 'beauty, intelligence and wit': they were of legendary loveliness, outstanding in an age of great beauties; writing of her fictitious heroine in *Love in a Cold Climate*, Polly Hampton, Nancy Mitford said 'Polly's beauty was greatly remarked upon, especially by those of a former generation, who were all saying that since Lady Helen Vincent, since the Wyndham sisters, nothing so perfect had been seen in London'.

The individual members of the Souls are recorded, like the dramatis personae of a play, in the guest lists of the two parties given for them by George Curzon in 1889 and 1890, and in the party they gave for him in 1898 to honour his appointment as Viceroy of India. At the core of the group were certain families; Wyndhams, Charterises, Tennants, Custs, Windsors and Grenfells. A. J. Balfour was the quintessential Soul, sometimes even being referred to as 'King Arthur'. These remained at the heart of the circle. The cast list was flexible, as younger charmers such as Lady Islington and Maurice Baring were to be welcomed by the group, whilst some early members lapsed. Mary Ponsonby, for instance, married and went to live in Ireland. Other famous names appear and disappear – Lady Randolph Churchill, the Marquis de Soveral, Oscar Wilde – like leading actors in a walk-on role. Some became Souls through marriage, though others did not; certain husbands, or wives, lacked the *esprit* – or the desire – to participate in the activities of the coterie: Mary Curzon was too shy, Nina Cust too serious, Lord Granby not interested.

A houseparty at Taplow Court in 1887. Front row: The Duchess of Leinster(?), Willy Grenfell, Margot Tennant. Back row: St John Brodrick, Mrs Willy Grenfell, Lord Elcho, George Curzon, unknown

The Souls crystallized as a group around the mid-eighties. In 1883 Mary Wyndham married Lord Elcho, and in 1887 Ettie Fane married William Grenfell. Lady Elcho and Mrs Grenfell (later to become Lady Desborough) were the two great hostesses of the Souls, and their parties at Stanway and Taplow gathered the Souls together. The Tennant sisters were a catalyst, for Margot Tennant was perhaps the most vital and enthusiastic early member of the group: 'nobody has made or unmade more "Souls" than Margot Tennant'.

There are two versions of the origin of the 'Souls' title. Lady Elcho and Lady Desborough both thought that it was coined by that wag Lord Charles Beresford in the late eighties. 'You are all talking about each others' Souls, then I shall call you the "Souls" from henceforth.' Lord Curzon preserved a press cutting which claimed it was his invention. Taken from the *Portsmouth Evening News* in 1908, it read: 'As a matter of fact it owes its origin to Lord Curzon, who at dinner one day to the members brought out the essential point that in order to become one of the coterie it was necessary to possess a soul above the ordinary.' Both 'Gang' and 'Soul' occur in the poem George Curzon wrote for the dinner party of 1889, but 'Souls' was the name which stuck, the name which was used by Society, by the press, and which was so accepted that Jacques-Emile Blanche could mention the Souls in a book published in 1937 and assume that the general reader – for it is a book of discursive memoirs – knew who the Souls were without explanation.

The Souls have often been contrasted with the most famous group of the time, the Marlborough House Set. Such a distinction is too facile; London Society in the eighties was small, and all the members of the Souls knew the Prince and Princess of Wales and attended parties at Court. The beautiful Countess of Warwick, one-time friend of the Prince of Wales, attended the Souls banquet for Curzon in 1898. She wrote: 'There was a coterie which shot up in London in the eighties which for want of a better designation was called the "Souls". Although far too cosmopolitan myself to belong to any clique, I was intimate with several of these young people. This little coterie of "Souls" loved literature and art, and perhaps were more pagan than soulful.'

Lady Warwick considered that it was their intellectual and aesthetic tastes that set the Souls apart. She records the 'dismay aroused by the intellectual attainments of that delightful woman, Violet, Duchess of Rutland. Our unenlightened aristocracy was actually perturbed by the discovery that there were clever women in its ranks.' The beautiful young Mary Wyndham, as a debutante, alarmed a prospective suitor, who said that she was 'a very nice filly, but she's read too many books for me'. Female Souls were all avid readers, and some Souls men were classical scholars. They enjoyed contemporary novels, especially the works of Edith Wharton and Henry James. Favourite writers were authors of the English classics: Dickens, Carlyle, Meredith, Tennyson, Browning, and later A. E. Housman; Shakespeare was known by the Souls and their children virtually by heart. They were all seduced by Gilbert Murray's translations of Greek drama which were published in the early 1900s: perhaps this is why Daisy Warwick thought them 'pagan'.

Their taste in art was avant-garde, if somewhat insular; many were habitués of the Grosvenor Gallery, and commissioned pictures by Burne-Jones, Sargent, Watts and Whistler. Lesser artists like Ellis Roberts, Edward Clifford and Ralph Peacock were patronized. Violet, Duchess of Rutland was herself a portrait artist and sculptress of high distinction; others were amateur artists of talent, Mrs Percy Wyndham firing enamels and Mrs Graham Smith filling sketch books with watercolour portraits.

Music was a third interest. A. J. Balfour's passion for Handel was infectious; Lady Windsor, in her bedroom at Hewell Grange, had an overwhelming procession of figures painted in the frieze, intended to symbolize Beethoven's 'Pastoral Symphony'.

The Souls could be described as anti-Philistine. They disapproved of many of the aimless and extravagant pursuits of their social contemporaries. They disliked card games, and had a contempt of gambling and high play. Racing was regarded as both vulgar and extravagant. (George V was amazed to see Curzon at Ascot, and thought it was an excellent joke; Curzon had been persuaded to attend, once, by his second wife.) None of their hobbies was expensive. They were fond of golf, tennis and bicycling. When travelling by train they often went third class. Their food was simple, almost frugal – with the exception of Lady Horner's memorable table – and the supply of wine was far from copious. Lady Desborough and Violet, Duchess of Rutland were teetotallers; the Duchess campaigned for prohibition during the First War. Souls women dressed prettily and charmingly, patronizing modest dressmakers who were often former lady's maids. They eschewed grand couturiers and 'the cosy swansdowns and sables of society'. The two wives of Lord Curzon, neither of whom were Souls, dazzled in gorgeous toilettes from Worth, for this was a period of amazingly lavish expenditure on dress. Lady Cynthia Asquith said it was rumoured that Lady Wimborne spent over £10,000 a year on clothes; she herself managed on a dress allowance of £100 a year, and with imagination and improvization looked delightful. 'The Souls,' said Lady Tweedsmuir, 'dressed with a kind of aesthetic smartness all their own.' The most gentle and uncritical of women, Lady Tweedsmuir found the Souls disconcerting: 'They were a little suspect as not conforming to the rules of the social game.' There was a flavour of the arcane about the Souls. They devised their own entertainments, their own language, and even thought of starting their own magazine.

Their passion for pencil games was obsessive. Instead of the despised baccarat or bridge, or instead of listening to Viennese waltzes after dinner, a Souls evening would culminate in the 'Games'. Many of these, like Charades, Telegrams and 'Clumps' (an advanced form of Twenty Questions) are still played today. The games varied with house and hostess: the Tennant sisters scribbled essays in the styles of certain writers and wrote rather embarrassingly confidential 'character sketches'; Lady Desborough's games were witty, and played at lightning speed; those at Stanway were more hilarious and often ended in peals of laughter. Most of the games required a knowledge of literature, history and languages – 'Scrabble' was played in French or German – and could be alarming to the uninitiated.

In their own company the Souls used their particular slang, known as 'Gang language', which was based on Baring and Ponsonby family vocabulary and on in-jokes. They used it in their letters, and in their diaries, and doubtless constantly in conversation. They passed round an examination paper on it in 1893. Such behaviour did encourage the impression that the Souls were a sect.

A photograph of Lady Desborough from a Taplow Court Visitor's Book

It was inevitable that the Souls should be a little teased. Jokes descended to the pun of devising a coat of arms for the group composed of delicious fish. In 1892 E. F. Benson wrote *Dodo*, which caricatured Margot Asquith as the heroine, and mimicked the Souls: E. F. Benson dubs them the 'apostles'. They are shown as clever, possessed of great social gifts, but, in the last analysis, as self-indulgently intellectual. One character says, 'I would not mind being acutely unhappy if I could dissect my own emotions and have them photographed and sent round to my friends.' (Margot Tennant did write character sketches and circulate them round the group, so perhaps E. F. Benson was justified.) The chaffing continued for a long time though the point was often missed. When Lady Elcho's daughter, Bibs, married the son of Lord Plymouth it was described in the local press as the marriage of two children of the Sorrels!

The notion that the group was exclusive was displeasing to Lady Elcho, the 'least exclusive' of people. Her daughter Cynthia, when a debutante, wrote to her:

> But honestly I promise you that you are barking up the wrong tree when you accuse me of being 'cliquey'. It isn't in the least a spontaneous bark either – don't think I don't know who put you up to it – nor does it come well from one who for all her famous catholicity *was* herself labelled a 'Soul'. Haven't you yourself always told me – truthfully I'm sure – that there was nothing in the least deliberate, self-conscious, exclusive or superior about the 'Souls' – who were merely a group of very intelligent articulate people who happened to be friends and to share a love of good talk; and that in so far as they were a charmed circle, the line was drawn by those outside, not inside the circle.

Lady Elcho herself, ever hospitable, introduced new members into the group, and so did Lady Desborough. Initiates such as Maurice Baring and Pearl Craigie could be called latter-day Souls. But the truth was that the group was perfectly formed by about 1890; it needed no additions; it was in itself an entity, a society for mutual enjoyment. Disparate as the group may look from outside, it was its variety that gave it the necessary tensions to keep the company always stimulating. Lady Desborough was a brilliant hostess, adroit, charming, worldly-wise. The Duchess of Rutland was the artist and the beauty. George Curzon provided brilliant conversation and much merriment. Lady Elcho was sympathy incarnate, warm hearted, high spirited, with 'dancing gaiety' in her eyes. Harry Cust and George Wyndham were poets and romantics, and Godfrey Webb was the reliable old friend, the constant wit. Margot Tennant produced an 'electric charge', and the Americans introduced into the group, the Harry Whites and Amélie Rives, provided Transatlantic novelty. No one was more English and deliciously droll than Lord Elcho. And presiding over this band of brilliant diverse people was the ever calming and benign presence of Arthur Balfour. The Souls and their families so delighted in each other's company that there were at least seven marriages in the second generation of the group and several in the third; four of Lady Elcho's children married children of Souls, and the romances and alliances in the group are of amazing complexity. In love, as in companionship, they were not tempted beyond the charmed borders of their circle.

It was A. J. Balfour who told Margot Asquith that no history of the times would be complete until the history of the Souls was written, and it was Mary Elcho whom he persuaded to attempt this task; her children remember her walking round the house leaving half written pages on chairs.

A page from a Taplow Court Visitor's Book, signed by guests at two Sunday luncheon parties. Lady Desborough always illustrated her Visitor's Books with photographs of guests

Various people who knew the Souls have described the effect they had on contemporary society. Daisy Warwick talked of their love of books and art: 'They were clever and well-read, and exercised great influence on London society for five or six years. I think they sent us all back to reading more than we otherwise would have done, and this was an excellent thing for us.' The Souls made it socially acceptable to talk about books and art and history, not at all in a pedantic way, but with a delicious frivolity. Their influence lasted far longer than a few years. 'Thanks to the "Souls" ', said Lady Violet Bonham Carter, 'it was no longer fashionable to be dull.'

An essential feature of Souls' society was the dominance of women. Lady Desborough and Lady Elcho were maintaining traditional roles as great hostesses, but under their aegis the women ruled. There was no segregation of sexes and the men did not, as was the custom in England at that date, linger long hours over port. What is of much more significance was the development of a greater freedom for women, probably initiated by the Tennant sisters. 'It is a theory of the "Souls", and a delightful one, that the two sexes can associate without any thought of earthly sentiments or any social danger.' In her memoirs Margot mentions that she has a supper *à deux* with Godfrey Webb in his flat. Edith Wharton's heroine, Lily Bart in *House of Mirth*, was ostracized by New York Society when she was seen leaving a bachelor's flat alone after afternoon tea in 1905. Within the Souls it was possible to have platonic friendships without scandal. Arthur Balfour took Mary Curzon to lunch, Ettie Desborough was escorted to Ascot and to the opera by men friends. The Souls impact on Society was 'liberating and civilising', wrote Lady Violet Bonham Carter. 'How much of our fun and freedom was a direct heritage from them.'

No account of the Souls would be complete without mentioning their philosophy of life founded on Christianity, patriotism and the triumph of optimism. The virtue which they most admired was courage. Most of the Souls had known great personal suffering: Balfour's fiancée, May Lyttelton, died of diphtheria, causing a grief from which he never recovered. Lady Elcho's beloved son Colin died at the age of three, and Ego and Ivo Charteris were killed in the Great War. Curzon was persecuted in his childhood by a sadistic governess, and grieved by the early deaths of both his mother and his first wife. The toll of the Great War was appalling. Courage was a virtue needed to sustain one through life, the courage to bear one's own woes, then to hide them and be able to give strength to others. Lady Desborough's unflinching optimism was known as Ettie's 'stubborn gospel of joy'; at first the younger generation found this unrealistic, but later they came to admire her courage greatly.

There was a feeling amongst the children of the Souls that they could never vie with the brilliance of their parents. Billy Grenfell wrote ruefully to his mother: 'There is no fear, believe me, of the older generation being trodden down. They have their feet too firmly on our necks, what with references to the beauties like the Duchess of Leinster, and living genii like Lord Curzon.' For a brief time the children of the Souls rebelled, and formed the 'Corrupt Coterie', which included Edward Horner, the Grenfell brothers, Raymond Asquith and the daughters of Violet, Duchess of Rutland. The coterie was soon diminished by the tragic deaths of many of the members. Those who survived no longer rebelled, but admired the enduring virtues of the Souls. 'I give Ettie top marks in war time', said Cynthia Asquith. And Lady Diana Cooper, the beautiful ringleader of the coterie, wrote in admiration of the Souls: 'This group of intelligent, cultured men and women, who knew how to live and love and serve and savour the best.'

Those who remember the Souls talk of them in lyrical terms; they recall the joy of their company, but find it hard to describe them. 'Lady Desborough was absolutely marvellous, unique, but she was so subtle one cannot describe what she was really like', has been the answer of many to a researcher's plea. The Souls talked of each other in eulogies, flattering and imprecise. People were 'glorious' or sometimes, as Cynthia Asquith said of Billy Grenfell, they were a 'luxury'. 'Golden' was always a favourite adjective. Looking back at the life of the Souls before the Great War, it does indeed seem golden to us. They met during the legendary long summers of late Victorian and Edwardian times. The Souls' season began with Easter houseparties at Clouds. In London, they met for dinners at the Tennants' in Grosvenor Square, and at the Cowpers' house, 4 St James's Square, where Julian Grenfell was born. The Wyndhams were 'At Home' in Belgrave Square, and Violet, Duchess of Rutland had an informal salon in her studio in her wonderful William Kent house in Arlington Street. There were 'Saturdays-to-Mondays', walking in the park at Wrest, strolling over the lawns at Stanway, or joining in the Thames-side life at Taplow, where each summer in succession was so lovely that almost every meal was a picnic. The season might end with a visit to the Tennants at The Glen. (The Souls were not *aficionados* of huge autumnal shooting parties.) Julian Grenfell did at one moment rebel against such an idyllic life, criticizing his mother, according to L. E. Jones, for 'her deft manipulation of a procession of week-end parties, lightly skimming the cream from the surface of life'. So too did Lord Haldane, who at one time was 'taken up' by the Souls. In an extract from his memoirs, published in *The Times* of 17 January 1929, he attacked the group – citing no valid reason – for their exclusive and intellectual pretensions. He attacked foolishly. Four days later there appeared in *The Times* an anonymous letter widely attributed to Lady Desborough which totally routed Lord Haldane, making his comments appear petty and ungrateful. But the letter is interesting in that it is a loyal and golden account of the Souls by one of its foremost members.

Sir,

In the section from Lord Haldane's memoirs in your issue of January 17th he speaks of the 'Souls', and I would like to say a few words about that happy friendship among a number of young people forty years ago. They were nicknamed the 'Souls' by Lord Charles Beresford, amid laughter, at a dinner party at Lord and Lady Brownlow's house in the early summer of 1888. 'You all sit and talk about each other's souls – I shall call you the "Souls" '. It was a modest joke enough, but it persisted – on ever declining levels of wit – for many years, and out of it there gradually grew, I think, an erroneous and rather heavy and pretentious impression of the little group concerned; and they were both attacked and defended by those who did not know very much about them.

Never can there have been people less desirous of forming a clique in any sense of the word. They were great friends – the men all hard at work, in different ways, the women occupied and busy – who often met together to talk and play, and who enjoyed every minute of their pastimes. They all mingled in a number of the different small 'sets' of the day. Society was very inter-changeable: members of all the various sets, including the racing world, were often to be met at the country houses singled out by Lord Haldane as those frequented by the 'Souls', and the latter regarded any chaff about the close bonds of friendship among themselves with the most serene indifference.

Lord Haldane says that they took themselves too seriously, but one might have expected criticism to leap to the very opposite point of attack and to complain that they never took themselves at all [sic] and that lightness of touch was perhaps carried to the extreme limit. Certainly any idea of exclusiveness or arrogance or sententiousness would have been abhorrent to them, for such moods of the mind were foreign to their whole outlook upon life.

It is a shock to read that one so beloved by many of the friends as was Lord Haldane should have doubted whether their influence was on balance good. I do not suppose that it was a question they ever considered, for, as I have tried to say, they never thought of themselves as a clique at all, nor did they dream of influencing anybody. But when they are remembered as individuals it would be hard to deny not only the brilliance and achievements, but the courage and kindness and high sense of honour, the wit and gaiety and grace and gentleness that they shed round them into life, and passed on to their sons, so many of whom were to die in the very zenith of youth. They belonged to the two generations who were to bear the sharpest anguish of the war and they stood the test.

Many of the little group still live, still close-bound in affection, and well able to speak for themselves. But many are gone from sight, and it is for their sakes that one would like to recall the joys, imponderable as gossamer and dew, the laughter and delight and the steadfast loyalty of friendship that those far-way days enclosed.

Yours faithfully,

X

✿ ONE

Lord Curzon

Ho! list to a lay
Of that company gay
Compounded of gallants and graces
Who gathered to dine,
In the year '89,
In a haunt that in Hamilton Place is.

There, there where they met
And the banquet was set
At the bidding of Georgius Curzon;
Brave youth! tis his pride,
When he errs, that the side
Of respectable licence he errs on.

Around him that night –
Was there e'er such a sight?
Souls sparkled and spirits expanded;
For of them critics sang,
That tho' christened the Gang,
By a spiritual link they were banded.

George Curzon

The Bachelors' Club was situated at 8 Hamilton Place, near the corner of Piccadilly and Park Lane, set amidst the vast Victorian mansions of Rothschilds and Sassoons. In Griffiths *Club Guide* of 1907, it is described as a 'modern club of fashion and distinction, much favoured by the *jeunesse dorée*. Play prevails to a high extent.' Bachelors only were admitted as members; were they to marry they had to seek re-election, and pay a fine of £25. However, ladies were allowed as guests, which was rare among London clubs. The Bachelors' Club was immortalized by P. G. Wodehouse as the Drones. It has another claim to fame as being the venue for the two dinner parties which George Curzon gave for the 'Souls' in 1889 and in 1890.

In 1889 George Curzon was still a bachelor. Although he was heir to Kedleston in Derbyshire, perhaps the most perfect eighteenth-century house in England, his father, Lord Scarsdale, was known for his austere temperament – 'a despot from the thirteenth century', Mary Curzon was to say in an extreme moment of despair. There was absolutely no question of George Curzon's being allowed to invite his friends to his splendid home. His own London lodgings were modest, a set of bachelor's rooms in St Ermin's Mansions, Westminster. There was little he could to repay all the hospitality he had received at Taplow, Ashridge, Wilton, Hewell, Wrest, and the other country houses of his friends; his solution was to give a dinner for them at the height of the season, when they were all in London. It was at this party that the name 'Souls' was (according to one story), half-teasingly, semi-officially, given to the group. The host wrote a rhyming panegyric to his guests, copies of which were placed on their chairs before dinner, which praises their individual and collective charms – 'Souls sparkled and spirits expanded'.

Various stanzas from the poem have been used as chapter headings in this book. The verses were first published when they were quoted by Margot Asquith in her autobiography of 1920. She neglected to ask Curzon's consent to do so, and he was annoyed that what were intended to be flippant and ephemeral rhymes should be in print. However, the dinner party of 10 July 1889 is so crucial in the history of the Souls that perhaps Lord Curzon will forgive his high spirited rhymes ('doggerel appalling' he described them) once more making an appearance.

At the time of the first 'Souls' dinner in 1889 Curzon was twenty-nine, and had for two years been Tory Member of Parliament for Southport. All the triumphs of the future lay ahead, but they were to come quickly, and only nine years after this gathering of Souls, George Curzon had been appointed Viceroy of India. From early youth he had dedicated himself to a life of service for his country; in an epitaph which he composed for himself he wrote:

As Explorer, Writer, Administrator and Ruler of Men,
He sought to serve his country
And add honour to an ancient name.

His days at Eton were a record of scholastic brilliance; he won more prizes than any one else in the history of the school. The years at Oxford were distinguished by the Arnold and Lothian prizes, and though he missed a much coveted First in Greats, he was recompensed by being elected a Fellow of All Souls in 1883. Since Eton he had been spoken of as a potential Prime Minister. Once he entered politics, he found that his interests were more in sympathy with foreign affairs than with Westminster. To make himself master of his subject, he embarked on a series of arduous journeys round the world: between 1887 and 1889 he visited Canada, America, Japan, India, Russia and Samarkand. The Souls dinner of 1889 was held on the eve of his most famous journey, the Persian expedition; the book he subsequently wrote on Persia was acknowledged as a masterpiece.

On 9 July 1890, Curzon gave a second dinner for his friends at the Bachelors' Club. On this occasion, the guests presented their host with a commemorative album, handsomely bound, containing autographed photographs of themselves. The volume was prefaced with a grandiloquent inscription in Latin (perhaps written by Harry Cust), which must have entertained Curzon greatly:

SODALI HOSPITI AMICO

NEC NON EIDEM ORATORI ET POETAE

OPTIMO MAXIMO

GEORGIO NATHANEEL CURZON

QUI

ULYSSEN VIIS INGENIO TULLIUM ALKIBIADEN SPLENDORE SUPEREMINES

TERRAS CORDA ARTES

QUOT VIDIT VICIT

UT SESE SPOLIIS QUAM PLURIMUS

OPIMIS AUCTUM

REI PUBLICAE PRAESIDIUM SUIS DELICIAS OSTENDERET

HANC PINACOTHECAM

AMICITIAE VEL SI SIT AMORIS PIGNUS
DONO DEDERUNT
SOCII
QUORUM VEL QUARUM CORPORA EPULIS PLUS SIMPLICI VICE
ANIMAS CONSILIIS FACUNDIA RISU
MILLIES RECREAVIT*

Forty-nine of Curzon's friends are portrayed in the album. If one is to analyze who were members of the Souls, it is surely these forty-nine who are the kernel of the group:

Margaret White	Duchess of Sutherland	Ettie Grenfell
Lord Pembroke	with Mrs Ralph Sneyd	Lady Windsor
Lady Granby	and their dogs	Lady Hilda Brodrick
Lord Cowper	K. Lyttelton	Lady Pembroke
Lady Cowper	Evan Charteris	Lord Wenlock
Ernest Beckett	Alfred Lyttelton	Wallace Cochrane Baillie
Schomberg McDonnell	Godfrey Webb	Lady Ponsonby
A. J. Balfour	St John Brodrick	Lady Sybil St Clair Erskine
D. D. Balfour	F. Rothschild	Alan Charteris
Lady Wenlock	Lord Ribblesdale	Sibell Grosvenor
George Wyndham	A. G. C. Liddell	(two photographs)
Lord Granby	Charty Ribblesdale	Lady Brownlow
Willy Grenfell	Mrs Graham Smith	Lord Brownlow
Henry White	Margot Tennant	Lady de Grey
Lord Cranborne	Spencer Lyttelton	Amélie Chanler
Lord Elcho	Lady Elcho	K. Drummond
Henry Chaplin	(drawing by Violet Granby)	Duchess of Westminster
Duchess of Sutherland	Harry Cust	

There are a few unexpected names – more friends of Curzon's than of the group. The Duchess of Westminster was the former mother-in-law of Sibell Grosvenor, whom Curzon had long loved. Wallace Cochrane Baillie, later Lord Lamington, was an old Oxford friend, and was to be Curzon's best man at his wedding to Mary Leiter in 1895. Baron Ferdinand de Rothschild was a munificent host to many at Waddesdon, his palatial mansion near Aylesbury, filled with wonderful eighteenth-century works of art. Mrs Chanler was an American girl from Virginia, who wrote sentimental historical novels under her maiden name of Amélie Rives. She later married Prince Pierre Troubetskoy, the painter, and brother of the sculptor. The drawing of her by Violet, Duchess of Rutland shows her to be a girl of arresting good looks, with adventure in her eyes.

The album was assembled with affection and with care; some of the photographs had been specially taken, and those of Lady Windsor, Lady Wenlock and Mrs Graham Smith are the

*To our friend, our carousing companion, our host tonight, Also an orator and a poet too George Nathaniel Curzon, Great and Good, who Has excelled Ulysses in his voyages, Tully in his genius, and Alcibiades in his glory Who, like Caesar, has seen and conquered lands, arts, and hearts His friends present him with the gift of this album of pictures As a pledge of friendship, affection and love so that he can be seen, adorned by many trophies, to be The guardian of the nation and the pride of his friends We, men and women alike, have been his guests, and the fare of his banquets has been surpassed When he has refreshed our souls a thousand times With sympathy, eloquence and laughter

work of the same photographer; his subtle use of lighting has produced portraits with a glamour that makes his sitters diaphonously dreamy, and he has skilfully portrayed the reticence of Lady Windsor, the gentleness of Mrs Graham Smith, and the distinction of Lady Wenlock. Mary Elcho, liking no photograph of herself enough, presented a reproduction of the lovely drawing of her done by Violet, Duchess of Rutland, in 1886. Opposite the photograph of Sibell Grosvenor, Curzon has pasted in another of her: obviously at this time she still held a special place in his heart.

Curzon treasured this album. With the scholarly attention to detail which characterized every aspect of his life, from government administration to decoration of his houses, he kept the volume as an archive of the Souls. The end-papers at the front give guest lists for the two Bachelors' Club dinners and those at the back record the Hotel Cecil dinner of 1898, and the housewarming party at 1 Carlton House Terrace in 1912. He also garnered a quantity of press cuttings about the activities of the Souls, and pasted these into the empty pages at the front of the album, inscribing on each in his elegant and lucid hand the name of the publication and the date.

These press cuttings are mainly from the early 1890s, but continue until 1908. They come from papers as varied as *The New York Herald*, *The News of the World*, *The Birmingham Gazette*, *The Glasgow Herald*, and *The Queen*. Obviously such a group of glamorous and glittering people were eminently newsworthy, but it is surprising that their activities spread to the provincial newspapers. In 1892 *England* gave a description of the leading Souls, and their account of George Curzon conveys the impression he made on those who did not know him well.

The dinner party given by the Souls for Lord Curzon to honour his appointment as Viceroy of India. It was held at the Hotel Cecil on 9 December 1898. The Duchess of Rutland is on Curzon's left

He is, in conversation probably the most brilliant of all the Souls, and at the same time, the most reckless. . . . There is a diablerie about Mr Curzon's dialogue. Both Mr Curzon and Mr Cust have a somewhat exaggerated idea of their own importance and a too pronounced cynicism towards those who are outside their coterie to be absolutely popular; but time will mellow and perhaps destroy these undesirable mannerisms.

Curzon had a great ability to laugh at himself and it is obvious that he collected and preserved this body of often comical cuttings with amusement.

In December 1898 a third dinner party was held, given by the Souls in honour of Curzon's appointment as Viceroy of India. It took place in the Hotel Cecil, in the Strand, which had opened only two years before. The decor was opulent, even grandiose, and the large hotel had sufficient space and a chef capable of providing a suitably sumptuous dinner for the seventy-one guests invited. The company were seated at small tables, and the *placement* was changed before the dessert, when the party was photographed. The evening was concluded by George Wyndham reciting a poem to Curzon, and Curzon thanking his hosts, who were 'the friends of a tumultuous but absolutely unrepentant youth; the comrades of a more sober and orderly middle age – and when I return five years hence, what I hope may be the props and solace of dull and declining years.'

Those who view the statue by Sir Bertram Mackennal, which shows Lord Curzon dressed in the robes of the Star of India, and which haunts Carlton House Terrace with the grandeur of past Imperial magnificence, may find it hard to reconcile this patrician statesman with a merry member of the company of Souls. Curzon's splendid achievements have been recorded for posterity by Lord Ronaldshay, Sir Harold Nicolson and, more recently, Mr Kenneth Rose. A writer of quite a different kind, the romantic novelist Elinor Glyn, who loved Lord Curzon for years, wrote of Curzon the statesman: 'My whole conception of the duty of the individual to the state, of man to humanity, was profoundly changed by my friendship with Lord Curzon.'

Mrs Glyn, whose heroes had hitherto been dashing cavalry officers, continued:

I came to understand that charm and gallantry are not enough, and that true romance inhabits nobler mansions than the fairy-tale palaces of my childish dreams. Curzon's untiring devotion to self-imposed duty throughout long, arduous, days – pain-ridden days – his thoroughness, his cheerful assumption of an ever-increasing burden of responsibility, above all, his noble disregard of personal advantage in the pursuit of what he believed to be the good of the country which he loved so passionately in his odd reserved way, made all my previous ideals of how a man should live, and what he should do, seem utterly inadequate.

She praises 'his selflessness in public life', and concludes that his failure to gain the premiership was trivial in comparison to his achievements: 'Far from failing to achieve leadership, it was his peculiar destiny to set the new standard of untiring personal industry and complete devotion to duty which is now demanded from all national leaders of the twentieth century – and to set it high.' His friend Sir Edgar Vincent said that Curzon's epitaph should be 'Immense orgueil, justifié'.

Curzon made a sharp division between his dedicated public life and the social life he greatly enjoyed. One of the Souls press cuttings he preserved states: 'He practically lives two lives, one among the Souls, and one for the outer world.' In this separation of work and pleasure, work always came first; when his future fiancée, Mary Leiter, was in London in 1891, Curzon had hidden himself at an anonymous address in Norwood to write his three-volume work on Persia; only for a brief afternoon did he emerge to see her. 'Complete devotion to duty' was foremost; friendships, loves and laughter, however cherished, were relegated to what moments of leisure he might find.

Harold Nicolson quotes a remark which Curzon made to Lord Riddell in the 1920s: 'I have always taken a humorous view of life.' When an undergraduate he was a prankster; he became one of the larkiest members of the Crabbet Club. The Souls cosseted him for his irrepressible sense of fun, and an essay written by Billy Grenfell, aged five, reveals a little-known Curzon: 'Of the company who often comes here [to Taplow Court], we like George Curzon best, what gives us fruit under the table. We like him very much, he gives us more than we ought to have of fruit. He is merry and very fond of travelling. He writes books.' Years later, his three Duggan step-children, who adored him, and whom he cherished as his own, would recall how he made them laugh with the anecdotes of his travels, and often recounted hilarious stories against himself. Even when he was Foreign Secretary, he found time every evening to talk and read to them, and he kindled their interest in books and in history.

Those who knew Lord Curzon well commented on his shyness and reserve with strangers. With his family and his close friends he was light-hearted and humorous. In public he was shy and reserved to a point when he became glacial, and because of this Daisy Warwick described him as 'one of the most tragically misunderstood of men'. This chill showed itself most with his subordinates; Lord Curzon had little patience with those whose work was slipshod and fell below the impossibly high standards which he himself had attained. Nor did the world know of the constant pain he suffered. When an undergraduate it was discovered that he had developed a curvature of the spine, caused by relentless overwork. Riding became a penance; the formal duties of the Viceregal court were sometimes torture. Daisy Warwick said Curzon accepted this pain without resentment: 'When you are sufficiently absorbed in a big problem, you can forget yourself, and in that forgetfulness comes release, he said.'

Women never failed to give their sympathy to George Curzon, and the Souls was a group dominated by intelligent women. He was one of those rare Englishmen who positively enjoyed the society of women, their sympathy, their gentleness, their intuition. All the female Souls were his friends, sometimes platonically, sometimes with a filament of flirtation.

The Tennant sisters, for whom generally and severally he had a warm affection, were particularly susceptible to his charm. The letters he sent to Mrs Grenfell show that he held a special niche in her heart. He fell deeply in love with Sibell Grosvenor, the lovely and sweet-natured widow of Lord Grosvenor, son of the Duke of Westminster, and was severely wounded when in 1887 she married George Wyndham, her other serious suitor, in preference to him. It was some years before his heart was quite whole, and it was not until 1895 that he married. But he had the great art of keeping his former 'spangles' as friends, and he and George Wyndham and Sibell always remained on the happiest of terms.

George Curzon had also always had a penchant for female writers, however varied their

Lord Curzon at the time when he was Viceroy of India.
This was a favourite photograph of the family

talents. He helped Ouida in her penurious old age with an allowance from his income. His association with Elinor Glyn has been recounted in the biography by her nephew – but Mrs Glyn was never a Soul. Amélie Rives became a Soul through the introduction of George Curzon and so did the novelist, Pearl Craigie, who wrote under the pseudonym of John Oliver Hobbes. Had she met Curzon earlier, she would undoubtedly have been invited to the dinners. She was a woman of fragile loveliness and fastidious taste. Her American parents had made a fortune from a proprietary medicine, and moved to London, where they had a vast house in Lancaster Gate. Pearl Craigie's marriage was miserable; her husband was a drunkard, and she was forced to seek a divorce. Her sophisticated novels and plays had much contemporary acclaim; they were written in epigrammatic form, and in their cleverness have a flavour of Oscar Wilde, but are threaded through with despair. Both George and Mary Curzon liked her immensely, and invited her to the Delhi Durbar, and she was a frequent guest at Taplow. She died suddenly in 1906, just one month after the death of Mary Curzon, and George Curzon arranged for a memorial to be carved in her memory. At the unveiling he quoted a line from one of her novels: 'There is only one obligation in life, and that is courage.' This was the true stoical philosophy of the Souls.

Lord Curzon and his bride Mary Leiter at Kedleston in May 1895. They had been married in Washington on 27 April. When they came home the route from Derby station was lined by cheering spectators

It was not, however, amongst the band of Souls that Curzon was to find a bride. His first wife was a beautiful American girl, Mary Leiter, who worshipped him. She had first met him in London in 1890. Her mother was taking her on a European tour where, in the tradition of American heiresses (her father was a founder of the famed Marshall Field department store in Chicago, and had amassed an immense fortune) in the 1890s, she received several glamorous proposals. But she had fallen in love with George Curzon at first sight. Although she had been fêted as a debutante in Washington, praised and socially pursued on visits to London, buttressed by the love of her parents, and launched in life with the aid of their enormous wealth, she was still a shy and diffident young bride; she could not compete with the self-assurance and spirited sallies of the Souls. They had invited her before her engagement – indeed she had first met Curzon at a weekend party at the Brownlows' house, Ashridge – but the Souls were reluctant to admit outsiders into their charmed circle, and she was not welcomed by the group until she was Vicereine of India. Both the responsibilities and the romance of this great position inspired noble qualities in Lady Curzon; her devotion to duty equalled that of her husband, and in her great role she found a fulfilled beauty and distinction which were victorious.

During the seven years that he was in India, Lord Curzon was able to demonstrate for the

Lady Curzon in the 'Peacock Dress' designed by Worth for the Coronation Durbar of 1903. Inspired by traditional Indian embroidery, the pattern of peacock feathers is worked in three shades of gold thread and the hem is composed of hundreds of cream linen roses

Lord Curzon in the robes of the Star of India at the Coronation Durbar

first time his lifelong passion for art and architecture. That the Souls loved and encouraged art is one of the themes of this book. Of all the Souls Curzon was the widest travelled; he had seen, and understood, the cultures and arts of many nations. He might have thought the very English taste of the other Souls a little parochial; not for him the encouragement of arts and crafts, or the gentle patronage of the minor painters. For him art was without boundary of country or date. As Viceroy of India he spent much time and money on restoring the ancient temples and monuments of the past. For the future, he planned the building of the Victoria Memorial Hall at Calcutta, which he wanted to be a 'magnificent shell, pure and serene in its simplicity . . . a Valhalla of all Indian heroes and worthies, with the Queen in the centre'. When criticized for the expenditure he had incurred, he answered in a speech at Delhi: 'Art and beauty, and the reverence that is owing to all that has evoked human genius, and has inspired human faith, are independent of creeds, and, in so far as they touch the sphere of religion, are embraced by the common religion of all mankind.' Art he saw as an Olympic torch of civilization; to preserve it was 'an offering of reverence to the past, and a gift of recovered beauty to the future'.

In August 1905, Curzon resigned as Viceroy, and returned to England; his last two years had been made miserable by a series of misunderstandings and eventual quarrels – which never healed – with Balfour and St John Brodrick, his secretary for India. In the autumn election the Tories, under Balfour, were defeated by the Liberal party led by H. H. Asquith. It was eleven years before Curzon was again to hold office, in Lloyd George's coalition government of 1916. It was a period of political exile and great personal loneliness, for Mary Curzon died suddenly in the June of 1906.

As a sad widower Curzon found consolation in building a Memorial Chapel for Mary and himself. It lies in the church at Kedleston; six years were spent in its perfection. In the centre is a marble effigy of husband and wife, protected by two sorrowing angels. The monument was carved by Sir Bertram Mackennal; his instructions were 'to show the pathos of Lady Curzon's early death' and to depict 'the deepest emotion'. To set off the white marble best, Lord Curzon chose 'a beautiful translucent quartz known as aventurine', and two years' search was necessary to find a green of sufficient intensity. The history of the construction of the chapel was described by Lord Curzon in a volume on Kedleston Church, which was published in 1922, and presented to the London Library by the author.

For Lord Curzon the long years without political appointment were lonely, but never idle. In 1907 he was appointed Chancellor of Oxford University, and he found in this exalted office a compensation for his misfortunes, and a great position from which to exercise his intellectual powers. Other honours accrued. In 1911 he was invited to be President of the Royal Geographical Society. In the same year he accepted a Trusteeship of the National Gallery, and later became a most distinguished Chairman. As a guardian of the art treasures of the nation, and decades before the idea was realized, Lord Curzon saw the necessity of establishing a National

The memorial to Mary Curzon in the thirteenth-century church at Kedleston. The base is inscribed with lines from D.G. Rossetti's *Blessed Damozel*:

There will I ask of Christ the Lord
  This much for him and me
Only to live as once on earth
  With love only to be
As then awhile, forever now,
  Together, I and he

Heritage Fund to staunch the flow of paintings from the country. Various ideas were put forward for its funding: it should receive the proceeds of entrance fees to the gallery (6d was charged on two days of the week); that the death duties which had been paid on works of art should accrue to this fund rather than to the Treasury; and also that a tax on auction sales be introduced. Such ideas have been mooted in our day. When in 1916 huge death duties compelled Lord Ellesmere to consider the sale of his Titians, Lord Curzon produced a revolutionary and brilliant report. He suggested that the nation should buy not one of Lord Ellesmere's celebrated Titians, but the three best: 'My own view is, we should play a much bolder hand, and aim at a larger quarry.' The necessary monies, he suggested, should be raised by selling some of the lesser Dutch paintings from the National Gallery and the Wallace Collection, or, preferably, some of our vast hoard of Turners. (Turner's testamentary dispositions were vague, and encumbered by codicils; Lord Curzon's interpretation was that only the completed works had been left to the nation.) Such a policy of 'de-acquisitioning' exists in many American museums, but is rare here. To sell off paintings to establish a Heritage Fund would probably not be acceptable in England today; fortunately such a Fund as Lord Curzon envisaged more than sixty years ago has now been established by the government.

Lord Curzon played no small part himself in preserving the national heritage. From his own pocket he bought and restored Tattershall Castle, in Lincolnshire, and Bodiam, in Sussex, and bequeathed both to the National Trust. So great was his affection for Bodiam, which looked like a chateau in a mediaeval illumination, that when he wanted to propose to Mrs Duggan he took her to see this romantic ruin he had preserved – 'A fairy tale castle, I can find no words to describe the beauty,' she wrote. Afterwards they drove to nearby Winchelsea church, where she accepted his suit.

It was in 1915 that Violet, Duchess of Rutland had introduced Lord Curzon to Mrs Alfred Duggan, a beautiful cosmopolitan widow of American descent. He was at once captivated by her appearance, and soon conquered by her good sense, her good humour, and her zest for life. Mrs Duggan was a blossom of society: endowed with lovely looks, an exquisite taste in dress, a great talent for entertaining, and a large fortune, she was the perfect wife for the Foreign Secretary, a post which Lord Curzon held between 1918 and 1924. Their London house was 1 Carlton House Terrace, and here they entertained in splendour; often, in the middle of a formal dinner, Gracie Curzon (as she was always affectionately known) would receive a note from her husband, delivered on a salver by the footman, congratulating her on the arrangement of the party. In spite of the grandeur of her early life, friends remember Gracie, 'always a very good sport', teaching herself how to cook during the Second War, and coping wonderfully. The second Lady Curzon brought much happiness to her husband.

The Curzons resided in two country houses – Montacute, in Somerset, which Lord Curzon could not resist as he thought it the most perfect Jacobean house in England, and the more convenient Hackwood Park. Hackwood is a large Palladian house near Basingstoke. Lord Curzon took pleasure in finding furniture and tapestries of the appropriate date with which to embellish it. Such was his enthusiasm for works of art that Lady Curzon teasingly said he would spend £10,000 on a painting, and not replace his old dressing gown.

It was a most endearing trait of Curzon's that he commissioned portraits of the women whose beauty he admired; to paraphrase his words, it was a gift of beauty for the future. He chose artists of international fame. To portray Mary Curzon he selected the Munich artist Lenbach, who gave his sitter the appearance of a vivacious ghost. Curzon's choice was inspired: Lenbach was captivated by Mary's wide-eyed and fragile face, and painted twelve sketches of her. De Laszlo, the Hungarian painter who came to live in England, but whose reputation was European, was a favourite painter of Curzon's. From him, he requested a regal portrait of Elinor Glyn, telling the artist he could 'make a splendid thing of her, with her white skin, dark eyebrows, green eyes and Venetian red hair'. After his marriage to Mrs Duggan (who had been previously painted by de Laszlo, looking touching in her widow's weeds), Curzon was most anxious that she should be portrayed by Sargent, but he had now retired; through the intercessions of Evan Charteris, he was persuaded to paint Gracie, and produced a most lively portrait. Curzon was modest about being painted himself; the first official portrait is a de Laszlo sketch of 1913 which hangs at Balliol. Harold Nicolson considered 'his personal appearance was better observed in photographs'.

In 1916, when Lord Scarsdale died at the age of eighty-four, Curzon at last inherited Kedleston. It is a Palladian house of great beauty, and the interiors designed by Robert Adam are perfectly preserved. He spent many weeks and weekends there in the remaining years of his life, renovating, restoring, and perfecting in every detail the house which so suited his own personality, and which he so greatly loved.

Lady Curzon preferred life at Hackwood, and it was here that she and her husband entertained the Souls friends of his youth. In her autobiography, she described small dinner parties, 'with Harry Cust at his most brilliant' and 'wonderful women like Ettie Desborough and Mary Elcho'. Curzon always remained devoted to Lady Desborough; on the death of Billy Grenfell in July 1915 he rushed at once to Taplow to be by her side, to find the King and Queen had also come to offer solace. The death of Alfred Lyttelton, in 1913, from a cricket injury was a great loss. Curzon made a particularly eloquent address at the funeral of this old friend of his youth.

It became the custom for the Curzons to hold Whitsuntide parties at Hackwood, which, Lady Diana Cooper recalls, as she was invited together with her mother, were 'very elderly parties, made up of the Souls, and Cabinet Ministers with their wives or the ladies they loved. They strolled high-heeled, with parasols, on the lawn, through the aisle of beeches.' In one of the 'Games', Curzon chose Lady Diana as the ideal travelling companion, as she was 'both gentle and vivacious'.

In the last years of his life Lord Curzon was denied the Premiership, given instead to Stanley Baldwin. His disappointment was bitter, but brief. He continued for some time to hold office as Foreign Secretary, and then as Lord Privy Seal. He found solace in the happiness of his family. He also worked with his usual application in researching and writing the histories of the houses he had lived in or restored – Bodiam, Tattershall, Walmer Castle (his residence as Warden of the Cinque Ports), Montacute, Hackwood and Kedleston. When he visited Madame Balsan (the former Consuelo, Duchess of Marlborough) in the south of France a few weeks before his death, he stayed up into the small hours striving to complete his manuscripts. At Kedleston he sorted diligently through several generations of documents, and preserved in his library the album of the Souls parties, a souvenir of the merry youth of this noble and eminent English statesman.

❧ TWO
Arthur Balfour

There was seen at that feast
Of this band, the High Priest,
The heart that to all hearts is nearest;
Him may nobody steal
From the true common weal,
Tho' to each is dear Arthur the dearest.

George Curzon

Arthur Balfour was the undisputed centre of the Souls' circle and by far the best known for his achievements outside that circle: as a statesman and politician, and to some extent as a philosopher. In fact these aspects of his life were so important that he cannot be described merely in terms of his dealings with the other Souls: an account, however brief, of his public career must be given to assist in understanding the whole man.

Balfour's paternal grandfather had made a very large fortune as a contractor in India, and bought the Whittingehame estate in East Lothian on which he erected a grand neo-classical mansion designed by Robert Smirke. Balfour inherited the estate directly at his coming-of-age in 1869, his father having died in 1856. His mother was a daughter of the second Marquess of Salisbury and sister of the third, who was the Conservative Prime Minister. He was educated at Eton and Trinity College, Cambridge, where, though academically undistinguished, he discovered a talent for metaphysical speculation which led him to write his *Defence of Philosophical Doubt*, published in 1878. Parts of this work had already appeared in the *Fortnightly Review*, the editor of which, John Morley, told him roundly that he could not understand a word of it. It was in fact chiefly an attempt to reconcile religion and science. To those who had not read the book, the title was misleading, and gave its author the reputation of a philosophical *fainéant*. This was perhaps the origin of the legend, current in his later years, that Balfour would stand at the top of the double staircase of his house in Carlton Gardens unable to descend because he could not make up his mind which side to take.

He entered Parliament as a Conservative in 1874 – at first rather tentatively, for it was two years before he made his maiden speech. However, in 1885, when after five years out of office his party returned to power under Lord Salisbury, Balfour was appointed Secretary for Scotland; he achieved Cabinet rank later in the same year. The turning-point of his political career came in 1887, when he accepted the most difficult, and most dangerous, post in the Government, that of Chief Secretary for Ireland. The appointment was greeted with derision as an example of

Arthur Balfour as a young man, drawn by George Richmond and dated 1877

The Rt Hon. Arthur Balfour, M.P. by Onslow Ford. A bronze bust from the plaster portrait exhibited at the Royal Academy in 1892. In 1891 Balfour had become First Lord of the Treasury and Leader of the House of Commons, and was recognized as heir apparent to the Conservative leadership

nepotism on Lord Salisbury's part; but Balfour's languid manner and air of dilettantish affectation were deceptive. The resolute and ruthless steps that he took to suppress the Land League agitation soon changed his original nickname, 'Miss Fanny', to a new one, 'Bloody Balfour'. By 1891, as First Lord of the Treasury (a nominal title usually held by the Prime Minister) and Leader of the House of Commons, he was recognized as heir apparent to the Conservative leadership.

In 1895 he published his second philosophical work, *The Foundations of Belief*, a pessimistic and baffling treatise on the same theme as its predecessor. Lord Esher took him to task:

> It is really hard, when you are the apostle of a charming sect, to trouble their minds with abstract speculations . . . However Mrs Grenfell and the others will no doubt feel that no one is likely to tackle them about details, so they can pretend to know all about it.

Balfour himself later discovered the truth of this; after discussing the book with Lady Desborough, his hostess at Taplow, he told Lady Elcho that 'she [Ettie Desborough] had got stuck in some very unexpected places'.

In 1902 Balfour succeeded his uncle as Prime Minister. Uniquely among twentieth-century statesmen, when his political career is surveyed as a whole, his Premiership appears as an

A drypoint portrait of Balfour by Mortimer Menpes, *c*.1900. This shows him at the most crucial time of his political career, just before he became Prime Minister

episode rather than a climax. It was his misfortune to take office when his party had been uninterruptedly in power for seven years. Ministers were jaded, and the electoral pendulum was beginning to turn against them. The party was also divided between the supporters of Free Trade and of Protection, so that Balfour was obliged to devote much of his time, and all his powers of dialectical subtlety, to the task of devising a policy acceptable to both sides.

A further difficulty – though one of which he himself made light – lay in his relationship with King Edward VII. He had got on very well with Queen Victoria, who praised his 'extreme fairness, impartiality, and large-mindedness'. She went on: 'He sees all sides of the question, is wonderfully generous in his feelings towards others, and very gentle and good-tempered.' But the King, in Harold Nicolson's words, 'never really cared for Mr Balfour, whose imperturbable, impersonal and indeed indiscriminate politeness, whose bland unawareness of grandeur, filled him with a certain disquiet'. The disdain felt by Balfour and his circle for what seemed to them the unrefined amusements and materialistic preoccupations of the 'Marlborough House Set' led him to underestimate the value of the King's shrewdness, knowledge of the world, and long experience of affairs. Sir Lionel Cust wrote:

> Of all men [he was] the least able to bring his intellect down to what he no doubt conceived the low level of the King's. The King to Balfour was at first just one of those irritating factors in general politics, which you cannot ignore, and which you must treat with dismal and ficticious solemnity.

Balfour's administration, short-lived though it was, brought real achievements. He was not only a skilful politician but a statesman of foresight. He began to reform the War Office; encouraged the setting up of the Committee of Imperial Defence; and, seeing the growing German threat, moved towards a rapprochement with France. However, most of these plans came to fruition only under a different administration, for the election of January 1906 brought the Liberals to power. Balfour himself lost the seat at East Manchester which he had held since 1885. Philosophical detachment and the ability to see both sides of a question are not qualities appreciated by an opposition party smarting under defeat. Something more aggressive is looked for, and in 1911 Balfour resigned the leadership. But when war broke out he rejoined the Committee of Imperial Defence and was also invited by the Prime Minister, Asquith, to join an informal, inner 'War Council'. In 1915 he returned to office as First Lord of the Admiralty in the Coalition Government. After the only major naval engagement of the war, the indecisive Battle of Jutland in May 1916, Balfour's disinterested attachment to truth, and his patrician inability to enter into the feelings of the man in the street, led to his drafting an official communiqué which gave the impression that the Royal Navy had suffered a decisive defeat. In the second Coalition, later in the same year, when Lloyd George replaced Asquith as Prime Minister, Balfour accepted the Foreign Office. As Winston Churchill said, 'he passed from one Cabinet to the other, from the Prime Minister who was his champion to the Prime Minister who had been his most severe critic, like a powerful graceful cat walking delicately and unsoiled across a rather muddy street' – a remark possibly coloured by envy, for he himself had been omitted from the new Government largely because of Conservative opposition and was not without *partipris*; a more charitable interpretation of Balfour's acceptance of office under Lloyd George is that he regarded his duty to his country as of paramount importance.

As Foreign Secretary Balfour was one of the British delegates to the Peace Conference in

Paris. He had now become in fact what he had long been by temperament – an elder statesman: to this role his intellect, his persuasive charm and his dispassionate approach to problems were perfectly suited. Clemenceau once described him as the 'Richelieu of the Conference'. On the conclusion of the peace negotiations he handed over the Foreign Office to Lord Curzon, but remained in the Cabinet in the non-departmental post of Lord President of the Council. At the break-up of the Coalition in 1922 he followed Lloyd George out of office, but in 1925 returned to the Cabinet under Baldwin, again as Lord President, a post which he retained until the year before his death.

In 1923, Lloyd George's successor Bonar Law, then gravely ill, had resigned. In the circumstances he declined to advise the King on the choice of his own successor. Lord Curzon, who had just scored a brilliant diplomatic triumph at the Lausanne Conference, had every reason to suppose that he would be chosen. Balfour was one of the senior Conservative statesmen summoned by the King to give his opinion, and he travelled to London from Sheringham in Norfolk where he had been on a golfing holiday with a party of friends. On his return, one of them asked him, 'And will dear George be Prime Minister?'

Balfour replied, 'No, dear George will not.'

Balfour advised against Lord Curzon's appointment because his own uncle, Lord Salisbury, had found being in the Lords such a problem during his Premiership.

In his last years Balfour suffered from deafness and towards the end of the twenties his physical strength declined rapidly. He was also beset by financial worries. He had been a very rich man – his inheritance was reputed to be worth a million pounds – but injudicious speculation in a company intending to produce industrial fuel from peat had brought heavy loss. At his death this disaster, coupled with neglect of the agricultural potential of the Whittingehame estate and the beginnings of the world depression, left his family seriously in debt. For Balfour himself it was a case of *'Après moi le déluge'*. His sister Alice said to Lady Wemyss, 'I can only leave Arthur to put his mind to the matter or not, as he likes.' Balfour did not like: he had other things to think about. His last two years were spent at his brother's house, Fisher's Hill at Woking, surrounded by friends and with the never-failing solace of listening to music; he died on 30 March 1930, in his eighty-second year.

Beatrice Webb, very much outside any of the circles in which Balfour moved, saw him perceptively but unkindly as:

> . . . the ideal Tory: every inch a fine gentleman with a big dash of the scholar and dilettante
> metaphysician who favours the Christian hypothesis. He is strong-willed, swift in execution,
> utterly cynical and honestly contemptuous of that pitiful myth, 'Democracy'.

To his friends Balfour revealed a completely different face. His Souls' life was for him a complete relaxation from the political arena. Indulging in idle or amusing chatter, playing tennis with more enthusiasm than skill and bridge without seriousness, competing at the famous after-dinner games with which the Souls amused themselves and terrorized their friends, he was at ease. Balfour was the undisputed idol of the Souls: in Curzon's words, 'To each is dear Arthur the dearest.' The feeling was mutual, for no man long remains the idol of a group of people whom he does not cherish and regard as important to himself. It was he who was said to have made the often-quoted remark: 'No history of our time will be complete unless the influence of the Souls upon society is accurately and dispassionately recorded.'

Without Balfour the Souls would not have existed. His public stature, his formidable intellect – Alfred Lyttelton wrote: 'I can imagine no intellectual dilemma from which Arthur Balfour could not emerge with triumph' – and his celebrated charm lifted their group above a merely social standing. In 1892 *England* published an article purporting to be an interview with a Soul; it shows the popular view of the members and of their relative importance.

> Among the males there stands conspicuous and foremost the ethereal, mysterious and
> ever-interesting figure of Mr Arthur Balfour. He may be described as a fixed Sun round which the
> lesser luminaries revolve. I doubt, indeed, if he were extinguished, whether the society could exist
> without the clear electric light which they derive from his *spirituelle* nature.

In his perceptive account of Balfour written for the *Dictionary of National Biography*, Algernon Cecil has given great prominence to this involvement with the Souls, recognizing the important role they played in Balfour's life:

> The memory of the 'Souls' is intimately associated with his name. They formed a coterie for which it
> might be difficult to find a parallel in English history. Free from any disastrous exclusiveness either
> social or conversational, interested in really interesting things, alive to the claims of art and not dead to
> those of morals, blending politics with fashion and fashion with philanthropy, they contrived,
> without incurring too much ridicule, to sacrifice to Beauty, Truth, and Goodness against a
> background of West-end dinner-parties and great English country-houses. Of this circle of clever
> men and often brilliant and beautiful women Balfour seemed made to be the *arbiter elegantarium*.

Balfour clearly voiced his preference for a life of undisturbed philosophical speculation; yet fate forced him into the political arena. Once there, his outstanding intellectual ability was bound to take him to the greatest heights, making such a hermit's life even more difficult to attain.

The verdict of posterity on his philosophical writing is severe: in spite of the power of his prose at its best, his achievement as a metaphysician fell short of the most profound understanding; indeed many of his contemporaries were likewise inclined to dismiss him as an amateur. In attempting to reconcile the irreconcilable – the opposing claims of science and religion – he became incomprehensible. Nevertheless, a much-quoted passage from the first chapter of *The Foundations of Belief* has considerable literary effect and compels respect, if only for the unrelieved pessimism of the author's conclusions.

> Man, so far as natural science by itself is able to teach us, is no longer the final cause of the universe,
> the Heaven-descended heir of all the ages. His very existence is an accident, his story a brief and
> transitory episode in the life of one of the meanest of the planets. Of the combination of causes which
> first converted a dead organic compound into the living progenitors of humanity, science, indeed, as
> yet knows nothing. It is enough that from such beginnings famine, disease, and mutual slaughter, fit
> nurses of the future lords of creation, have gradually evolved, after infinite travail, a race with
> conscience enough to feel that it is vile, and intelligence enough to know that it is insignificant. We
> survey the past, and see that its history is of blood and tears, of helpless blundering, of wild revolt, of
> stupid acquiescence, of empty aspirations. We sound the future, and learn that after a period, long

compared with the individual life, but short indeed compared with the divisions of time open to our investigation, the energies of our system will decay, the glory of the sun will be dimmed, and the earth, tideless and inert, will no longer tolerate the race which has for the moment disturbed its solitude. Man will go down into the pit, and all his thoughts will perish. The uneasy consciousness, which in this obscure corner has for a brief space broken the contented silence of the universe, will be at rest. Matter will know itself no longer. 'Imperishable monuments' and 'immortal deeds', death itself, and love stronger than death will be as though they had never been. Nor will anything that *is* be better or worse for all that the labour, genius, devotion, and suffering of man have striven through countless generations to effect.

Over half a century later George Lyttelton remarked to Rupert Hart-Davis: 'Nowhere that I know is the stark factuality of science so majestically garbed in language.'

To attempt to penetrate the secrets of a man who has learnt such an awesome lesson from life is a daunting prospect, but it is against this background of profound pessimism that Balfour's personality, or as much of his personality as he chose to reveal, should be considered. So much of the interest and charming attention that he showed to his friends and political associates in the everyday concerns of their lives must have masked an unshakeable belief in their total lack of importance to the perishable universe. This was the man who, in George Wyndham's words, 'knows there has been one ice-age; and [he] thinks there is going to be another'. Yet he rarely dropped his mask, even in autobiography. Most works in this genre are at least to some extent unintentionally revealing; yet Balfour's *Chapters in Autobiography* are quite the reverse; intentionally unrevealing, this book allows no hint of emotional turmoil to penetrate the urbane façade which he had spent years constructing and perfecting.

As a young man Balfour was emotionally vulnerable, moved to melodramatic gestures, particularly in affairs of the heart. Yet one cannot view his emotions as straightforward: even then Balfour could rarely be taken at face value. In spite of the apparent profundity of the feelings which prompted him to the public display of grief or love, his favourite niece and first biographer, Blanche Dugdale, who was exceptionally close to him, wrote of him:

> His power of becoming aloof at will was perhaps the most important thing for an understanding of his character and the only way of explaining a paradox that lurked in the depths. He basked all his days in affection, and repaid it to the full. Yet no misfortune, no bereavement, could have broken him, for he was solitary at heart.

Certainly Balfour himself liked to increase this impression of emotional invulnerability. The story of his joking response to a piece of sentimental coat-trailing on the part of Margot Asquith has often been told to demonstrate his heartlessness. (There are a number of different versions in which the dramatis personae change, but this is from *Off the Record*, one of Mrs Asquith's own books of reminiscences.)

> [Margot Asquith:] 'If Mary, Etty and I died you would not miss us. I know you are devoted to Mary Wemyss, but for us others, you don't care two hoots! You have a taste for us as you might have in clocks and furniture.' [Balfour:] 'I should mind if you all died on the same day.'

Balfour was asked once if the rumour that he intended to marry Margot was true. 'No,' he replied, 'I rather think of having a career of my own.' No such neatly deflating response would have sprung to his lips had the memory of May Lyttelton been invoked; for Balfour this was sacred territory on which no one might trespass.

The two years after Balfour was elected to Parliament in 1874 were for him a period of considerable emotional stress, marked by the death in 1875 of May, sister of his great friend Spencer Lyttelton and the woman whom he had confidently expected to make his wife. Her loss was to haunt him for the rest of his life: indeed, one of his last actions was to 'communicate' with her through Mrs Willett, the popular medium, who had been summoned to his death-bed. At this distance of time it is difficult to unravel fact from fantasy in this affair. As far as Balfour himself was concerned, it seems that he believed that a proposal of marriage had been accepted and that May's death had deprived him of a future wife. No such certainty attaches to May Lyttelton's interpretation: although Balfour's attentions had been pressing she had other suitors and had twice hoped to marry, both before and during Balfour's courtship. Her first love, Edward Dennison, died in 1870. By 1871 Balfour, an habitué of the Lyttelton circle since his friendship at Cambridge with Spencer, was in love with her, although he had already given a clear impression of being interested in May's cousin, Mary Gladstone (daughter of W.E.), an interest that was wholeheartedly returned. Whether May Lyttelton took him seriously is open to question. Her brother Neville remarked of him: 'I don't think much of Spencer's friend, he was always hanging around the girls.' She may have thought that he was simply showing a characteristic preference for feminine company. In any case it was at this time that May Lyttelton met and fell deeply in love with Rutherford Graham, Frances Horner's somewhat ne'er-do-well brother. The match was not welcomed by her family but might eventually have been tolerated had the young man 'made good', as was his intention when he set out for the United States in October 1872. In Liverpool he contracted diphtheria and died. With renewed hope Balfour continued to press his attentions on May, and was later to maintain that they had become engaged at a weekend party in December 1874. When May died in March the following year he caused an emerald ring which had belonged to his mother to be placed in the coffin, a pledge and a proof of their betrothal.

The Hon. Mary (May) Lyttelton, from a newspaper cutting dating from the time of the publication of Balfour's *Chapters in Autobiography*

38   THE SOULS

It is curious that this most suitable betrothal was not made public. May did not write of it to her closest women friends. Shortly before her death she said to Margaret Leicester Warren that she felt there was a fate about her. 'It was a strange life crossed always by Death.' She had bestowed her affection successively on three men and had just then heard of the death of the third, a man named Marshall who was killed in the Alps. None of the men she named was Balfour.

For Balfour himself the emotional distress caused by her death was real enough: but it was also to be exploited as a line of retreat in his subsequent romantic affairs. He remarked to Lady Elcho that he had only loved 'in that way' once (meaning with physical passion). She was in no doubt that he referred to his relationship with May Lyttelton. A rumoured attachment, which seemed likely to result in marriage, to Lady Jenny Lindsay, the daughter of the Earl of Crawford, foundered all too easily on some quite trivial religious differences. After that he seems to have had no temptation to exchange his emotional freedom for the commitments of matrimony.

After May Lyttelton's death Balfour went abroad with Spencer Lyttelton and Mary Gladstone; the party was chaperoned to Düsseldorf for the Musical Festival by Mary Ponsonby, the wife of the Queen's Private Secretary, Sir Henry Ponsonby, a shrewd commentator who kept a diary of their progress. It is full of amusing observations:

> Mr Balfour's dressing-case was certainly the most elaborate thing I have ever seen, and somehow unlike him, I should have thought, to think so much of his personal arrangements. I suppose it is really a symptom of laziness.

The moodiness of her companions struck her forcibly and she was sometimes pleased to escape for solitary sightseeing; the prevailing atmosphere alternated between schoolboy hilarity (Spencer Lyttelton addressed his friend: 'Balfour, I don't know if it is the vulgarity of your manners, or the ugliness of your appearance which is attracting public notice, but we are the centre of attraction for all observers') and the profoundest gloom. She paints an uncharacteristic picture of the charming and urbane Balfour. Few of the friends of his middle years can have remembered him thus:

> Mr Balfour I think the cleverest, but he does not give himself the trouble to know one exists, half the time, and there is no affectation of any sort in him, but when he rouses himself to say anything deliberately he expresses himself more clearly and forcibly than most people. It is ill-health that makes him languid and limp – but he has conquered it to a great degree, and never wastes his strength on things that are not worth it. The net result is that he is formidable, as one is always afraid of boring him.

In later years Balfour was to be noted for his air of consuming interest in the conversation of his companions, so that they sparkled with wit and interest in return.

For Mary Gladstone the trip to Düsseldorf may have rekindled past hopes. She had had to watch his pursuit of her cousin May. Perhaps shared grief would now bind them together. Earlier hints in her diary show how seriously her affections had been engaged. During 1871 she had a number of reasons for believing that Balfour himself was 'showing a preference'. When she was staying at Whittingehame he sought her company constantly and on more than one occasion he appeared, uncharacteristically early in the morning, to take breakfast with her. They shared a sense of humour: sitting together at a dinner party in London she remembered that they 'talked a good deal of nonsense as usual, and he [Balfour] laughed so immoderately as to be forced to starve'. More importantly they were drawn together by a passion for music. Balfour played the piano and the concertina (affectionately known as the 'infernal'); Mary Gladstone herself was a talented pianist. She practised seriously for many hours each day and, although her performances were erratic, at her best she was brilliant. Balfour's interest in music was consuming, and his stamina when it came to listening to performances of his beloved Handel was remarkable. Like so many who are seriously interested in music, he attended rehearsals, sometimes of interminable length. On the trip to Düsseldorf Mary Ponsonby, who was herself a fine musician, writes, with a certain air of stoicism, 'we had altogether eight hours of music today', and she recalls Balfour's intentions, stated on arrival – 'I announce that I go to see no churches, no pictures, and no monuments' – thus leaving the days entirely free for music. Some years earlier Mary Gladstone, observing him at a concert at the Crystal Palace, noted 'the appreciation so keen and intense as almost amounted to pain'.

The trip to Düsseldorf was followed by journeys to the United States, the Antipodes and the Far East. Eventually returning home, Balfour was confronted with the urgent necessity to attend to his neglected political career. As Lady Salisbury forcefully pointed out, he was now into his third session without having so much as spoken in the House. Even with this formidable spur to his conscience, political duties were not allowed to take up his full time. Never in the whole of his career was Balfour entirely to neglect intellectual and aesthetic interests. During these next few years he constructed the personality that he presented to the world in his maturity.

As a young man Balfour had satisfied his artistic inclinations by making a collection of blue and white porcelain, but now he embarked on a more serious form of patronage. Soon after May Lyttelton's death, when all his friends united to find distractions for him, Lady Airlie took him to meet Burne-Jones in his studio. Balfour was immediately attracted to both the painter and his works and a major commission – to decorate the walls of the music-room at Balfour's London house at 4 Carlton Gardens – was offered and accepted. The scheme, produced by Burne-Jones and William Morris together, was for a series of panel-paintings illustrating the legend of Perseus, which were to be framed by plasterwork in an acanthus design, and below them panelling of unstained oak, a style of decoration remarkably unsuited to the house. Progress was slow, and only four of the panels were ever completed. These, with other pictures by the artist which Balfour had bought, were displayed at Carlton Gardens for a short time, and then at Downing Street where they seem to have created an unfavourable impression. The newly elected Unionist M.P. Willie Bridgeman, on being summoned to a meeting at Downing Street in January 1906, viewed them with considerable distaste: 'The room was full of very excellent Burne-Jones pictures, whose anaemic and unmanly forms seemed to give the meeting a nerveless and flabby character, and were to me painfully symbolic of their owner.' Burne-Jones died with the Perseus pictures still uncompleted. A portrait of him painted in the last year of his life shows the half-finished panel of *The Arming of Perseus* behind the painter, who is working at his easel. The work had haunted Burne-Jones for over twenty years: he must have been happy enough to be able to look still on the image of his beloved Frances Graham (Lady Horner) whose serene profile is on the extreme right of this panel.

The enamelled overmantel by Alexander Fisher, made for Whittingehame, Balfour's house in Scotland

Undaunted by this frustrating experience, Balfour again ventured on large-scale patronage by commissioning an elaborate mantelpiece from Alexander Fisher, the jeweller and enamellist from whom Madeline Wyndham learned her skills in these crafts. This was one of Fisher's most ambitious projects because of its unusually large scale, and it looked very impressive when it was installed at Whittingehame; A. C. Benson remembers 'a splendid dining-room, richly panelled in light oak, with a big piece of metalwork at one end of a Burne-Jones type'.

Once initiated into the pleasures of visiting studios, Balfour came to know several prominent artists of the period. One such visit was to provide a lasting distraction that was to sustain Balfour for the rest of his life. In about 1879 he met Mrs Percy Wyndham and her two eldest children, Mary and George, at Frederic Leighton's studio in Kensington. Invitations were soon exchanged: Balfour was asked to musical parties at the Wyndhams' London house in Belgrave Square, and in return Mrs Wyndham and her daughter were asked to stay in Scotland. Balfour was thirty-one and already well embarked on a promising political career. Not surprisingly, he was regarded with favour as a suitor by Mary and her mother. No obstacles were put in the way of a proposal, which Mary later told him would certainly have been accepted; but none was forthcoming. 'Mama wanted you to marry me,' she remembered; 'You got some silly notion in your head because circumstances threw Hugo and me together and accidents kept us apart – you were the only man I wanted for my husband.' 'Hugo' was Lord Elcho, a rival and more energetic suitor. Such were the pressures of convention in the eighties that if an eligible husband presented himself with a firm proposal of marriage there was little chance of escape.

Hugo Elcho was not a faithful husband: 'He goes his way,' as Mary was to explain to Wilfrid Blunt when she was staying with him in the desert in Egypt in 1895. Blunt had noticed during his first visit to the Wyndhams at Clouds in 1887 that 'He [Balfour] has a *grande-passion* for Mary – that is quite clear – and it is equally clear that she has a tenderness for him. But what their exact relations may be I cannot determine. Perhaps it is better not to be too wise and as all the house accepts the position as the most natural in the world there let us leave it!' Blunt eventually settled for a neat diagnosis of the situation: '. . . their love should be within certain limits – a little more than friendship a little less than love.'

This relationship was the most complicated and delicately balanced of the many that Balfour entered into, and the demands that it made on both sides were considerable. Balfour was technically quite free, a situation of which he was often tempted to take advantage, enjoying delightful interludes with, for instance, Laura Lyttelton, or Mary Curzon, home from India without her husband. Momentarily the fragile structure would tremble and passionate accusations would be made; but both had too much to lose and it would be repaired once more. After nearly a quarter of a century Mary Elcho could view their mutual dependence with a dispassionate eye:

> The thing I am most grateful for is that you do not humbug me or tell sham things to flatter me. We do trust each other more sensibly than that . . . You know, I never want to know anything for the sake of knowing or to gratify a shallow vanity – but it is different and it's the most exquisite pleasure that I can have – that if you are worried, about money, politics, enemies, friends or – loves! I never want you to say anything you are not in the mood to say and I always respect you! Above all I should deplore anything that might spoil our relations which have worn for more than a dozen years.

This was written in 1904. At Balfour's death, twenty-six years later, she wrote: 'I cannot yet realise how great the blank will be – but I can only feel grateful to have had such a friend for fifty years.'

One more episode in the long friendship was still to come. A small black despatch-case which he had entrusted to his sister-in-law when he departed for Ireland in 1887, to be opened only in the event of his death, could at long last be unpacked. There was no key, and the side had to be slit open, as Balfour had instructed. Inside there was a diamond brooch accompanied by a letter of explanation.

At that now distant date Balfour had envisaged the possibility that Mary Elcho would have to mourn him in secret; in old age she faced a very different predicament, as she thought that news of his death might make people talk of the past:

> They would say – How pathetic to see Arthur Balfour and Mary Wemyss. How sad is the end of life – the necessary onslaught of illness and old age. How sad to outlive Romance. I believe they were lovers once – tho' nobody knows – no-one ever knew the truth about these things.

The truth is that this relationship sustained them both through busy and emotionally taxing lives. Balfour needed a refuge from his professional life, a sympathetic and discreet confidant; Mary Elcho needed emotional and moral support to sustain her through the quicksands of her family life.

Balfour, at least, had managed to make his family life a bulwark against the outside world. His relatives and their many children, one of whom, his niece Blanche, he loved as if she were his own, were encouraged to accept freely the open-handed hospitality which he dispensed at Whittingehame. In 1904 A.C. Benson bicycled over to Whittingehame in response to an invitation to lunch:

Golf became a consuming passion for Balfour. When he was out of office he established a routine which allowed him to play every weekday

We put our bicycles by the door; and then saw the Prime Minister approaching across the grass, swinging a golf-club – in rough coat and waistcoat, the latter open; a cloth cap, flannel trousers; and large black boots, much too heavy and big for his willowy figure. He slouched and lounged as he walked. He gave us the warmest greeting, with a simple and childlike smile which is a great charm indeed. I was conscious at once of *charm* more than anything.

Many people were struck by Balfour's physical appearance, among them the painter Jacques-Emile Blanche, who conjures up the whole flavour of the man in his observations:

There was Arthur Balfour with his flowing morning coat, very tall and stooping, his arms of extraordinary length, impersonal, graceful, with the Englishman's youthful look and the charm that belongs to those happy mortals to whom dealing with their fellows has brought sympathy. His culture and lack of pride were evident to anyone fortunate to have a few minutes' conversation with him. Max Beerbohm's drawings made him look floppy and rather too fatherly, somewhat like Thackeray's divines, with George Moore's gestures, I wondered if he knew them. One day I asked him: Had he sat for competent artists? Watts and Burne-Jones were the great painters for the 'Souls' and for Mr Balfour, Lady Elcho's great friend. He replied, 'I have nothing to take hold of; Mr Sargent goes mad when he tries to draw me.' Certainly Balfour was 'all expression', as good people say. But it was just that which struck one. It was easy to give his head that air of irresponsibility women who knew him gave him in their drawings, reminiscent of Burne-Jones or Sargent. For there was the slapdash method of Sargent or Laszlo, and the *Soul*ful one.

'*Etude de Mr Balfour, souvenir de Ph. de Laszlo*'.
This portrait was presented to the National Portrait Gallery by Lady Wemyss (Mary Elcho) in 1935

In spite of Balfour's distaste for being portrayed his position made it inevitable that he would have to submit a number of times, the most celebrated portrait of him being the magnificent full-length by Sargent which is now in the Carlton Club. A more unconventional treatment, very much in the 'Soulful' manner mentioned by Blanche, was used by Alma-Tadema, showing Balfour seated in his most characteristic position, almost lying on the base of his spine. Official portraiture, however, was not well suited to catch the flavour of Balfour's subtle and elusive personality. The conventional – and fashionable – viewpoint adopted by both Sargent and de Laszlo give a much less searching picture of the man than the marvellous series of drawings by Max Beerbohm.

Beerbohm was fascinated by Balfour, almost it might be said obsessed, particularly by the contrast of the apparent fragility and vagueness of his character with his ruthlessness as a politician. He drew Balfour repeatedly; the most elegant and decorative evocation of his subject must surely be 'Balfour, a frieze' which was included in *Fifty Caricatures* (1913), and which expressed so much about Balfour without crude ridicule. The most shrewdly analytical of the captioned drawings must be 'The Old Self and the Young Self' which is reproduced in colour as the frontispiece to *Observations* (1925). The caption runs:

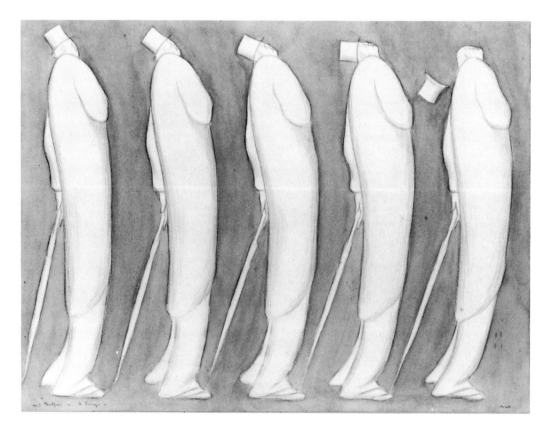

Mr Balfour – a Frieze, c. 1912, by Max Beerbohm. Beerbohm was fascinated by Balfour and caricatured him repeatedly

Young self (faintly): 'Who are you? You look rather like Uncle Salisbury, shaved. And what is that curious thing you are holding? [A tennis racket] And won't you catch cold with so little on? But don't answer: I don't really care. And don't let me talk: I don't fancy I've long to live; and I want to devote the time to thinking – not that I suppose my thoughts to be of much value, but – oh, do, please, go away.'

The knockabout humour of the drawings showing Balfour professing ignorance of the whereabouts of 10 Downing Street or the function of the Houses of Parliament gets less to the heart of the matter, though anyone with an appreciation of Balfour's tortuous personality would assume that he has a good but secret reason for these apparent idiocies.

Kenneth Young gave to his biography of Balfour a sub-title, 'The happy life of the politician. Prime Minister, Statesman and philosopher'. This gives an over-simplified view of the position. Balfour was too intelligent to be happy, but he was probably too philosophical to be unhappy. He had been sustained through a busy life by relationships which left him content, and he had learnt to avoid being overwhelmed by emotion. He knew which pleasures endured: when he was on his deathbed and barely conscious he returned to the greatest solace of his youth, and the joy of his whole life, music. While he was still just able to express a desire he asked that Charles, the talented son of Reginald McKenna, should be brought to his bedside to sing. Charles McKenna remembers this incident of half a century ago; in March 1930, when in his last year at Eton, he was taken by his mother to Woking. Arthur Balfour was propped up on a couch. Charles McKenna sang Purcell's 'Evening Hymn' and Handel's 'Where e'er you walk'. He had also prepared 'Waft her, angels', but he was not asked for it. Arthur Balfour could no longer speak, but 'gurgled' his appreciation. He died about ten days later.

⚘ THREE
Violet, Duchess of Rutland

And my Lord and my Lady Granby;
Is there one of the Gang
Has not wept at the pang
That he never can Violet's man be?
George Curzon

In her entry in *Who's Who* Violet, Duchess of Rutland described herself in a single word: 'artist'. Under the section devoted to recreations she stated: 'portraits, drawing, sculpture'. This is precise and just; the Duchess was a most talented artist, and expressed her gifts in portrait drawing and sculpture. She was a true aesthete; 'she liked only the beautiful in everything', and her whole life was dominated by this cult of beauty of which she was the living embodiment, for she was widely regarded as one of the most exquisite women of her time.

It was natural that Violet Rutland should have been among the leading Souls. 'The most delicate and artistic of all the female Souls . . . that slender and ethereal figure, those dark, sad, beautiful eyes, that graceful and refined mien.' The Duchess had a lovely singing voice, and was said also to have entertained the Souls by her graceful dancing. 'She was one of the most cultured young women in Victorian society,' wrote her friend Daisy Warwick. 'Her love of art made her a number of enemies among those who disliked the idea of women developing an intellectual standard.' But she was greatly admired by the Souls for her talents, and they regarded her as their 'Egeria', their wise nymph (according to Curzon's press cuttings); she and Mr Balfour were their two deities. As befits this role, the Duchess seems distant and remote, and even the Souls found she had 'a certain mysterious detachment'.

The Duchess had spectacular beauty, with auburn hair and a camellia complexion inherited from her Irish mother. Her extreme slenderness of figure was modern rather than Victorian. Her face looked sometimes Greek, sometimes mediaeval. But, according to Lady Cynthia Asquith, 'the faintly sinister strangeness of her eyes so deeply set in shadowy caverns' transformed what would otherwise be classical beauty into something haunting. As Bacon remarked: 'There is no excellent beauty that hath not some strangeness in the proportion.'

She was an inspiration to many painters. G. F. Watts was obsessed by her and painted her as a Virgin of the Rocks, in a Prussian blue gown. In a second portrait he produced, full-face, the huge gaze of a pagan goddess looking at the world from afar. J. J. Shannon painted her several times, occasionally in 1890s' guise, in a chiffon and lace tea-gown, shadowy, and once as an Art Nouveau priestess in a Mucha-style head-dress. Jacques-Emile Blanche made two portraits of

46

Portrait by G. F. Watts, *c*. 1879. The colouring echoes the sitter's own tastes: her auburn hair is complemented by her rust coloured dress and the cream chiffon scarf draped loosely round her neck.

This studio photograph shows the
Duchess in her favourite style of dress: a
cream blouse trimmed with lace, and
with open cuffs, worn with a wide
petersham belt

her in later years as insubstantial as pale smoke from a fading fire. So outstanding was the
Duchess's beauty that when she was at Balmoral it was remarked on by Queen Victoria, who
made a charming watercolour sketch of her when she and her parents were staying there.

The Duchess had strict aesthetic tastes, delightfully described by her daughter, Lady
Diana Cooper, in her memoirs. In colour she liked only the faded and subdued. Even too-vivid
curtains were placed on the lawn in summer to fade. For her clothes she chose non-colours:
creams, fawns, soft blue-greys and blue-greens, the hues of Chinese ceramics. She adapted the
contents of the family jewel-chest in a charming and haphazard manner: the great badge of the
Order of the Garter (not at that time borne by a member of the family) became a necklace; she
wore her tiara back to front, enclosing her Grecian chignon. Diamond insects and stars seemed
to hover around her diaphanous dresses. Everything floated and trailed: veils, streamers of lace
around the head, scarves round the neck, ribbons, long trains unsupported by illogical bustles
which concealed the natural grace of the figure. Such a style enhanced her beauty, and was in
accordance with her dislike of the trends of fashion in life or in art.

Of painters she loved the Italian masters Botticelli, Crivelli and Mantegna, and hung reproductions of them in her children's schoolroom. She also taught them to appreciate nineteenth-century artists: Turner, Millais, Burne-Jones, Leighton. Her children inherited her taste, sometimes dramatic, always imaginative; her daughter Marjorie, who attended the Byam Shaw School, was a draughtsman as gifted as her mother.

Violet Rutland had been born a Lindsay, a family inheriting through many generations a great love of art. It is said that her father recognized her precocious talent for drawing when she was only five and sought counsel of Burne-Jones, who advised against formal instruction. She travelled to Italy in her early teens, and by the age of twenty-two she was already exhibiting her work professionally. In 1877 the Grosvenor Gallery – the avant-garde home of Burne-Jones, Watts and Whistler – had been opened by a cousin, Sir Coutts Lindsay. Here Violet Lindsay showed both drawings and sculpture, and in 1879 she exhibited a statuette of a friend and fellow sculptress, Princess Louise, Queen Victoria's fourth daughter. From 1881 she also showed at the Royal Academy portraits of Souls and friends of the Souls such as Mrs Edmund Bourke (known as Daisy to fellow-Souls) and Viscount Peel, father of the popular young Soul, Julia. In 1902 she exhibited two hundred of her portrait drawings at the New Gallery, and three of them – including portraits of Harry Cust and the novelist Amélie Rives – were purchased by the Musée du Luxembourg of Paris for their collection of modern art.

The Duchess's self-portrait of 1893 shows her as Margot Asquith described her – 'A Burne-Jones Medusa'

The Duchess's costume for the Devonshire House Ball in 1897 (she was then Lady Granby) is based on an eighteenth-century portrait

In 1882 Violet Lindsay married Henry Manners, the heir to the Duke of Rutland. Her husband was an extremely handsome man, whose interests lay partly in politics (he was, at the time of their marriage, private secretary to Lord Salisbury, then not in office), but mainly in sport and agriculture. Of all the husbands of the female Souls, he was the least concerned with the activities of the group. The Duchess did not regard such a dynastic marriage as in any way conflicting with her artistic career. Every afternoon she worked in her studio, and continued to exhibit as before. In an age of amateur lady artists, the Duchess was a true professional, and praised as such by Auguste Rodin and Jacques-Emile Blanche; yet, as her obituary was to admit, 'There can be little doubt that the Duchess lost, rather than gained, in reputation by her rank.'

The Duchess's speciality was portrait heads, executed in soft pencil. The drawings are delicate, and as the Duchess best portrayed loveliness, fragility and pathos, her female portraits are naturally the most successful; though she endows her male sitters with distinction and sensibility. The women look ethereal, large-eyed; she confessed that her artist's licence often made eyes wider to flatter the beauty of the sitter. Nevertheless, as portraits her drawings are very true. Lady Elcho so preferred the Duchess's portrait of her to any photograph that she chose it to portray her in the album that the Souls presented to George Curzon. It captures her particular gentleness of expression. The Duchess became virtually the portrait artist by appointment to all the Souls, and also to their children. Few escaped her enthusiastic pencil; Billy Grenfell wrote what a flattering drawing 'Violet Duchess' made of him, and that of Julian Grenfell was chosen by Lady Desborough as the frontispiece to her *Pages from a Family Journal*.

The Duchess considered that her greatest work of art was her memorial to her son, Lord Haddon, who died tragically at the age of nine. Lady Diana Cooper wrote:

> My mother was in such an anguish of grief that she withdrew into a studio in London, where in her dreadful pain she was able to sculpt a recumbent figure of her dead son. . . . All her artistic soul went into this tomb.

This plaster of the memorial to
Lord Haddon, who died in 1894
aged nine, was modelled by his
mother immediately after his death

The little boy lies in his nightshirt, his head resting on a pillow and his hands clasped over the sheet which enfolds his body. The parallel lines of the linen drapery, straight, rigid, unruffled, emphasize the stillness of death. The work is natural, classic and timeless. On a plinth at one end the Duchess has written: 'Hope of my Eyes, Something is broken that we cannot mend', and added in small letters 'entirely designed and modelled by his mother', as if it were the last present she could give him. The sculpture was greatly admired by Alfred Gilbert, and by Rodin, whom Jacques-Emile Blanche took to see it. A marble version was made by another hand, and placed in the chapel at Haddon; the Duchess kept the plaster in her house, too precious to part with. She made an elaborate base on which she worked for years, set with relief portraits of all her family in roundels, she herself with her hair tied back in the scarf she wore when sculpting. This effigy was to initiate a cult of memorial sculpture amongst the Souls. It inspired the monuments to Lord Curzon and his wife, to Harry Cust, and to those who died in the Great War.

The Rutland family had a palatial William Kent mansion, 16 Arlington Street, overlooking Green Park. The house retained all its marvellous original plaster work and panelling. The Duchess turned most of it, in a charmingly Bohemian way, into her studio. Her busts of her children were placed on the landing of the grand staircase. Her own drawings were hung all over the walls of her boudoir, with a carefree lack of concern about their conservation. 'In the so-called ballroom a spot of oil on the floor, or paint rags lying about, did not astonish the domestics, for it was a workshop in which hat-boxes and opened parcels lay about.'

The drawing room at 16 Arlington Street. On the left hangs a portrait of the Duchess by J. J. Shannon and on the console table are three of her own sculptures

At this house she enjoyed giving luncheon parties, and welcomed impromptu visits to the studio. Blanche remembers meeting there Lady Horner, Lady Desborough and Lady Helen Vincent. A true romantic, the Duchess was a match-maker amongst the Souls; she would have agreed with Lady Horner that to remove romance from life was 'to replace the sky with a ceiling'. It was at one of the Arlington Street parties that Curzon was invited to come and meet that 'very pretty Mrs Duggan', as the Duchess described her, and he very soon married her. A romantic himself, he insisted that his wife appeared every year on the anniversary of that luncheon in the same blue dress and hat that she had then worn. A letter from the Duchess to Mrs Patrick Campbell – whom she had introduced into the Souls' world – on her marriage to George Cornwallis West in 1914 shows how warmly she felt for the happiness of her friends:

> Oh my dear,
>   My joy was great, and I feel so interested in life when I think of you, at last brilliantly contented too.
>   Soon I hope to see happy faces.
>   How glad I am he talked to me at Alice Keppel's. It makes all the difference to have heard from him what adoration and devotion he has for you.
>   His people must love him because of his 'expression' if nothing else, and if they love him they must know how happy he is.
>   Bless you both.
>   V.R.

The Duchess must have delighted in the beauty of her own daughters. The eldest, Marjorie, later Lady Anglesey, was a brunette with huge eyes and a face of a shape so exquisite that it was several times sculpted by the Duchess. Letty, the second daughter, who married the Elchos' eldest son, Ego Charteris, had a pale fragility perfectly caught for posterity by Sargent. The youngest daughter, Lady Diana Cooper, remains a legend for her golden beauty. The three daughters were less members of the Souls than the younger, more unruly group known as the 'Corrupt Coterie', which flourished briefly in the hectic days before and during the Great War. Admiring good looks in others, the Duchess made protégés of several lovely young girls, and introduced them into society. The ravishing Pamela Plowden, later Lady Lytton, was a favourite of the Duchess. So was Anne Dundas, later Lady Islington, who in that way became a latter-day member of the Souls' circle in the nineties. A third initiate was the Duchess's relative and neighbour, Nina Welby-Gregory (later Mrs Cust), whose entry into society was to have a strange sequel. The Duchess included portraits of these three girls in the album of drawings she published in 1900.

Another friend and beneficiary of her generosity was Alfred Gilbert, whom the Duchess regarded as England's leading sculptor. She introduced him to Nina soon after her marriage to Harry Cust, and he made a beautiful bust of her, her head inclined like a drooping flower. Gilbert's professional life was always badly organized; he fell into arrears with commissions and worked for ten years on the tomb of the Duke of Clarence leaving it incomplete. His marriage broke down, and a romance with the beautiful but unstable Mrs Eliza Macloghlin, who had commissioned from him a memorial to her husband, led to hideous recriminations. He retired to Bruges in despair and poverty. It is to the great credit of the Duchess that she tried to rehabilitate him and restore his confidence. 'I am determined that future generations of English men and women shall possess and admire his work,' she said to Lady Warwick. The Duke commissioned from him a war memorial for Leicester, but sadly this project too was never finished.

After the death of her husband in 1925 the Duchess sold 16 Arlington Street, and moved to Chapel Street, where she turned two houses into one and built a large studio out into the garden. There she worked much as before. She made no concessions either to age or to fashion, wearing the clothes of her youth, the cream blouses, the lace scarves. Her style was unchanged, and her great beauty lingered. In 1935 Chips Channon went to a ball at Belvoir: 'The women were magnificent – but I thought that old Violet Duchess looked the best, tired, eighty, and in white; she was a romantic, rather triste figure in a castle where she had reigned so long.'

In 1933 the Duchess gave an exhibition of her portrait drawings at the Russell-Coates Museum in Bournemouth. In November 1937 she had another exhibition at Chapel Street; all her friends came – Lady Horner, Lady Desborough, Lady Lytton – it was an autumnal reunion of Souls. The drawings were for sale and the proceeds were to go to St George's Hospital to fund a cot in Haddon's name. The plaster of Haddon was on view, and to her extreme delight it was accepted by the Tate Gallery.

Just before Christmas of that year the Duchess died. Knowing how her mother would have been saddened by the thought that mourning would prevent the family festivities at Belvoir, her daughter Diana announced her death afterwards.

Of all the Souls the Duchess is perhaps the most elusive to describe. Immense beauty tends to overshadow personality. Moreover, the Duchess was a very private person; she was devoted to her family, loving to her friends, passionately dedicated to her art. It is her own art, her perceptive portraits, that best illustrate her friendship with the Souls.

A studio portrait of the Duchess in the 1890s. She habitually wore a sprig of bay pinned to her collar

❧FOUR
Lady Desborough

Very dear are the pair
He so strong, she so fair
Renowned as the *Taplovite Winnies*;
Ah! he roamed far and wide,
Till in *Etty* he spied
A treasure more golden than guineas
George Curzon

In a tribute to Lady Desborough which Lady Diana Cooper wrote for *The Times*, she spoke of

> . . . the years before 1914 when Lady Desborough held a position in the worlds of wit and fashion that nobody has occupied since. Some of them, very few, will recall the closing years of the last century when so many of those who gave colour to the epoch were her most frequent visitors. As a hostess she was an inspiration.

The Duke of Portland, in his memoirs of 1937, encapsulated the compliment: 'Her reputation as a hostess is unrivalled.' It therefore seems fitting that Lady Desborough should be on the cover of this book, posing with her guests after a Sunday luncheon in the summer of 1898.

The joy of Lady Desborough's parties was the brilliance of the talk, its wit, its speed, its fun. Her son-in-law, Lord Gage, said that he had 'never before or since' heard such 'witty, amusing conversation' as he had at Taplow Court. Lady Desborough had the rare gift of inspiring her guests to their most vivacious; even the young and timid found themselves burgeoning into wit under her particular sorcery. Focusing all her short-sighted gaze on her neighbour, as if she were blinkered to the rest of the party, she would ask him some direct and disarming questions to assess his character; such was her perception and skill that the newcomer soon shared his hostess's effervescence. Lady Desborough herself said that one of the qualities she most admired in Oscar Wilde was that he would seek out the most prosaic person in the room and conjure him into being a wit; she herself emulated this, though there can have been few boring guests at the parties she attended. Lady Cynthia Asquith thought it was unlikely that Lady Desborough ever saw people in their duller or more dismal moments, because she herself made them such star performers. She was always said to be 'the making of every party'. 'Ettie was the tuning fork', 'Ettie always at concert pitch', wrote Cynthia Asquith. People talked of her in terms of magnetism, electricity, bright light. Even breakfasts at Taplow, Lady Cynthia recalled, 'were more lively than champagne dinners elsewhere'.

54

Mrs William Grenfell (later Lady Desborough) in 1890. This is the photograph she chose to be included in the album presented to Lord Curzon in 1890

Lady Desborough loved to be surrounded by people – she liked a procession of parties. Orphaned at the age of five, she had been brought up by her aunt, Lady Cowper, and her uncle, both of whom she adored. Lady Cowper was a famed hostess at her country houses, Panshanger, Brocket and Wrest, and Ettie Fane's social gifts were nurtured in a world of houseparties full of celebrities. At the time of her marriage at the age of twenty she knew all London society, old and young, and all the Souls-to-be.

As a debutante, Ettie Fane was greatly admired and courted. Her attractiveness had the allure of an air at the same time vulnerable and aloof. Her graceful figure enhanced her elegance, and she was vivacious and witty. 'Her charm was magnetic,' said the Duke of Portland. Her diaries reveal that she was also susceptible. 'O Heart Leap,' she wrote after one beau came to sit beside her on the sofa. After about a year of temptation and indecision she married for love, and lived happily ever after.

She became engaged to William Grenfell and their marriage took place on 17 February 1887 at St George's, Hanover Square. *The Times* commented on the size and splendour of the congregation, which included the Duke of Clarence. Willy Grenfell was not by worldly standards the most brilliant match. He was not an aristocrat. He did not own a great house; but he had a large estate at Taplow on the Thames near Henley, surrounding a bright modern villa. His family money came from tin mines in Cornwall which had flourished in the 1840s and 1850s and gave him an income which was comfortable though not limitless. But for Ettie Fane he was an ideal husband: he adored her and put her on a pedestal for ever; he was of sterling quality, 'the finest kind of Englishman' who could always be relied on to behave with perfect integrity. Betty Montgomery, the closest friend of Lady Desborough's youth, described him as 'a perfect angel'. With such a husband his diamond-like wife could sparkle: 'She who has her husband with her may turn the moon round her finger,' as Ouida had written.

Besides these fine qualities of character, Willy Grenfell had all the glamour of a hero. He was fabled for his strength, courage and athletic prowess. He was six feet five inches tall, with the physique of a Titan. He swam twice across the pool at the base of Niagara Falls: once for fun and once, during a snow-storm, to prove to a doubting friend that such a feat was possible. The list of his other triumphs fills a whole page of the Duke of Portland's memoirs. To detail a few, he was punting champion of the Thames three years in succession, and he rowed for Oxford in the Boat Race. He was a champion fencer, representing England in the Olympic Games in 1908. His athletic victories tended to dwarf his public work. He was first a Liberal and then a Tory M.P.; he was secretary to Sir William Harcourt, Chancellor of the Exchequer, and he became chairman of 115 committees, including one on that mid-nineteenth-century fascination, bimetallism. One feels that he must have been a little bewildered by the brilliance of his wife – 'Dear Miss Fane, you make me feel like an owl' – but he would have endorsed the words of the Duke of Portland: 'The crowning achievement of his life, athletic or otherwise, was his marriage to Ettie Fane.' Those who knew Lord Desborough recall him as being a very kindly, gentle man. If some of the young and shy found his wife's brilliance too blinding, he would take them off for a walk and a gentle chat. The marriage, apparently of opposites, was one of extreme happiness: 'Ettie absolutely adored old Willy,' said one of her friends.

A woman as alluring as Lady Desborough naturally attracted many admirers. Two Souls adored her all her life: Evan Charteris and John Revelstoke. They admired and respected the great happiness of her marriage; with her they enjoyed that delightful relationship described by Margaret Lane as 'amitié amoureuse', friendship spiced with flirtation. Lord Revelstoke once fell deeply in love with another woman, Nancy Shaw, who, believing him to be in love with Lady Desborough, rejected his proposals and married Waldorf Astor. (Nancy Astor thus became, as mistress of Cliveden, the Desboroughs' neighbour; they occasionally entertained each other, and Lady Astor became a special friend of the young Billy Grenfell.) Evan Charteris, later in life, married Lady Dorothy Grosvenor, who became a latter-day Soul and a good friend of the Desboroughs.

Her son-in-law wrote of her domination over her admirers: 'She had men friends and was highly possessive of them; and that was that.' The long absences of Lord Desborough on committees here and abroad meant that Lady Desborough required escorts. She needed the company and compliments of men, and told Cynthia Asquith that '. . . she was not monogamous in the strict sense of the word, and had never been in love in the way which excluded other personal relationships. To be at her best with one man she must see a great many others.' For enjoyment she needed the society of many friends.

For such an enthusiastic hostess, Taplow Court was a good base for hospitality. Trains from London were frequent, and Taplow was only twenty minutes from Paddington, so guests could come from Saturday to Monday, or even for a Sunday luncheon party. The platform at Taplow station was, by strange coincidence, the longest in England, perfectly suiting the huge number of Lady Desborough's guests. (When the Desboroughs went to London, a special messenger was sent to the station, and the next train – even an express – would be specially stopped. Mr Good, whose father was butler at Taplow, remembers as a very little boy being taken to Taplow as a treat to see the train halted for Lord Desborough.) During the summer Lady Desborough would give perhaps ten Saturday-to-Monday parties, and several Sunday luncheon-parties followed by punting on the Thames or tennis. She also entertained in various houses she took in Mayfair for the season, or in Lady Cowper's house at 4 St James's Square.

As her children grew up she held parties for the Eton boys, sometimes crammed four into a room, and she would also give one or two balls each January for more than one hundred guests. Much of Lady Desborough's entertaining was done for the sake of her children. In 1905 she held a fancy-dress party for the children: her elder daughter Monica, aged eleven, was dressed as a snake-charmer, and opened the cotillon with Archie Gordon; kittens were given as cotillon presents. She was greatly ambitious for them and envisaged brilliant careers and brilliant marriages. Her three sons died tragically young – the eldest two in the Great War – but not before they had fallen in love with children of other Souls, not wholly to her approval – Julian with Lady Marjorie Manners, and Billy with Cynthia Charteris. In 1912 Lady Desborough gave a January fancy-dress ball with 150 guests, who were photographed at the party; Billy was dressed as a Roman centurion, a most impressive figure with his great height. Lady Diana Manners was memorable in her adaptation of the tulle-and-roses costume worn by the dancer Karsavina in Le Spectre de la Rose. The following year at the last winter ball, Monica was carried in in a basket covered with flowers; she jumped out through the petals, and performed a solo dance.

Lady Desborough at Ascot in 1909, escorted by Lord Revelstoke. She was the only Soul who enjoyed racing – most thought it a Philistine pastime

Lady Desborough also gave parties for Ascot; the Souls disliked racing and the racing set, but her worldliness won. 'How *could* you go to Ascot three days, it beats me?' wrote Julian. More than any of the other Souls, Lady Desborough moved in Royal circles. The Prince and Princess of Wales (later Edward VII and Queen Alexandra) came from Windsor to have luncheon at Taplow almost every summer. The Queen was Godmother to her younger daughter Imogen who was born in 1905. In 1911 Lady Desborough became a Lady-in-Waiting to Queen Mary; she accompanied the King and Queen on their state visit to Paris in 1924. She must have been a great asset in court circles; as Margot Asquith said: 'She should have been born in the days of the great kings' mistresses.' One feels that she would have been much at home at Versailles; performing her court duties and at the same time holding a salon, entertaining the most amusing writers and intellectuals of the day. She liked life to be a balance of formality and fun.

From the first years of her marriage Lady Desborough was a hostess to the Souls; her visitors' books show that her weekend parties were a house full of Charterises, Wyndhams, Ribblesdales and Barings – and of course those highly desirable, most eligible bachelors Arthur Balfour, George Curzon and Harry Cust. Balfour had his own room at Taplow Court, the Upper Turret Room; it was always referred to as 'Mr Balfour's room', and other guests had to be content with the Chintz Room, the Alphabet Room or the Japanese Room.

Taplow Court in 1887. The gardens run down to the Thames on the right and the Desboroughs' own first floor rooms overlook the river

Taplow is a strange house, curiously urban. The small forecourt is dwarfed by the tall, looming neo-Tudor villa in bright red brick cruelly unmellowed by time. 'Taplow is a very big house, it looks red outside,' wrote Billy Grenfell, aged four. The house was bought by the Grenfells from the Orkneys in the 1850s, when it was still being remodelled by William Burn, so the Grenfell device is everywhere inserted in patterns above brick windows, doors, porticos. For a house on a country estate the garden is surprisingly small, like a neat municipal park. There is no attempt at a garden in the English sense of the word; according to Billy there were flower beds, 'some in the shape of stars and other round pieces', filled with bright-coloured hardy plants. The lawn was appropriated for croquet or tennis. A Swiss-style chalet was built for Lord Desborough, incorporating a real-tennis court and a gymnasium. The only place where it is possible to stroll is along the celebrated 'Cedar Walk' down to the Thames; but this itself is a history lesson, for every tree was planted by an eminent guest – royalty, diplomats, writers. There is no part of the garden where one can relax and read.

Above. The Library at Taplow Court. The ceiling is of embossed paper, simulating Jacobean plaster

Left. The central hall at Taplow Court. The stags' heads and the elephant-foot vases on the right are Lord Desborough's hunting trophies

Lady Desborough's boudoir, adorned with drawings and photographs of her children. 'A very private sitting room,' said Lady Aberconway, 'where no one, even her family, came uninvited. To be asked there for an intimate talk was the greatest treat and the envy of all fellow guests'

The house inside is equally untranquil. It is built round a high entrance hall, in an ecclesiastical Romanesque style, open and arcaded; every room is visible from the hall. There are no rambling corridors or attic rooms, no sense of privacy at all. The Desboroughs had their own suite, bedroom, dressing-room, bathroom and boudoir, at the back of the house and separated from the other bedrooms on the first floor by a platform and a short flight of stairs. There was nowhere to retreat except for the large ground-floor library, but even this served as a passage between hall and drawing-room. One guest said that the house reminded her of an hotel. Nor did Lady Desborough's taste in décor add any calm to the interior. She liked colours to be vivid. The bedrooms were described as being 'done up' in marigold yellows, orange (her favourite colour), fuchsia-pink and reds. The cushions and curtains were often made from Lady Desborough's discarded evening dresses. Flowers were sometimes artificial. But uncomfortable houses, like uncomfortable chairs, often provoke good conversation; beautiful surroundings can be more soothing than stimulating. Taplow Court was perfectly suited to Lady Desborough's brilliant houseparties.

Taplow is now used as an office building by Plessey; but they have taken good care of it, allowing only minor alterations such as temporary plywood partitions. In many ways it is much as it was in Lady Desborough's heyday: pastel portraits of her and her husband dominate the first-floor gallery; the library, with deep bookshelves and embossed Lincrusta papered ceiling, is little changed since the Souls sat there and played their pencil games.

We know from an article published by Henry Labouchère in his satirical paper, *Truth*, that Lady Desborough sat for an examination in 'Souls' language' in 1893. Like all people who see a lot of each other, and who share the same tastes, and above all the same jokes, the Souls had their own argot, which was known as 'Gang-language'. It was largely based on the Baring and Ponsonby family vocabularies, and much used by that delightful and irreverent tease, Maurice Baring. Obviously the examination paper, which *Truth* quotes, must have been quite difficult to have merited its existence. 'Manchettes', 'eternity soup' and 'six cloisters' all remain obscure. 'Having a dentist' became commonplace in their vocabulary; it meant a heart-to-heart talk, possibly an uncomfortable one. 'Floater', a howler so dreadful that it never sinks into oblivion, is too good not to be in present use. 'Swimgloat' means a gorgeous carefree time. Her son Julian wrote to Lady Desborough that he feared she would give him an 'Archbaker'; Baker had been the gardener at the Barings' house, Membland, and was famous for his loquacity. The common use of 'Gang-language' by the Grenfell and Charteris children as late as the First World War indicates that much of it was everyday parlance.

In that second arcane cult, the 'Games', Lady Desborough was a prize performer. She excelled at any form of charade, for she acted very amusingly. 'I shall always remember with almost more pleasure than anything else you writhing and twisting on the parquet floor in red velvet, your conception of the serpent's tail being one of the greatest triumphs of modern art,' said an admirer. 'Clumps' and 'Telegrams' were played at Panshanger during her later years, and she invented a game of guessing what people might have left behind them after a weekend party which hovered between frankness and fun.

In her account of the Souls Margot Asquith wrote of Lady Desborough that she was '. . . a woman of genius, who, if subtly and accurately described, either in her mode of life, her charm, wits or character would have made the fortune of any novelist'. In talking of Lady Desborough,

her friends automatically use the words 'intelligence', 'charm', 'intuition', until they are tired and tepid. A letter from Julian, written in 1910, evokes some of her fascination:

Mother darling,

You *are* wonderful, your wonder is inexhaustible, and keeps coming on me with the shock of newness every time. I've never had such a good ten minutes as on Friday, and never such a good hour as on Saturday. Your dark depths and your surface fun are so perfectly blended that you can laugh at the deepest and weigh the lightest; and it all runs on a connected and continuous line, a perfect picture with its light and shade. And your sympathy, which gives not only meaning, but the half-tone and the shades of the meaning before it is said, sometimes makes it silly to talk at all. I want to see you again soon because you are far better than anyone else. I don't want to see you again ever, because everyone is like flat soda after you. Advise me what to do . . .

She retained this magic to the end of her life. A grand-daughter's young fiancé who met her in the 1940s was equally captivated: 'Lady Desborough was simply bewitching.'

Ettie Desborough herself would have been the first to admit, with a smile, that she was inartistic. She did not like music at all, and was able to laugh at her dreadful 'floater' when at the age of seventeen she sat next to Sir Hubert Parry, the composer, at a dinner, and opened the conversation by saying, 'I do hate music, don't you?' She was the only Soul to be totally uninterested in the visual arts: not for her William Morris or the Grosvenor Gallery. When in 1891 she and her husband decided to commission portraits of themselves, they chose Ellis Roberts, a minor artist, though he was known among the Souls for having painted Lady Evelyn Charteris and Millicent Sutherland. He produced the two life-size pastels which still hang at Taplow. The representation of Willy Grenfell is conventional. It shows him in a tweed suit with an ulster, and one sees in this early picture how much his son, Julian, came to resemble him. The portrait of Lady Desborough is a shock. It is a pure pastiche of a Gainsborough. She stands in the same pose as the Hon. Mrs Graham, one elbow resting on a column. Her clothes are entirely eighteenth-century: the robe, the dress, the plumed hat. The sole anachronism is her mantle, which has slightly raised shoulders as in the fashion of the late 1880s. It is a mystery why she chose to be depicted in antique dress. For once, and quite untypically, she looks directly at the artist, who has given her huge brown eyes – but the portrait is unrecognizable. The charcoal drawing by Sargent of 1909 (which was probably a gift, for he gave her one of Willy later for their silver wedding) is described by all those who knew her as an excellent likeness; and they remark on the typical way in which her lips are about to break into laughter. 'Lady Desborough, always smiling,' said Anita Leslie, 'always with a twinkle in her eye.'

Lady Desborough was most distinguished in appearance. She was tall, about five feet ten inches, and of an enviable slenderness and grace. People remarked on her dignity of carriage; like the ladies at Versailles, she walked with tiny gliding steps. She always spoke very slowly and very gently; 'Ettie's float voice', Cynthia Asquith called it. She had an abundance of soft, dark hair, which was always beautifully coiffed, either in the chignons of her girlhood or the wide halo style of the 1900s. Photographs of her as a young woman show a face with the elusive shyness of a gazelle. But later photographs, and the Sargent drawing, reveal a face of great character, with deeply-lidded eyes. Her individual looks make her recognizable in any houseparty group. She was short-sighted and rarely looked directly at the camera: the Souls were born before the days of the obligatory smile.

Lady Desborough in 1909, a charcoal drawing by John Singer Sargent.
Those who knew her considered the drawing an excellent likeness

She was lucky to have been born into her epoch, for the fashions of her prime suited her perfectly. Curzon comments on how charmingly she was attired, 'always incomparably dressed, and an epicure's feast for the eye'. Her clothes emphasized her slenderness. Until the First World War, women tended to restrict their choice of colours: they wore white, cream, or stone, or sometimes grey, mauve, or dark blue. White suited her best. One dress of white lace brought forth a note of filial approval. Julian wrote to her in 1915: 'Do get a new gown for when I come, like that one made of lace that you had for my last fourth of June at Eton; when you came over from Versailles for the day, and got marks for it from me and Billa.' Photographs of her at home show her in the white shirts and tightly belted dark skirts which were the informal daytime wear of that date.

Her clothes were made by simple dressmakers, or possibly her maid: Lady Desborough was economical. Grand couturiers she would have regarded as ostentatious. Most of her jewellery had been stolen during a burglary at Taplow soon after her marriage, but later John Revelstoke gave her some beautiful pearls. The diamond crescent shown in the Sargent drawing was a favourite hair-ornament, but she was never adorned in the dog-collar and sautoirs of the Marlborough House set. Her one extravagance was hats; she adored the huge flower-tray bedecked hats favoured in that period, and they suited her admirably.

After the First World War, fashion went rainbow riot. Lady Desborough's clothes (now generously donated to the Brighton Museum) were the colours of semi-precious stones: garnet, coral, turquoise, topaz, often brightened with silver or gold thread. She probably wore her dresses for several years, as they bear traces of remodelling. In the early twenties she patronized the Martine boutique which Poiret had opened at 15 Baker Street, and was influenced by the 'Fauve' colours of the fabrics which he showed. Poiret was much favoured by the Souls, especially Margot Asquith and the daughters of Violet Rutland.

Lady Desborough with her daughter Imogen in about 1912. She is wearing a dress inspired by Poiret, and the photographs show her unvarying elegance

Lady Desborough's choice of dress, in an age when women spent fortunes on clothes, and bought a new wardrobe every season, was symptomatic of a basic sense of thrift. She was very careful about money, though she laughed at her economies. She herself recounted how once she and her husband were travelling to Scotland by night, and went third class; at Norwich Lord Desborough could bear it no longer, and moved into a first-class sleeper. She was quite happy to stay in simple houses, and was much amused when Margot Asquith, invited to a tiny farmhouse Lady Desborough had leased in Scotland, asked, 'Has any gentleman's family ever lived here before?' Country inns did not deter her, and she planned a bicycling holiday in France, in which the Souls should travel on wheel, and the servants follow them by train. She was naturally frugal, a teetotaller, and never smoked. She ate little: a slice of pheasant and a potato sufficed, for she regarded food as sustenance, no more. This quiet and deliberate avoidance of opulence was symptomatic of the Souls' whole way of life.

Extreme self-discipline, even self-denial, was a virtue to the Souls. Of this Curzon is the chief exemplar with his arduous journeys across Persia, his unending attention to work while in constant pain. Lady Desborough had apparently suffered from depression in her youth, and had overcome it by sheer willpower. Her passion for company may have been an antidote. Julian wrote to her about the formation of character:

> I think any doctrine of predestination about character is obviously untrue. Character is *the* thing that you can make and mould for yourself; it is the result of continuous working upon the faculties which one starts with.

Lady Desborough's philosophy excluded sadness and despair; she liked clouds to have golden rather than silver linings; in Margot Asquith's words, 'Her genius lay in a penetrating understanding of the human heart and a determination to redress the balance of life's unhappiness.' This attitude led to what Cynthia Asquith called 'Ettie's stubborn gospel of joy'. Even death itself was not a tragedy; it was to be welcomed as natural. She instilled this doctrine early into her children. When their old Nanny died, Billy wrote from Eton: 'I do hope you are not too sad. Death was for her the true Greek ideal, the kind yet inexorable messenger. She is happy now, I am sure.' Such a philosophy helped Lady Desborough enormously in time to come.

Much of the information we have about the Desborough family comes from *Pages from a Family Journal*, which covers the period from 1888 to 1915. It was published in June 1916, only eleven months after Billy's death. It was intended, said Lord Desborough in a preface, 'for Julian and Billy's brother and sister, and for their most intimate friends'. In fact Ettie's book became, as Lady Cynthia Asquith wrote, 'the topic'. It is oddly disjointed; Lady Desborough refers to herself throughout as 'Julian's mother' or 'Imogen's mother' or whichever is appropriate. The early chapters might be entitled 'Sayings of the Children' (the title of a book later published by Pamela Glenconner); some of their observations are trite, but some amusing. 'Mama, why did you say I might never see that lady again?' Julian asked very loudly in front of Queen Victoria in 1895. 'I do so like reading the Bible, there are such very naughty people in it,' Monica declared. It recounts the holidays she took with the children, the books she read to them, *Treasure Island*, Kipling, Rider Haggard. It tells of the fun they had together: buying shrimps at a fishmonger in Bond Street for the children's tea, staving off Ivo's hunger at the

The family at Taplow, *c*. 1909. The group shows Billy Grenfell (b. 1890), Ivo (b. 1898), Monica (b. 1893), Lady Desborough, Lord Desborough, Julian (b. 1888) and Imogen (b. 1905)

coronation of George V with biscuits and chocolate which she had concealed in her coronet. Other parts of the book could be called 'Lady Desborough's Social Journal'; here are described the countless parties at Taplow, with lists of the eminent guests. Lady Desborough would probably have edited this – fascinating reading though it is for us – if the book had not been produced in such a hurry. She appears as a most loving mother as well as a proud one: no trouble was too great for her to take for her children. When they fulfilled her ambition for them, she was elated. Monica was a swimming champion, and won the Bath Club trophy three years running; this triple triumph was telegraphed to Julian in South Africa.

Julian and Billy were expected to be both academically brilliant and to emulate the athletic feats of their father. Julian won the prize for Latin verse at Eton; at Balliol he rowed and boxed, and starved to jockey weight to ride in point-to-points. Perhaps because of this, his health broke down, and eventually he took a Pass Degree. Billy and Julian were only two years apart in age. Billy was a brilliant scholar and won the Newcastle Scholarship, the highest Eton honour for Classics; the pressure at home must have been intense: 'They had been sleepless for days, almost weeks about it.' Although Billy won the Craven, the greatest Oxford Latin prize, he too failed to get a First. He was tempted by too many talents, and could not fulfil them all. He was also, like his father, an athlete; he ran, and he twice played tennis for Oxford. Teasingly, he once wrote 'These blasted bogus books ruin all', but his true ambition was a Fellowship of All Souls.

Julian had joined the Army in 1910; Billy volunteered in August 1914. It was then thought that 'The whole War might be a matter of months or even weeks.' In 1915 both were fighting in France. Julian enjoyed the war; he liked the danger and the excitement of challenge. He had written poetry for years, in the style of Gilbert Murray's translations of Greek dramas, with their irresistible swaying Swinburnian rhythms; his favourite play was *Hippolytus*. In April 1915 he wrote a poem which his mother liked so much she sent it (having made some minor alterations) to *The Times* where it was published under the title of 'Into Battle'. The first stanza praises the glory of dying for one's country:

> The naked earth is warm with spring
> And with green grass and bursting trees
> Leans to the sun's kiss glorying,
> And quivers in the loving breeze;
> And life is Colour and Warmth and Light
> And a striving evermore for these;
> And he is dead who will not fight;
> And who dies fighting has increase.

The last verses of the poem describe the thrill of battle:

> And when the burning moment breaks
> And all things else are out of mind,
> And Joy of Battle only takes
> Him by the throat and makes him blind
> The thundering line of battle stands
> And in the air Death moans and sings;
> And Day shall clasp him with strong hands,
> And night shall fold him with soft wings.

The poem was Julian's masterpiece. Henry James praised its 'extraordinary ringing and stinging verses'. Many considered it the finest poem of the Great War.

In May 1915 Julian was hit by a shell; he received a wound in the brain which was at first considered not grave, but after a few days it was apparent it might be fatal. Lord and Lady Desborough and Monica, now aged twenty-three and a nurse at Wimereux, were all the time at Julian's bedside. Billy sent a philosophical letter from Hooge trying to comfort his parents: '*Sed miles, sed pro patria*'. Lady Desborough's deliberately unemotional, bravely objective account of Julian's death still reduces the reader to tears. She printed some of the letters of sympathy she received; some are heart-rending, others congratulate her on sacrificing her son for her country. In July Billy was killed, instantly, leading a charge at Hooge.

Lady Desborough published her Journal; she built a war memorial for the boys in the garden, with a statue of Apollo in his chariot, and 'Phoebus Apollo', Julian's last words, carved underneath. On the back of the memorial was inscribed Julian's poem.

'It is the end of one's youth, all this,' wrote Cynthia Asquith. 'Ettie and poor Willy. How can they face such utter desolation, such extinction of joy, glamour and hope. I remember them [Julian and Billy] so well as little curly-headed boys in white the first time they came to Stanway.' But Lady Desborough's wonderful valour helped her to overcome the tragedy:

She inspires one with tremendous admiration. There seems nothing stained and artificial about her marvellous courage, just a sort of alchemy which has translated tragedy to the exclusion of all gloom. . . . Her determination to go on fighting with broken tools and to save whatever was still worth keeping was wholly admirable.

She refused to wear mourning, she went on seeing her friends, and chatting and making jokes. Her courage was an inspiration: Letty Elcho said that Lady Desborough had greatly comforted her wild grief when her husband was killed, and Mary Elcho's daughter remembers with admiration her braveness at this time.

In 1926 her youngest son Ivo was killed in a car crash at the age of twenty-eight. Those who knew her well said that this useless tragedy saddened her far more than the deaths of Julian and Billy in the glory of battle.

Lady Desborough lived until 1952, and the legend of the Souls lived with her. In 1913 she inherited Panshanger from her aunt Lady Cowper, and from then on the Desboroughs lived there in the winter. She put in a tremendous central heating system, bathrooms, and five tennis courts, but would return to Taplow at Easter for the summer, giving, incongruously, a Christmas party at Easter for the Taplow tenants. She continued to entertain old Souls friends, and the amusing and promising young.

Weekend parties at Taplow in the twenties and thirties were recalled with nostalgia by the guests: 'It was all such fun.' The hostess expended her legendary charm on her old friends and her youthful guests alike. Newcomers on approbation were taken by Lady Desborough for a walk in the garden 'to have a dentist', so she could discover and assess their talents. The weekend was fully organized. Nine-o'clock breakfast began the day, the hostess presiding at the table in sparkling form till the last sleepy guest came down. Various sports were suggested, croquet or punting parties on the Thames. Lady Desborough herself would play tennis in a long white flannel skirt, partnered by a former Davis Cup player whose practised strokes fortified her gentle lobs. The legendary 'Games' continued, played in the afternoon and after dinner. There was an imaginative mixture of guests; girls and boys of eighteen were invited with politicians, writers and painters. A debutante might find herself seated next to Mr Balfour or Rudyard Kipling at dinner, a juxtaposition that delighted each equally.

Lady Desborough managed the transition from the elegance of her youth to the hideous fashions of the twenties with great style, by simply taking no notice. For the daytime she adopted a slim hobble skirt in the style of 1912, its hem just above the ankle. She preserved all her distinction of appearance, but even in smiling photographs her face shows the evidence of many tears.

Lord Desborough died in 1945, and Lady Desborough moved permanently to Panshanger, where, as her aunt 'Ka' Cowper had done in her widowhood, she lived in a small sitting-room at the back of the house. Visitors came: Queen Mary, Winston Churchill, Harold Macmillan. The family stayed, and talked and laughed. The 'Games' continued: rhyming games, 'Telegrams', 'Clumps'. A grandchild who played them said that success came not from erudition, but from vivacity and wit. These two qualities always remained with Lady Desborough, as did a greater one, her indomitable uncomplaining courage.

✿ FIVE
Harry and Nina Cust

Harry Cust could display
Scalps as many, I lay
From Paris as in Piccadilly.
    George Curzon

The first time I ever saw Harry Cust was in Grosvenor Square, where he had come to see my sister Laura. A few weeks later I found her making a sachet, which was an unusual occupation for her, she told me it was for 'Mr Cust', who was going to Australia for his health.

So wrote Margot Asquith, painting a picture of the perfect Victorian present being confected for the perfect Victorian cavalier. None the less it is not surprising to find that Laura, the most enslaving young woman of her time, had herself been enslaved. The first, almost hypnotic, impression of Harry Cust must always have been of the piercing blue stare from his beautiful eyes; but he was notorious for his immaculate – even dandified – clothes and his negligent yet always unruffled elegance. Lady Diana Cooper remembers, in an affectionate picture of the man now acknowledged to be her father:

Very beautiful, I thought him, with noble hands and impeccable filbert-shaped nails. He wore a coat such as I never saw another wear – dark blue cloth, flaring full, with a flat sable Eton collar. It was like Holbein's *Ambassadors*.

This cool exterior masked a turbulent and compulsive *homme à femmes*; for him the consuming love-affair was as necessary to his survival as breathing. Inevitably people with a more conventionally regulated life were bound to disapprove. The strait-laced members of his circle, who could not bring themselves to mention his romantic escapades, took refuge in deploring the way he did his hair; the quiff carelessly flung back from his forehead they considered vulgar.

At Eton Cust had been Captain of the Oppidans (the main body of the school, as distinct from the scholars). In his brilliant early years he excelled with incomparable ease and grace at both intellectual and athletic pursuits. At Trinity College, Cambridge, he was judged (in the words of his obituary) to be 'a man possessed of excellent brains and a tongue that could say sharp things if the owner pleased'. His literary executor, Charles Whibley, called him 'this gay and gracious spoilt child of Eton and Cambridge'. He was called to the English Bar, but went on to take the French *Baccalauréat en Droit* because it was more difficult and also 'more fun'. He also served two terms as a Unionist Member of Parliament, only finally losing his seat in the Liberal landslide of 1906. His political career hardly lived up to the expectations of one of his Eton masters who, according to A. C. Benson, had picked out Cust in preference to Rosebery and Curzon as the most likely to become Prime Minister. Yet he would have been most unsuitable for that high office. He often indulged in rashly flippant political quips, one of the most famous being on the subject of Tariff Reform, of which he remarked: 'My position is quite clear, I have nailed my colours to the fence.'

Cust was a poet of some distinction. His 'Non Nobis Domine' was included, at first anonymously, in the *Oxford Book of Verse* during his lifetime, and a selection of his poems, many of which had appeared as 'occasional verses' in the *Pall Mall Gazette*, was published the year after his death in a small volume edited by his wife and his nephew, Sir Ronald Storrs. His editorship of the *Pall Mall Gazette*, which began in 1892 and ended in 1896, was a brief but memorable episode in the annals of journalism.

His amorous exploits were as numerous as they were well known. They resulted in a number of unacknowledged children. In 1893 he was more or less forced to marry the silent and reserved Emmeline (Nina) Welby-Gregory; he submitted only after intense social pressure from the 'highest quarters'. The union was a miserable one until the last years of his life, when, ill and disappointed, he finally established a rapport with his wife.

Cust's life was dominated – and to a great extent blighted – by the constantly present mirage of his expectations. As the heir to his cousin Lord Brownlow, a man who was his near contemporary, he felt wealth and position were tantalizingly near; yet in fact they were ungraspable. Much of his life was frittered away in waiting for an inheritance which he did not live to enjoy. His political career and his editorship of the *Pall Mall Gazette*, to which his talents were so perfectly suited, should have engaged his serious attention, but they were to him mere stop-gaps while he awaited the ownership of Belton and Ashridge.

A sculpture of Harry Cust
by his wife Nina. It stands
on the staircase of Belton
House, the seat of his cousin,
Lord Brownlow

Right. Harry Cust by
Violet Granby (later
Duchess of Rutland),
signed with initials and
dated 1892. This was
one of the drawings included
in the album of portraits by
the Duchess which appeared
in 1900

18G92

It was inevitable that with his looks – as a youth he had been described as having the profile of a Greek coin – his reckless wit and disarming charm Harry Cust would be in the very centre of the Souls' circle. Margot Asquith wrote of him that he was 'in some ways the rarest and most brilliant of them all'. In his obituary notice in *The Times*, Lord Curzon wrote:

> He was the unchallenged leader of the dinner-table. Quip, retort, repartee, quotation, allusion, epigram, jest – all flashed with lightning-like speed from that active workshop, his brain.

Harry Cust became a member of Wilfrid Blunt's Crabbet Club through his friendship with George Wyndham and George Curzon, and attended his first 'Saturday-to-Monday' at Crabbet in July 1891. Lady Anne Blunt, organizing with some difficulty accommodation for this invasion of twenty young men, speculated on whether Cust would expect a room to himself. The sybaritic Oscar Wilde, who was a guest on the same occasion, had of course to have his own room, but George Leveson Gower remembered sleeping three to a room, an arrangement clearly only for the hardy.

Harry Cust at Aston Clinton, *c*.1890, from Lady Battersea's photograph album. All the visitors were elaborately posed for the portraits in it and the whole operation must have been a feature of that particular visit

Cust inevitably excelled in the Club's poetic contests; yet perhaps his most significant poem, on 'Marriage', written in 1892, was only runner-up. It begins:

Cust, who at sundry times in manners many
Spake unto women – and is speaking still –
Eager to find if ever or if any
One would obey and hearken to his will . . .

In the third and last verse he assumes – rashly as things turned out – that his agreeable career of philandering bachelorhood would continue:

Yet even cursed Cust, who may not nibble
These darling dainties made for married man,
May envy still the spouse of Lady Sibell
And bow before the Lord of Lady Anne.
Various vigorous virgins may have panted,
Willing widows wilted in the dust: –
To no female has the great God granted
Grace sufficient to be Mrs Cust.

The poem is full of unintentional irony, for in the following year Cust found himself forced to 'nibble those darling dainties made for married men' with a wife he had not chosen and could not love. Arthur Balfour had more than once been given the unwelcome task of intervening to prevent some disaster brought about by Cust's insatiable appetites, and this time he had to insist that Cust should marry Miss Welby-Gregory although he was then in love with Pamela Wyndham. He submitted, but with a bad grace, and continued to lead his accustomed social life almost entirely without his wife's assistance. Harry Cust wrote to Sibell Grosvenor, his confidante at this trying time, of his feelings:

Except by English law I am not one bit married save to Pamela only. Not before God and still less before my legal wife: of the ways of married women, of merest touch of hand or glance of eye there is not the faintest possible remotest question.

In 1892 Harry Cust had taken over the editorship of the *Pall Mall Gazette*, offered to him over the luncheon-table by the new owner, the American millionaire William Waldorf Astor. He had accepted, although, as his obituary makes plain, 'he knew nothing of newspapers and had never attempted journalism'. He proceeded during his sadly brief reign to gather a galaxy of talent around him. The manager, Henry Leslie, went so far as to say: 'He was the best editor the *Pall Mall* ever had.' The mordant wit, the sharp observation of the comments, the faintly satirical tone of the political reports, and the unusually literate style of the other articles, all reflect the brilliant personality of the editor. A passage from Curzon's Crabbet Club poem on 'Sin', the subject set for 1893, suggests how much the style of the paper had altered since the days of John Morley's highly respected editorship:

The *Pall Mall* under Cust
Shall ennoble forms of lust
That might have shocked the sensitive and
    squeamish soul of Stead.

The reference in the last line is to the notorious court case which resulted in the imprisonment of W. T. Stead after he published articles about child prostitution in the *Gazette*. But Cust's coat-trailing was of an entirely different order. A relentless flippancy masked the seriousness of his intentions, and it has often been said that he was deprived of his job because he was too funny for the taste of the owner. Astor seems to have sensed a more fundamental irresponsibility, as the following note, taxing Cust with his erratic attendance at the editorial offices, shows:

> Dear Mr Cust,
>
> I have decided to adopt your good suggestion that I should call 'any morning at 7.30' at the Gazette office, and see the busy morning's work commenced at that early hour. I intend to arrive there at 7.45 and wait ten minutes to see whoever is in charge. If no one of the staff of the paper can be found at 7.55 I shall leave this note. You always get the better of me on so many points that it makes me merry to be able to score now and then.

Astor scored only too effectively in 1896 when he dismissed Cust without even the usual month's notice. He gave a number of reasons, none of which seem convincing enough to explain his inflexible decision that Cust should leave forthwith. With hindsight it seems unnecessary to seek far for the real reason: Cust, with habitual recklessness, had rejected every one of the contributions submitted by his employer for publication. Astor was a published author of two historical works – *Valentine* (about Caesar Borgia) in 1885 and *Sforza* (1889) – if not an experienced journalist, and might have expected a more courteous hearing from his editor. So Cust's inflexible concern for quality cost him an occupation ideally suited to his talents and temperament.

H. G. Wells has a memorable passage in his *Experiment in Autobiography* describing the flamboyant style of life in Cust's office:

> I remember it as a magnificent drawing-room; Fleet Street hath not its like today. There was certainly one grand piano in it, and my memory is inclined to put in another. There was a vast editor's desk, marvellously equipped, like a desk out of Hollywood. There were chairs and sofas. But for a moment I saw nobody amidst these splendours. I advanced slowly across a space of noiseless carpet. Then I became aware of a sound of sobbing and I realised that someone almost completely hidden from me lay prostrate on a sofa indulging in paroxysms of grief.
>
> In the circumstances a cough seemed to be the best thing. There upon the sound from the sofa ceased abruptly and a tall blond young man sat up, stared and then stood up, put away his pocket handkerchief and became entirely friendly and self-possessed.

Wells never discovered what the bother was about; the mystery was not elucidated until many years later when Peter Quennell taxed his friend Richard Wyndham to provide an explanation for this untrammelled grief: he unhesitatingly replied, 'That must have been Aunt Pamela'.

The luxury of the office appointments was a typical Cust 'tease': no one was more adept at lavish spending, and he saw in Astor an immensely rich man whose money was simply there to be spent. There is no doubt that Astor had much to complain of, but his remedy was savage.

The years that followed were bleak and disappointing. Cust was no longer in Parliament. It was said that he lost his seat because he neglected it, but he had in any case become aware of the difficulty of combining his editorship with his parliamentary duties. He did not stand for Parliament again until 1900.

In the years after his departure from the *Gazette* there must, in spite of the stimulating company of the Souls, have been a fair number of unoccupied hours. Cust had one notable game for passing the time in dull company: 'Boring the Bore'. Walter Raleigh describes this grinding experience in a letter: 'He does it by flat interminable reminiscences of his childhood, till even the Bore screams.' This ploy was certainly the more effective as it was in such painful contrast to his usual flashing wit. As Charles Whibley said of him: 'Cust was the best talker of his day.'

In 1902 Harry Cust was host at the famous dinner-party immortalized by H. G. Wells in his political novel *The New Machiavelli*. The occasion was enlivened by an outbreak of fire on an upper floor of the house; when informed, the host simply replied: 'We have not finished dinner; bring on the next course and ring up the fire brigade.' When a member of the fire brigade suggested that the party should disperse, Cust is said to have expostulated: 'What, send my guests away before dinner is over? I never heard of such a thing!' As water poured through the ceiling the remainder of the evening was spent with the accompaniment of bath-towels and footbaths. The entertainment of the conversation may well have overcome anyone's desire to escape the discomfort of being soaked with dirty water. The main subject of discussion was in fact not in itself very alluring: it was Government policy on education, so it is tempting to see the gesture as simply an attempt to add to the store of Cust myths. H. G. Wells actually said in the novel: 'I remember that afterwards Tarville was accused of having planned the fire to make his dinner a marvel and a memory.' The artist in Wells supplied a more likely reason for this feat of endurance on the part of Tarville's guests. He made the subject of conversation the very much more exciting one of the sacking of the Summer Palace in Peking in 1900 after the suppression of the Boxer Rising, with gruesome descriptions of the looting and pillaging by respectable European wives, who are described as casting aside lengths of silk with exclamations of disgust when they are found to be bloodstained.

Harry Cust died of heart failure in 1917 at the early age of fifty-five. During the war years he had served with distinction as Chairman of the fund-raising Central Committee for National Patriotic Organizations. He is buried at Belton, the beautiful Lincolnshire property which he did not live to inherit, and is commemorated by a life-size recumbent portrait figure carved in alabaster by his devoted wife, his pet bulldog at his feet. Lobengula, called after a bloodthirsty Matabele chieftain, became an habitué of the Pall Mall office, as much part of his master's editorial image as the immaculate shirtsleeves and the cigarette in an elegant holder immortalized by Spy in a *Vanity Fair* cartoon of 1894. It is appropriate that he should take the place of the crusader's hound on the monument.

The story of Nina Cust is one of obsessive love. The beautiful, intellectual, shy wife of Harry Cust devoted all her married life – and the thirty-seven years of her widowhood – to the total worship of one who treated her with humiliation and neglect and who kept her concealed as if she were a not very reputable mistress, so much so that some of the second generation of Souls did not even know that Harry Cust had ever married.

Nina Welby-Gregory was the daughter of Sir Glyn Welby-Gregory and Victoria Stuart Wortley. Her father's estate, Denton near Grantham in Lincolnshire, lay between the Belton estates of Lord Brownlow and the vast acres of the Vale of Belvoir: Lady Welby-Gregory was

Nina Welby-Gregory before
her engagement to Harry
Cust, photographed by Lord
Battersea at an Aston Clinton
houseparty

herself a grand-daughter of the fifth Duke of Rutland. Before her marriage she had been a Maid of Honour to Queen Victoria and had the reputation of an intellectual, writing, according to Lady Tweedsmuir, philosophical books that were not very comprehensible to most of her relations and readers. She was a celebrated needlewoman, and founded and funded the Decorative Arts Needlework Society, an offshoot of the Royal School of Needlework. Her daughter inherited her interest in art and was sent to the Académie Jullian to study.

Nina was a beautiful girl, a brunette with huge bewildered eyes, and a graceful figure, thin rather than slender. Violet, Duchess of Rutland, both a cousin and a neighbour, early recognized her loveliness and made her a protégée: she drew a portrait of Nina in 1892 heavily veiled and with downcast eyes, depicting the innocence and reticence of the young girl. Two years later the Duchess was to encourage Alfred Gilbert to make a sculpture of Nina; the work shows her as pensive and soulful.

Nina Cust: one of several pencil drawings by Violet,
Duchess of Rutland. This drawing was also reproduced
in her album of portraits

The marriage of Harry and Nina took place quietly – indeed, for the heir of the Brownlows, almost furtively. There was a simple announcement in the *Morning Post* of 16 October 1893:

A marriage has recently taken place between Mr Henry Cust, M.P. and Miss Welby, daughter of Sir William and the Hon. Lady Welby-Gregory of Denton, Lincolnshire. Mr and Mrs Cust have left England for the Continent.

A few months later the gossip column of the *New York Herald* remarked on 25 February 1894:

A small cloud that appeared on the horizon a few weeks ago has assumed such thunder-like proportions that the 'Souls' are in doubt about themselves. Mr Henry Cust, M.P., the clever editor of the *Pall Mall Gazette*, is a 'Soul', but he took unto himself a wife, I believe not a 'Soul', which gave offence in the club. I don't know whether he has resigned yet, but he has given notice of resigning his seat in Parliament on account of his heavy journalistic work.

It seems that poor Nina was completely ostracized by the Souls, although by beauty, birth and talent no one was more equipped to enter the circle. Various reasons may be conjectured: there was perhaps a suspicion that she inveigled Harry into marriage when he was in love with Pamela Wyndham, and when it was thought they would become engaged. There might even have been a temporary resentment that someone outside the circle should have captured this dazzling bachelor, who was also one of the great *partis* of England: although Harry Cust was not a rich man, he was heir to Lord Brownlow, to palatial Ashridge in the Chilterns, a vast opulent house with a marble ballroom and sumptuous salons designed for entertaining, and to the beautiful seventeenth-century house Belton, set in many acres of green Lincolnshire countryside.

A plaster bust of Nina Cust by Alfred Gilbert. It was made between May and October 1894 and required twenty-four sittings

Nina could probably have been forgiven after a time, had Harry helped her; but he did not. He was not only unfaithful, but completely negligent; as if ashamed of her, he never took Nina out with him, but left her at home night after night in their Westminster house in Delahaye Street while he went to parties given by his old friends. Nina did not have the spirit to overcome this oblivion. She lacked social ambition, and had none of the intense zest for life which characterized the Souls. Without competitiveness, she was 'a presence in a room which made few demands on anyone'; she simply wanted to be a loving wife to the man she idolized.

Harry's neglect saddened Nina. Lady Tweedsmuir, who loved her, wrote:

> She had a kind of moonlight charm as she smiled slightly, like the moon coming out from behind a cloud. . . . Nina's smile was less amused and more ironic as the harshness of life pressed more strictly upon her.

She was obviously very lonely. Her cousin by marriage, Sybil Cust, who was pitying rather than admiring of Nina, described her in 1898 as 'Nina *in statu quo* who clings closer than a limpet'. Again she wrote somewhat condescendingly of her staying at Belton in 1915:

> Here is Nina, only I've not seen her yet; she's more ill than usual, having tired herself with sending thousands of written letters in all languages to every country in Europe, with a statement on the Mind of England about the War. It is pathetic, for I really don't think half of them will be read, or do any good if they are.

This photograph of Nina Cust belonged to Lady Tweedsmuir, who loved Nina and described her beauty as 'a moon behind a cloud'

Lord and Lady Brownlow, by compensation, liked Nina very much. She was often at Ashridge or Belton, with or without Harry. Two portraits of her, showing her in all her frail, vulnerable prettiness, hang in the Wyatt room at Belton, the house of which she would have been châtelaine. Lady Tweedsmuir's family, too, were very devoted to Nina, and they disliked Harry. Those who knew them both took sides; those who loved Nina found Harry cold and caustic; those who enjoyed Harry's company thought Nina shy and dull. But Nina was unswerving and loyal always in her love for Harry.

Towards the end of a life which had become dissipated by drink, he returned to the ever-open arms of Nina, who cherished him until his death in 1917. She then set about two acts of widow's piety. The poems of Harry – most of which were written to other women – she had privately printed under the guidance of Harry's nephew, Ronald Storrs. She then undertook a colossal labour, the carving of a life-size memorial to her husband. This eccentric work is now in the chapel at Belton. Harry Cust looks world-weary and no longer golden, wrapped in some quasi-ecclesiastical robes. The base is composed of an ornate intertwining of dense leaves, somewhat in the style of Grinling Gibbons, who had adorned some of the rooms at Belton with similar harvest festival swags. The effigy is inscribed as if it were to Sir Lancelot: 'Of all sorts enchantingly beloved. Full of noble device'. More strange, at the foot is the inscription '*Sed pro patria*'; but it was not fighting for his country in the Great War that Harry Cust died. Nina may have been influenced to make this memorial by the example of the Duchess of Rutland, whom she so much admired and envied, and in her admiration imitated. She made a copy of the effigy, and kept it in her drawing-room in Chancellor's House in Hyde Park Gate, the seventeenth-century house where they lived together at the end of Harry's life, and where Nina spent the long years of her widowhood.

The two effigies are rumoured to have taken seven long years to complete; Nina's sculpture was inspired more by devotion than talent. Visitors to her house in the twenties recall her draped in long black veils, sitting by the monument. Some found her grief disturbing, and Nina an insubstantial ghost. She lived to be nearly ninety, and when she died in 1955 she was buried with Harry in the tomb she had carved at Belton.

Harry Cust's tomb, carved by Nina Cust. She herself is now buried there. Above the monument is inscribed 'Of all sorts enchantingly beloved, Full of noble device', and on the base is written in Greek 'His posthumous reputation will be the height of great mindedness'

The sage comment of the worldly Lady Leslie on Nina Cust was 'A beautiful blue-stocking'. Nina's real world was the tempting escape-world of books and scholarly research into the past. Her study on the Teutonic mediaeval knights, *Gentlemen Errant*, was much praised for its erudition. The author was quite at home with the rugged German dialects of her sources, and read Latin with ease. The book recounts the various picaresque journeyings across Europe made by four German knights, whose achievements inspired her to passages of lyrical prose. 'They have seen and known much; cities of men and manners, courts and the ways of kings. They have tossed in ships, and made the long roads their home. They have loved in haste, and married at leisure, and on the ringing plains of Europe they have drunk delight.' Though it is a romance, the author has taken pains to acquaint herself with the necessary military technicalities, including such instruments of war as those vast battering rams, the Stork and the Cat, each of which contained three hundred men. Nor does she flinch from describing the brutality of warfare and the horrors of the plague. Yet what appeals to her is chivalry. Her favourite hero is Wilwolt of Schaumberg, who fell deeply in love with an unknown lady; 'high and holy were their vows of mutual affection'. To visit her he had to swim across a moat and climb a ladder attached to her high window; one stormy day the ladder blew away and she sheltered him for three days and nights, feeding him with Rhenish wine and sweetmeats she stole from the table. Alas, such *amour courtois* was not to be Nina's lot, and she wrote with feeling of the camp followers, 'the multifarious cloud of females which then invariably followed the armies of Europe', whose role was to 'nurse their owners in sickness and comfort them in health'.

In 1928 she published a now little-known account of the travels of her grandmother, Lady Emmeline Stuart-Wortley, and her mother, Victoria, called *The Wanderers*. It is a delightful description of the enterprising journeys of two aristocratic ladies to America, Spain, and the Holy Land, learned yet light and amusing. The anthology which she published when nearly ninety, *A Tub of Goldfishes* (a title which is a quotation from Keats), shows a most varied and up-to-date reading, and includes quotations from Edith Sitwell, Lawrence Durrell and Dilys Powell. Even this, published thirty-three years after his death, was dedicated to Harry Cust.

Hyde Park Gate had large and lofty rooms, and Nina's décor made it seem like a house in the country. The windows were shaded by trees, and in time the roses and magnolias in the 'Sleeping Beauty' garden grew wild and filled the London air with fragrance. Nina lived there peacefully, still wearing the trailing, lacy clothes of her girlhood, with her Edwardian straw hat on the chair beside her. In her old age she preserved the memories of her girlhood like a pot-pourri. She received a few close friends, but she was increasingly isolated from life by her deafness. When she died her house was demolished, and Enid Bagnold, who lived opposite, looked with horrified fascination at an equestrian sculpture of Harry, which had stood in Nina's bedroom, being pulverized by the electric drill of the contractors.

The tale of Nina Cust is a strange one; but it is not tragic. She found her vocation in life in her love for Harry; doubtless she was disillusioned and suffered much, but her memories of him in her long widowhood were loyal, happy, perhaps even golden. The remark which Harry made just before his death could be a fit epitaph for Nina:

There are vacancies which only silences may dare to inhabit, which set to those whose very own they are, give out a flooding of music all life long.

❧ SIX

The Wyndhams

The Wyndhams were truly a Souls' family; between them they could muster at least ten members of the very inner circle of friends, and the families were to be united by marriage in two generations. Pamela Wyndham and Edward Tennant were followed by young Percy Wyndham and Diana Lister, the Ribblesdales' daughter. But the Wyndhams differ from the Tennants in one important respect; the older generation was as important as the younger one. Percy and Madeline Wyndham were the pivot round which their famous Easter gatherings revolved. Among their contemporaries, the Pembrokes, the Brownlows and the Cowpers, the respected and sometimes awesome elders benignly presided over a decorous Saturday-to-Monday, the tranquil days punctuated by poetry-reading and strolling on the lawn in the sun, the ladies protected by parasols. But such elegant diversions were possible only because their households at Panshanger, Ashridge and Wilton were without children.

The Wyndhams' establishment at Clouds, on the other hand, teemed with children, and formidable children at that. They were notorious for their unruly behaviour and the other children who played in the gardens of Belgrave Square, where the Wyndhams had their London house, were warned not to play with 'those wild Wyndhams', for fear that the contamination would spread.

Bred with all the lack of self-consciousness that characterizes the old landed families, Percy Wyndham himself stood out as original among the individualistic aristocracy of his day, and even among his own notably eccentric family. The younger but favourite and indulged son of the first Lord Leconfield, he had early been able to bend life to his will, and he adopted a style of life which, unexceptional in his youth, became increasingly out of step with the times. Even his clothes, though immaculate, were quite unlike those worn by his contemporaries. He had found a type of trousers and jacket that he liked, and he saw no reason for wearing any other kind. The jacket was an odd – possibly unique – type of tailcoat; the trousers were of pale-coloured nankeen, a buff or yellow cotton cloth originally from Nanking in China, and much used in the early years of the nineteenth century. Sir Henry Newbolt, visiting Robert Bridges in 1896, noticed the poet's 'narrow lavender-grey trousers of nankeen, a material then so obsolete that I never saw it worn by any other man, except, I think, Mr Wyndham of Clouds'.

His conversation was punctuated with expletives and blasphemies in a way commonplace in his young days but remarkable in the more genteel climate of the late nineteenth century.

Madeline Wyndham, c.1860, from an album assembled by Rosalind Howard, Countess of Carlisle. The photographer has captured her shy beauty and charm

His wife, Madeline, the seventh daughter of Sir Guy and Lady Campbell, adorned his pleasant life with, to quote Edith Olivier, her 'captivating jumble of genius, beauty and charm'. No doubt she inherited these qualities from her celebrated grandparents, the ill-fated Irish patriot Lord Edward Fitzgerald and the legendary Pamela – *la belle Pamela* – supposed daughter of the renegade Bourbon prince, Philippe Egalité, and Mme de Genlis.

Madeline Wyndham's appearance was recorded in the magnificent portrait by G. F. Watts, painted in 1877 and shown at the inaugural exhibition of the Grosvenor Gallery, to which the Wyndhams also lent a Whistler, one of the then highly controversial 'Nocturnes'. Henry James, who noticed the Watts portrait in his review of the exhibition, records the comment of his companion: 'It is what they call a "sumptuous" picture. That is, the lady looks as if she had thirty thousand a year.' The subject must have been surprised by this reaction for her dress, while scarcely plain, is conspicuously 'aesthetic' in taste. It was Mrs Wyndham's aim to achieve her effects by means of taste rather than of lavish expenditure. She had a true genius for living, devoting her many gifts of mind and spirit to the enrichment of her own life and that of her family. Madeline Wyndham adored her children; yet while she is depicted by Watts as a monumental maternal figure, that image belies the sparkling beauty and ready wit remembered by her elder son, George.

She was an accomplished amateur artist, painting with easy skill views that pleased her, as well as lively and detailed pictures of the interiors at Petworth House in Sussex, the principal seat of the Wyndham family. She was also proficient at embroidery, which she designed as well as executed. A bookcase curtain worked by her, possibly to her own design, was included in the contribution sent by the Royal School of Needlework to the Philadelphia Centennial Exhibition in 1876. The Wyndhams had been involved in the founding of the School in the early seventies – it was almost monopolized by the friends who formed the early nucleus of the Souls' circle – and when it achieved charitable status in 1878 Percy Wyndham became one of the seven nominal shareholders. One of the most ambitious of Edward Burne-Jones's needlework designs for the School, the large-scale *Poesia* which was usually executed in outline in brown wool crewel-work, was worked in full colour for Clouds. The cartoon, owned by Percy Wyndham, was an enlargement of one of a series of designs for embroidery made by Burne-Jones for Frances Horner's sister Agnes Jekyll. The type of 'Art Needlework' evolved at the school and practised by Madeline Wyndham, her daughter Pamela and Frances Horner, was among the most successful of their many artistic efforts, a notable example being the huge angel with great red wings embroidered by Frances Horner after a design by Burne-Jones, which hangs in the church at Mells.

Madeline Wyndham also set herself to master the tricky technique of enamelling on metal. She became a pupil of Alexander Fisher, whose work she greatly admired, and became proficient at his method of jewel-like 'Limoges'-style work. It was a proud moment in 1898 when her enamel of 'St Francis receiving the Stigmata' was accepted for exhibition by the Royal Academy. In 1896 Wilfrid Blunt recorded in his *Diaries* having seen her at work:

> She took me away with her to see some enamelwork she is learning to do at the studio of one Fisher, and I was shown all the process of mixing the colours, ground glass with water, and arranging them on a silver plate and burning them on a small oven . . . the best thing there was one of Madeline's own, two peacocks.

Edith Olivier remembered:

> She loved the surprises which are created by the enamellist's oven when the original colours are almost completely changed as the fire takes the bit between its teeth.

Above. Enamel triptych by Madeline Wyndham in a chased silver frame. The influence of her master, Alexander Fisher, is apparent

Left. Cartoon for the embroidery *Poesia*, designed by Sir Edward Burne-Jones for the Royal School of Needlework, and executed in colour for Clouds

The Wyndhams' five children were all born at 44 Belgrave Square, their London house from the year of their marriage. The two eldest, Mary and George, and the youngest, Pamela, were all members of the Souls' circle; in fact the Wyndham family might almost be said to form the core of the group. This was partly due to Arthur Balfour's lifelong attachment to Mary (who became Lady Elcho) and his political involvement with George Wyndham, for whose career he was entirely responsible; but collectively the family represented every aspect of the ideal Soul.

The Wyndham children were brought up in an ideal climate of love and freedom in which optimism and self-confidence could flourish and their charm and latent talents could develop to their fullest extent. In every way far ahead of her time, Madeline Wyndham never muffled her children in the stiff, scratchy and stifling clothes of the miniature adult which were thought to be the appropriate wear in those days. The boys wore traditionally patterned navy jerseys and shorts; the girls simple dresses of plain cloth. Photographs show them looking free and at ease, the envy of their friends.

The children were fascinated by their romantic inheritance, the whisper of a half-told story, the heady mixture of French and Irish blood which gave them, rightly, a feeling of being out of the ordinary. A royal prince in the shadows, and the acknowledged descent from a legendary beauty, invested their own outstanding looks with a magical aura.

This large family attracted many visitors of all ages. Both Percy and Madeline had innumerable and interesting relatives, in addition to a host of friends. At Belgrave Square and at houseparties in the country, the Percy Wyndhams displayed their natural lavish and kindly instincts. Lady Cynthia Asquith remembers, with incredulity, the scale of her mother's hospitality at Belgrave Square:

> There, my governess and myself could always propose ourselves to luncheon, for – hospitality now difficult to credit – she kept open house for this meal to which numerous people could come any day without giving any notice whatever.

Although this habit of keeping 'open house' for luncheon was not unique at that time, it was becoming rare, and ceased at the time of the Great War, never to be revived. The informal meal was set out on a side table and the guests helped themselves from silver dishes kept warm on hot-plates.

As a favourite son of Lord Leconfield Percy Wyndham was eagerly welcomed by his father at Petworth in the years before he had a country house of his own, but it was at Clouds, which was said by W. R. Lethaby 'to have been imagined by its gifted hostess as a palace of week-ending for politicians', that the large hospitality of the Wyndhams was to have its finest flowering.

The site for Clouds was found in Wiltshire after a long search and acquired in 1876. The small house there was known after a former owner as 'Clowdes', which was changed to the more evocative name by the Wyndhams. The kind of house that Percy Wyndham had in mind could not be achieved by even the most radical alterations to the existing building, and so it was demolished. The site provided the ideal setting for a fine country house. Although it is set high up with a falling vista to the south-west over open meadows with a few fine trees, it is very private, even hard to find in the network of little lanes that lead to it. On the other three sides the house is closely surrounded by trees which come right to the edge of the rather small garden – now sadly overgrown but once famous for its original layout and unusual plants. The terraces and lawn are separated from the open meadow by a retaining wall of green sandstone. This local stone was also used for the main body of the house.

Philip Webb, the Wyndham's chosen architect, and a partner in Morris and Co., gave long and careful thought to the planning of the house, and it was not until 1881 that a scheme that both he and his patron could approve was finally worked out. Then the building went on apace and the house was at last habitable in 1885. The final result was exactly what was required: a ready-made ancestral home, large and dignified but not pretentious.

Clouds cost £80,000 to build; a century ago that amount of money bought a very great deal of house, and Clouds was enormous. Even now, with much of it demolished, the first and most lasting impression is of sheer size, of towering walls, huge, glittering, many-paned windows and flights of steps leading up and up to high terraces or down to the maze of utility rooms on the lower floor. Only after this vastness has been assimilated can the bemused viewer take an intelligent interest in the details of decoration and construction.

The mixture of local traditional style, Gothic Revival and monumental classicism subtly suggest a building that has reached its final form by a process of alteration and adaptation over a long period of time. This carefully contrived effect has survived the ruthless rationalization and demolition needed to make the house habitable in the present century; but the rambling domestic offices, built in the vernacular style much favoured by Webb, round a series of courtyards in which grew ancient trees from the original estate, have gone. Everywhere are reminders of the thought lavished on this great project: the pattern of the stone setts in the stableyard, the woodwork of the beams and doors of the outbuildings, and the neat pointed tiling protecting the wall and buttresses round the perimeter have all been individually considered. Even today, though the abandoned rooms look sad, when one gazes at the ghostly elegance of the fine intricate plasterwork and panelling it is easy to imagine the cool, flower-filled blue and white scheme, peopled with the Wyndham family and their friends: Oliver Lodge demonstrating the glowing miracle of radium to a group of excited small children; Arthur Balfour, almost lying in his chair in the characteristic Balfour manner, discussing philosophy and poetry (rarely politics) after a round on the private golf course; Harry Cust writing verses and languishing after his host's daughter Pamela; the irrepressible George discussing his latest literary preoccupations in the respectful silence ordained for all his utterances by his loving family. On one memorable occasion in August 1901 Wilfrid Blunt camped Arab-style in the park in the course of his summer driving tour, as he had done at other Souls' houses in earlier years. Burne-Jones was a beloved friend, and his children, Philip and Margaret, were like children of the house, according to Mary Elcho. Other artist friends frequented the house, at ease in the atmosphere of informality.

A special gathering of the Souls took place each Easter, when the days were crowned by the famous after-dinner games reputedly never more brilliant than here at Clouds, presided over by the beautiful and benign figure of the châtelaine, sitting at her 'scrattle' table (as she called her worktable) always engaged on some artistic project. Arthur Balfour wrote to thank for one such visit:

> My dear Percy
>
> I did not realise that before I returned from Golf you would be gone: so I did not say goodbye after luncheon. I must therefore tell you by letter what I would much rather have told you by word of mouth – namely how much I have enjoyed my visit here and how grateful I am to you for your hospitality. I am afraid even to attempt any enumeration of my Easter stays in your house. The memory of man hardly reaches back to the first of them. They began in the old house, then went on through the interregnum in the Offices, and they have been continuous year after year in the New House. All have been delightful, but none more delightful than the visit of 1907, now alas verging towards its final moments. With many thanks . . .

The 'interregnum in the Offices' (the servants' block) was necessitated by the fire which raged through the house on the night of 6 January 1889 and virtually destroyed it. This had been prophesied, though the Wyndhams themselves were unaware of it. One day when no member of the family was at Clouds, according to Edith Olivier,

> . . . legend says a mysterious old woman, clothed in shabby black, appeared . . . Holding up her hand like some ancient sorceress she said these words: 'In three years' time this house will not be standing.' She vanished and was never seen again.

On that dreadful night the fire engine did not arrive until Clouds was a tall pillar of fire. When the terrible devastation was surveyed it was found that some of the walls, three feet thick,

A photograph of Clouds taken very shortly after the fire

were intact. With dogged courage the Wyndhams set out to restore the house exactly as it had been and within three years, to quote Lady Paget who was there in 1893, the 'glorified Kate Greenaway affair, all blue and white inside, and all red and green outside' rose again from the ashes.

The Wyndhams were right to persist. Clouds was regarded as Webb's masterpiece: widely celebrated among the knowledgeable, it attracted visitors for its own sake during his lifetime. In 1898 the architect wrote to Percy Wyndham commiserating with him on the inconvenience so caused:

Let me hope the irrepressible sightseer from Yankee land and elsewhere is beginning to cease disturbing your peace with his curiosity as to the kind of house an English gentleman lives in?

In 1904 *Country Life* devoted an article to Clouds. It was written by Wilfrid Blunt who knew the house well and greatly admired it, so the descriptions are more than usually detailed.

The green sandstone, quarried in the neighbourhood, of which the house was built, combined with red brick, tiles and brown weatherboarding to make an extraordinarily harmonious colour scheme. Inside the absence of colour in the decoration was remarkable for the date: the panelling was of unstained oak; the walls were mainly white, with here and there a Morris paper; the curtains were of Morris's silk and wool woven 'tapestry' in shades of blue except in the drawing-room where they were plain white cloth. Morris carpets provided the only note of colour in the rooms. The large drawing-room carpet is unique; it was woven in 1887 after anxious letters had been exchanged by Morris and Percy Wyndham respecting the design. It was

Above. The drawing room at Clouds, all decorated in white. The rich effects of the decoration were provided by the plasterwork and the fretted ornaments about the panelled bookcases. A startling note of colour comes from the blue and pink and green intricacies of the carpet, specially woven by William Morris

Left. The boudoir. This room, almost more than any other at Clouds, gives the flavour of Madeline Wyndham's life

sold to the University of Cambridge in 1936, and has survived continuous use on the floor of the Combination Room in the Old Schools, a tribute to the durability of Morris's work. The brilliance of the colours is still stunning, and the rich texture of the close-woven wool gives a voluptuous sense of luxury. It is easy to imagine the effect of this splendour in the austerely white drawing-room.

Although Morris himself played an important part in the decoration of the interior of Clouds, the final result is very different from the usual Morris and Co. style, which inclined towards a more recognizably Victorian idea of dark and glowing richness, jewel-like lustreware gleaming in the penumbra of arras-hung rooms whose only illumination came from stained-glass windows. In the Wyndhams, Webb had at last found sympathetic patrons whose taste in interior decorations exactly matched his own. Indeed, some of the very deep-set windows with their impressive panelled cases were curtainless, probably at Webb's instigation. This must have been a rare treat for him, since in most of his houses this detail is obscured by the heavy draperies favoured by nineteenth-century taste. The simple white panelling in the morning-room was relieved by shelves above the bookcases, set with Oriental blue-and-white dishes and jars, and more Oriental porcelain decorated the panelled shelves in the dining-room, where the oak table and leather-upholstered chairs in a plain Gothic Revival style must have seemed austere after the elaborately gilded and painted Italianate furnishings at the other great house built by one of the Souls' group, the Windsors' Hewell (see Chapter Nine). The drawing-room was the most ornate, though the prevailing colours were still just blue and white. There was a deep frieze of plasterwork and pierced and fretted headings to the bookcases and the china cabinets whose doors had glazing-bars in a bold rococo inspired by Chippendale; the picture-hung walls, and yet more Oriental porcelain, vied for attention with furniture upholstered in a Morris design of bold meandering acanthus leaves and the plain eighteenth-century tables laden with vases of flowers, books and ornaments of every description. The impression was of a timeless taste. Mrs Wyndham was far ahead of her time in preferring to mix the antiques and curios, which she and her husband had collected throughout their married life for the embellishment of their dream house, with pieces of fine eighteenth-century furniture. In spite of the proliferation of objects, pictures and flowers the effect was still light and cool, and in letters and descriptions of life at Clouds the perfect taste of the owners is often remarked upon.

This 'artistic' style of decoration, inspired by the rather heterogeneous collection of furnishings, fabrics, curiosities and *objets d'art*, which might have been found in the studio of a successful Victorian artist, was hard to achieve without the aesthetic affectation which Du Maurier had ridiculed so remorselessly in his drawings for *Punch* in the 1870s. As early as 1890 in 'Oke of Okehurst', one of the ghost stories in the collection *Hauntings*, Vernon Lee was to write derisively of 'the picturesqueness which swell studios have taught to rich and aesthetic houses', suggesting that this eclectic taste had already been vulgarized. But if we are to look for a fictional equivalent of Clouds, it is surely to be found in Henry James's Poynton.

While the main theme of *The Spoils of Poynton* was inspired by a dispute between the members of a Scottish family which James was told of at a London dinner party in 1893, it is tempting to wonder whether, in some of the details of Poynton and of Mrs Gereth herself, James had Clouds and his old friend Mrs Wyndham in mind. Henry James describes Mrs Gereth amassing the contents of Poynton with:

. . . her husband's sympathy and generosity, his knowledge and love, their perfect accord and beautiful life together, twenty-six years of planning and seeking, a long sunny harvest of taste and curiosity. Lastly, she never denied, there had been her personal gift, the genius, the passion, the patience of the collector . . .

In the description of Poynton itself there is an authentic-sounding glimpse of Clouds:

Wandering through clear chambers where the general effect made preferences almost as impossible as if they had been shocks, pausing at open doors where vistas were long and bland, she would, even if she had not already known, have discovered for herself that Poynton was the record of a life. It was written in great syllables of colour and form, the tongues of other countries and the hands of rare artists . . . and in all the great wainscotted house there was not an inch of pasted paper.

This last touch strikes the reader with its sharpness of observation, encapsulating in a phrase the personal taste of a woman with the courage to ignore the decorating practice of her age.

No words, no photographs of unpeopled rooms at Clouds, nor of its peaceful park silent in clear unshadowed light, can convey the flavour of the inhabited house, full of vociferous and hilarious guests whose own exchanges were accompanied by the shrill cries of the peacocks who strutted round the house, and the maniac peals of mirth from a pair of 'African Laughing Jackasses' (presumably kookaburra birds), which were kept in a cage on the South Terrace. In many of the rooms Madeline Wyndham's doves were free to fly about, fluttering above the cushioned dog baskets for the pampered fox-terriers.

One of the features of Webb's plan was the large, nearly separate block of 'Offices', low-built, rambling, and wildly inconvenient. The kitchen was modelled, in fashionable affectation, on the mediaeval Abbot's Kitchen at Glastonbury, with the large central chimney masked from the outside by a neat arcaded clerestory in the steeply-pitched tiled roof. It can hardly have been an efficient place to cook in. At Madeline Wyndham's insistence, the fine mulberry which grew beside the old house was retained, having a most inconvenient effect on the plan of the servants' quarters. To convey food from the kitchen to the dining-room involved the use of two lifts and a railway track, passing through the attic storey of the Offices. This absurd contrivance stung Webb's biographer, Lethaby, into an unusually sharp comment:

It was the affectation of the time that work was done by magic; it was vulgar to recognise its existence or even to see anybody doing it.

During the rebuilding of the house, when the Wyndhams had to live in the Offices, they had good reason to be thankful that Webb had – by the standards of the time – considered the servants' comfort. This was put down to his socialist inclinations, and while the cause was deplored the effect was welcomed. This satisfaction with the amenities in the Offices seems a little surprising nowadays. There was accommodation for between fifteen and twenty servants in very small rooms, and not a single bathroom or water tap!

Before the fire the staircase wall of the house had been decorated with a 'great mural painting of a multitude of angels' – Edith Olivier's description of the cartoons for the 'Annunciation and the Angels' which Burne-Jones had designed for the mosaics in G. E. Street's American Church in Rome. She also records the regretful legend written by Madeline Wyndham on the back of a tiny photograph of the mural: 'All gone. Alas! Alas!' Perhaps

Millicent Duchess of Sutherland remembered Clouds when in 1902 she described a visit to 'Mrs Neyland's house' in one of her novels: 'Up the wide marble stairs, hung with masterpieces of Burne-Jones' women of romance – pale women of unsatisfied passion – she flitted.' In spite of this loss, which could never be repaired, Clouds regained most of its former self, but Lady Cynthia Asquith, the Elcho's eldest daughter, felt that the new house was ill-omened. The fire had taken place in the year that her brother Colin was born, but in the year that the rebuilding was completed he died, aged only three.

This restored glory was to last only a few decades, after which the great house was given up to institutional use. The trees optimistically planted with the pleasure of later generations in mind can be seen in their infancy in an early photograph of the house reputedly taken before the fire. They are now at the peak of their maturity, but no Wyndhams are there to enjoy them; what the fire could not achieve time has accomplished without effort.

Of the younger generation of Wyndhams who passed their days in these idyllic surroundings, the most prominent, both among the Souls and in public life, was George. Conspicuously good-looking, he was described as 'the handsomest man in England', and photographs of him confirm that opinion. His looks were both an advantage and a handicap, for some twist of human nature makes both friends and foes alike deal more hardly and critically with the smallest failings of such favoured beings. George Wyndham was, however, endowed with far greater gifts: he had wit, a far from negligible intellect, physical prowess and financial security. It might be thought that no more could be demanded of fortune than brains, looks, and money, but such bounty seems to be an irresistible temptation to the gods, and they were not slow to destroy it.

The Rt Hon. George Wyndham – 'the hand-somest man in England' – from the album presented to Lord Curzon in 1890

The facts of George Wyndham's life are unusually extensively documented for someone whose public career fell well short of greatness in the conventional sense: there are no fewer than four accounts of which the best is that in the two-volume *Life and Letters* edited by Burne-Jones's son-in-law J. W. Mackail and published in 1925. In particular, its picture of the Wyndham childrens' childhood is unforgettable, while the youth and the emerging public figure are strongly drawn.

Everything in George Wyndham's life fostered the brilliance which was his most noticeable quality. As Desmond MacCarthy remarked in his review of the *Life and Letters*, the word 'brilliant' was applied 'with every shade of admiration and detraction that adjective can acquire in different contexts'. He was educated at Eton and then went on to Sandhurst, too impatient to begin his army career to tolerate the length of a university education, a lack he was to regret in later life. In 1883 he went into the Coldstream Guards, and in 1885 he realized his ambition to see active service when he was sent out to Egypt. The circumstances of his departure were remembered in the 'Recollections of a friend' printed in *The Times* after his death in 1913. The correspondent and Wyndham were out hunting. 'I have seldom in a longish personal experience seen a hat or coat in the condition of Mr Wyndham's as we rode home together,' he wrote. When they returned to the house where they were staying a telegram was waiting bidding George Wyndham to rejoin his regiment at once, as his battalion was under orders to proceed to Egypt. ' "By Jove," he said, "I wish I'd known of this. I'd have ridden my other horse," and off he went, crushed hat, dirty coat, boots and breeches, and all, by a train he just caught, rejoicing in this new adventure.'

This was the level of excitement at which George Wyndham liked to live, and to a certain extent he contrived to do it, occupying positions of greater importance than his intellectual and emotional powers warranted. The year after the Egyptian expedition he met the ravishingly beautiful Sibell Grosvenor; after overcoming considerable opposition from the Duke of Westminster, her former father-in-law, on account of his youth and inexperience, they were married early in 1887. In the middle of their wedding tour a letter came from Arthur Balfour urging George to come home and act as his Private Secretary. He accepted this post, and embarked on a political career about which he seems to have had doubts for the rest of his life.

The Times had another obituary notice, entitled 'Personal characteristics – a friend's appreciation':

> On many occasions George Wyndham discussed with his intimate friends whether he had done well to embark on the stormy sea of politics, or whether, in the society of literary associates who surrounded and admired him, in the library which was his real spiritual home, he would have found a purer solace and achieved more enduring work.

As so often with the testimony of friends one wonders if George Wyndham had any need of enemies, for every tribute is tinged with wondering regret. For instance 'A colleague's tribute', written for *The Times* by Alfred Lyttelton on his speech-making, remarked:

> Wyndham's danger as a speaker in the House of Commons was in the first place a certain obscurity arising from the subtlety of his own thoughts, which was increased by the severe condensation which, contrary to his nature, he applied to them. But he had another defect remarkable in so buoyant and vigorous a speaker. He was apparently in genuine doubt as to whether this or that argument which he

was using was good or bad and was wont to refer the matter aloud to his colleagues behind him. 'Will that do, A?' he would ask, 'B, is that sound?' . . . Wyndham was at his very best at a tête-à-tête with a friend. In a larger company his exuberance and fertility were, it must be owned, a little excessive.

None the less George Wyndham's political career must be taken seriously, for he occupied positions of great responsibility, of sufficient importance to have disastrous repercussions when things went wrong. He was elected to Parliament in 1889 as member for Dover. The years that followed were occupied with a mixture of politics and literature, the latter often taking the greater part of his energy. He helped to edit the *New Review* and published a number of rather trivial books which enjoyed some reputation with his contemporaries. At last in 1898 he was offered, and immediately accepted, the Under-Secretaryship at the War Office vacated by St John Brodrick's elevation to Curzon's old position at the Foreign Office. Two years later he was made Chief Secretary to Ireland. In 1903 King Edward VII and Queen Alexandra were triumphantly entertained in Dublin; but in the following year things began to go badly awry. Nervous exhaustion caused George Wyndham to make a number of miscalculations in his conduct of events, one of which, the 'MacDonnell affair', concerned with the intricacies of the Home Rule policy, he so mishandled that early in 1905 Balfour had to ask for his resignation. Wyndham was not displeased to be out of office in spite of the distressing circumstances of his resignation. Indeed, by concentrating on his constituency, he was able to retain his seat at Dover in the débâcle of 1906 when no Conservative seat could be regarded as safe.

A bronze bust of George Wyndham
by Auguste Rodin

In 1911 Percy Wyndham died, and George succeeded to the estate at Clouds. He took up his new role with characteristic enthusiasm, continuing the benevolent plans of his father for improving the living accommodation in the village, and embarking on converting a range of bedrooms into a long library planned in bays in the old manner and running the whole width of the house on an upper floor of Clouds. The architect Detmar Blow was called in to design it. His work was well known to Wyndham as he had recently built Wilsford for George's sister Pamela and her husband Edward Tennant. Blow, taught by Ruskin and Philip Webb, should have been an ideal choice; but the scheme did not prosper and the remaining alterations were completed with the more sympathetic and less critical assistance of Mr Mallett, the estate carpenter. However, the Wyndhams' patronage of Blow was to lead to both the best and the worst thing in his professional career: his employment and ignominious dismissal by the extravagant Bendor, Duke of Westminster, George Wyndham's stepson.

In 1913, after only two years' enjoyment of his new role, and soon after the eminently satisfactory marriage of his son Percy to Diana Lister, daughter of Lord Ribblesdale, George Wyndham died in Paris. He had not even passed his fiftieth birthday and his untimely loss was acutely felt.

The legend composed by Balfour on the large east window, designed by Sir Ninian Comper and presented to East Knoyle Church by both Houses of Parliament in memory of George Wyndham, describes him as: 'Statesman, Orator, Man of Letters, Soldier'. Had Balfour been able to add the words, inappropriate to a memorial inscription, 'Sportsman, Wit, Handsome Charmer', he would have not only rounded off the description of George Wyndham, but at the same time defined the qualities of an ideal male Soul. Perhaps this unusual offering from both Houses came as a belated apology to the scapegoat of the MacDonnell affair: the design of the window refers to George Wyndham's links with both England and Ireland.

In many respects, and in marked contract to Curzon, George Wyndham never outgrew his 'tumultuous and unrepentant youth' – as Curzon himself put it. He had to a remarkable degree the capacity, often noticeable in young men of brilliant but undisciplined intellect, to sustain close friendships with much older men. Two great influences in his life were Arthur Balfour, whom he had known since he was barely seventeen and to whom he owed his political career – Balfour's biographer Max Egremont, a Wyndham himself, goes so far as to say that he was 'mesmerized' by Balfour – and his cousin Wilfrid Blunt. Blunt was a dangerously romantic mentor and his extravagant and chaotic way of life must have appealed to any adventurous young man; yet despite what Curzon wrote in his Crabbet Club poem on 'Sin' his was not a good example to follow:

> Our President shall set us
> An example that shall whet us
> To practice all the naughty things
>   he wrote of in his odes

Intensity of emotion matched with a faulty critical sense marred many of Blunt's literary and political achievements, and his reckless indifference to the consequences of his actions, which at one point landed him in prison in Ireland, made him a poor model for a man with so little capacity for self-criticism as a result of his indulgent upbringing.

None the less, who could resist Blunt's company? He persuaded George and his young friends to inject new life into his Crabbet Club, re-established after political dissension had dispersed many of the old group. Here George shone with particular brilliance, tossing off a poem in complicated metre between sets of tennis. His exuberant descriptions of Club meetings in his letters convey his enthusiastic participation.

George Wyndham's response to life was intensely romantic, and never more so than in his choice of a wife. The circumstances of Sibell Grosvenor's first marriage had been unpromising: she was married very young to the heir to the Duke of Westminster, the epileptic Lord Grosvenor. Even by the standards of the time, when arranged marriages were the rule, this was considered to be a cruel act on the part of her parents. Lady Antrim wrote in her *Recollections*:

> . . . some of the prettiest girls in London were invited to Cliveden for this party [Lord Grosvenor's coming-of-age ball], amongst them Sibell Lumley who shortly afterwards agreed to marry Lord Grosvenor. I believe the Duke of Westminster warned her mother, Lady Scarbrough, that he had epileptic fits, but this did not stop her from agreeing to the marriage. I can see Sibell standing close to her great lumbering fiancé at a ball at Lansdowne House where the engagement was announced, a pathetic little figure with sad star-like eyes bewildered by her congratulations.

Lady Antrim does both of the families involved less than justice. Sibell Grosvenor was never to suggest in word or deed that she regretted her decision. In fact she conducted her first marriage with conspicuous success, as is apparent from the way in which she won the heart of the Duke of Westminster, and she nursed Lord Grosvenor devotedly during his last illness. After his death in 1884, the Duke most carefully ensured that her second marriage was right for her by rigorous enquiries into George Wyndham's character. Both she and her family could afford to be choosy in the matter of a husband since she never lacked suitors of the most eligible kind, a passage from Henry James's *Notebooks* mentions that Lord Stafford, for instance, wanted to marry her. From this entry Henry James evolved his short story 'The Path of Duty'.

Many men were to see themselves as the one who would rescue Lady Grosvenor from her solitary widowhood; her brother Osric Lumley claimed that more than eighty men were in love with her at the time. Indeed one of her most ardent suitors was George Curzon; but Wyndham won.

Sibell Grosvenor's character is elusive. She was very beautiful, very good, and very religious. Nobody ever said that she was witty or clever; yet she was much loved in the Souls' circle where these gifts were so greatly valued. Perhaps her very lack of self-assertiveness was needed as a foil to the brilliance of her husband. Lady Paget said of her:

> Gentle and unselfish to the utmost, she has yet a great deal of character and much practical sense. Her opinions are firm though moderate, and her household is conducted with comfort and economy. Her beauty is one of colouring and expression solely, but it reminds one of the angels.

Sibell Grosvenor's looks were of the type known as *journalière*, 'changing with the day', depending on mood, the play of light, and, to a certain extent, the sympathy of the observer. She was like a painting rather than a piece of sculpture, and in many respects she resembled a portrait by Greuze – a painter whom she greatly admired – so the likeness may not have been entirely fortuitous. Edward Clifford's portrait of her also has a slight echo of Greuze, showing her in a

Sibell, Lady Grosvenor, a portrait by Edward Clifford dated 1887, the year of her marriage to George Wyndham

Antess
gnot

Edward CLIFFORD

misty muslin dress, slightly dishevelled in a way reminiscent of the eighteenth century, against a background of soft, pale green trees. Certainly the gauzy clothes were appropriate to the image. Her most frequently remarked feature, clearly seen in the painting, was the sweetness of her expression and it did not belie the owner's character.

At the time of her marriage to George Wyndham, Lady Grosvenor (as she was to remain) was living with her three children at Saighton Grange in Cheshire. This had been her home during her first marriage, and it was duly presented to the newly-married couple by the Duke of Westminster. She was deeply attached to the house, and even more to the garden whose flower-filled borders she had carefully planned. Edward Clifford also made a picture of the garden for her, which she had printed as a postcard to use for her correspondence. The Saighton flower garden was quite unlike the great formal parterres at Wrest and Ashridge or at Hewell Grange: it was of a type not then greatly in vogue, very unpretentious, and clearly expressing her personality. George Wyndham himself became greatly attached to the house. He made himself a retreat – a study and library up a precipitous winding staircase in a turret room – where he could find the peace to write, away from the rigours of parliamentary life.

Lady Grosvenor's natural sphere of influence was in her own home, arranging with discreet competence for the comfort of her family and the entertainment of her special friends. Guests would often find themselves alone with their host and hostess and the children, and even the shooting-parties were quite small. Wilfrid Blunt noted in his diary that a ball given in July 1895 was the first formal entertainment given by George Wyndham and his wife in London in the eight years since their marriage. She enjoyed the society of artists: Burne-Jones was a friend, as were his children, who had been the companions of George Wyndham's childhood. But she was especially attached to Edward Clifford with whom she shared an interest in religious matters. Clifford was a devout man, an admirer of Father Damien who ran the leper colony at Molokai, and he was also an active member of the Church Army. Sibell Grosvenor herself became even more deeply religious in later life when she joined the Anglo-Catholics. George Wyndham once said to Lady Paget that Sibell was 'a Roman Catholic in all but name'.

Life at Saighton was relatively easy to manage, since it did not entail the care of a large estate. When George Wyndham succeeded to Clouds in 1911 he was at first alarmed by the much larger scale on which it was run, with all the attendant organization, costs and wages. Nevertheless, he threw himself into the role of landowner with enthusiasm.

One of the most urgent matters which he had to occupy himself with at Clouds was the contriving of a chapel for Sibell. His son, Percy, suggested that once the electric light was installed the lamp-room, which would then be obsolete, might be adapted for this purpose. It is difficult to imagine what the Wyndhams' butler, who had his sitting-room next door, made of this innovation. Nevertheless, the white-vaulted room with its red-brick floor proved to be perfectly suitable, and once again a collaboration with the invaluable Mallett resulted in a further embellishment of the house. The family combined to present George and Sibell with a silver altar cross designed by Alexander Fisher to celebrate their silver wedding anniversary. Fisher had already been at work designing the cross which was to mark old Mr Wyndham's grave. A corner of the new cemetery at East Knoyle had been reserved to make a Wyndham family plot. A wall of the same green sandstone as the house was built round it, bearing flat stone tablets on which to record the names of the members of the family buried there. Almost all are still blank, and the metalwork of the graves, which are in the form of large plain crosses also designed by Fisher, and in the case of George, a sort of 'fence' of angels with their wings spread, is buckled and corroded with time. Nothing brings home more poignantly the brief reign of the Wyndhams at Clouds than this almost unused burial plot.

The Wyndham sisters, Mary, Madeline, and Pamela, were appropriately known as 'the Three Graces'. Beautiful and talented in art and literature, they brought to the Souls' circle an insouciant originality of mind.

The girls of the Wyndham family had shared with their brothers an upbringing wonderfully uncharacteristic of the period, and were allowed by their enlightened parents a quite unprecedented degree of freedom and indulgence. Far from 'spoiling the child' it seems to have given them the self-confidence to develop their individuality and creative gifts to a remarkable level. As adults they were to charm their friends with their many accomplishments, drawing, sewing, and embellishing their houses with a skill much greater than that usual even in the most well-brought-up young lady of that time when such talents were considered essential.

All the Wyndham children married and went their separate ways, but they remained very close and returned often to Clouds, gathering at any excuse such as a birthday or an anniversary. Mary (Lady Elcho) remembers that her birthday was always spent there. Those present were required to dine wearing wreaths of roses: 'George looked like a Roman emperor, my father more like Petrarch or Dante, and Arthur Balfour, with his big eyes and a very bunchy wreath, like a very nice owl in an ivy bush.' George, writing to Madeline from Saighton Grange in 1892 at Christmas, says: 'If only we could all be together! But even as it is I feel that Clouds, Babraham and Saighton are so many Leyden jars of electric love, with a strong current running round between them.'

The Wyndham sisters are forever united in the public imagination by the magnificent group portrait of them painted by Sargent in 1899. This picture, one of Sargent's great triumphs, was immediately dubbed *The Three Graces* by the Prince of Wales when it was exhibited at the Royal Academy in 1900. In March 1899 Wilfrid Blunt had seen Sargent at work on the very early stages of the picture: 'I . . . saw the first sketching in of Pamela's head which Sargent has just done in a couple of hours' work. It should make a remarkable picture, probably Sargent's best.' Sargent was less easily pleased; early in the following year after the picture was finished he happened to sit next to Pamela one evening at the Ribblesdales' and, as she wrote to her father, was '. . . very anxious for some more sittings from me, and enquired my plans most pertinaciously'. Evan Charteris said of the picture;

> Sargent has here isolated these sisters from the world and encompassed them with their own associations. They are back once again in the surroundings that made their common bond; their mother's picture by Watts is seen on the wall beyond, the noise of life is hushed for the moment.

He had good reason to know how truly this picture conveyed the common bond, for Mary Elcho was his sister-in-law.

By the time this portrait was painted all three sisters, even the youngest, Pamela, had been married for some time. Since 1883 Mary Elcho's influence had been transferred to Stanway, a

The Wyndham Sisters by John Singer Sargent, 1900, showing Lady Elcho (Mary), Mrs Tennant (Pamela) and Mrs Adeane (Madeline). In the background can be seen G. F. Watts's portrait of their mother, Mrs Percy Wyndham, painted in 1877

place of such crucial importance to the Souls that it has been treated separately from Clouds and the Wyndham family as a group. Madeline is in many ways the unknown Wyndham; she is referred to much less than the younger Pamela, who had a powerful, even attention-seeking personality. Pamela's greatest gift was for lively literary expression, and her letters are very entertaining. Many of them are marked for circulation around the family. She published a number of books, the best known a collection of observations and quotations entitled *The White Wallet* after the folder in which she kept her finds. She married Edward Tennant, brother of Charty, Laura and Margot, and a friend of her brother George, in 1895. She had, with good reason, expected to marry Harry Cust, and when these hopes were dashed she had a minor crisis of nerves. It is fruitless to speculate whether they would have been happy, but it seems unlikely.

When Pamela Wyndham married and went to live in the Tennant family house, The Glen, in Scotland, she took with her some of the flavour of Clouds' life. With a mixture of determination and tactful suggestion she effected some improvements in the gloomy rooms, and at the unimaginative meals; but it was with the building of their own house at Wilsford in Wiltshire that the recreation of the Wyndham way of life could be more completely realized. The house was designed by Detmar Blow. The influence of Webb is very apparent in the choice of a traditional stone-built vernacular style; but this is not a 'great house' like Clouds, it is more like a manor house in scale and appearance. The Tennants led a consciously simple life, often taking meals in the 'stone parlour', an open loggia with farmhouse furniture – a plate-bedecked pine dresser and rush-seated chairs made by Morris & Co. Blow was deeply imbued with Arts and Crafts values and his respect for the character of a region is reflected in his choice of local building materials. As with Clouds, the effect of a long-established building has been achieved. Pamela Tennant was widowed in 1920, and two years later she married her late husband's great friend, Sir Edward Grey, first Viscount Grey of Fallodon, who had already lived with them for some years.

Madeline married Charles Adeane in 1889 and went to live at Babraham in Cambridgeshire, outside the close circle of Souls and family, and in fact in the sporting and royal circles which the Souls avoided deliberately.

Pamela Wyndham, the youngest sister, who married Edward Tennant

✣ SEVEN

Lord and Lady Elcho

Lady Mary to-day
Should have beamed on a world that adores her
Of her spouse debonair
No woman has e'er
Been able to say that he bores her.

George Curzon

In 1883 Mary Wyndham, the eldest and most beautiful of the daughters of the Hon. Percy and Mrs Wyndham, married Hugo Charteris, Viscount Elcho, son and heir of the tenth Earl of Wemyss, and came to live at Stanway in Gloucestershire. Never can châtelaine and house have been more happily suited than Mary Elcho and her beloved Stanway. Her years as hostess there were legendary, extolled by H. G. Wells as 'the great days of Mary Elcho at Stanway'.

Stanway is a house like no other, isolated in its own loveliness and repose; it was once a rest-house for the Abbot of nearby Tewkesbury. The atmosphere of peace pervades the house, permeates the golden Cotswold stone, and is fostered by long lawns and ancient trees. In spring the gardens are fragrant with white and mauve lilac, in the summer all is a deep slumbrous green. The large oriel window in the great hall has mullioned panes tinted amber and gold with time, so that perpetual sunshine seems to fill the room. The Elchos' daughter, Lady Cynthia Asquith, wrote in *Remember and Be Glad:*

> I cannot remember anyone who didn't fall under the spell of Stanway. As a child I loved my home precisely as one loves a human being – loved it as I have loved very few human beings. I could never go away without a formal leave-taking. 'How are you?' I would ask on return, gazing up at the gabled front to absorb its beauty like a long, lovely draught, and I fancied that it smiled back a welcome.

Inside, Stanway has the pleasantly rambling form of a house that has grown over the centuries. On the ground floor are the great hall, drawing-room, and library; rooms for reading and resting, and rooms for talking lead into each other. On the floors above, long cool corridors lead to light, pretty bedrooms with pale, faded fabrics. Mary Elcho had been brought up in Clouds, a modern, 'aesthetic' house, idealistically planned to the smallest detail; yet she did not seek to alter Stanway. A few evidences of her taste are there, some William Morris fabrics covering chairs and several papers in the bedrooms, but she wisely let Stanway keep all its unselfconscious beauty, which remained intact even when the house was filled by her sociable children, their many guests, and her numerous chow dogs.

The front door of Stanway House seen through the gateway – said at one time to be the work of Inigo Jones

The Pyramid in the gardens at Stanway. A favourite walk was from the house up to the Pyramid

Stanway is a house made for hospitality, and never was there a hostess more generous than Mary Elcho. Summer weekend parties at Stanway were a cherished respite from the busyness of a London season. Trains to Cheltenham brought the guests. First and foremost were family, Lord Elcho's brother Evan Charteris and his two sisters, Lady de Vesci and Lady Hilda Brodrick, with her husband St John. Other visitors included Lady Elcho's brother George Wyndham and his wife Sibell Grosvenor, and less frequently her sister Pamela. Granbys and Grenfells were children's Godparents. It could be said that Stanway was the home of the Souls.

The weekend programme was gentle: walks in the garden with the chows, excursions into the Cotswold countryside – especially after the family acquired a motor car – and visits to the Arts and Crafts Guild founded by Charles Robert Ashbee in the East End of London and moved 'lock, stock and barrel' to Chipping Campden in 1902. The craftsmen found these sorties delightful but alarming. There was village cricket, croquet, and there were the famous 'Games'; but these were not taken nearly so seriously at Stanway as they were at other Souls' houses. Lady Elcho's favourite was called 'Unwinding'; one person chose a word, then another a word associated with it, and so on; and then each person had to unwind the words in reverse. In one popular game two people pretended to be historic personages meeting in Hades, and the others tried to guess who they were. There were acting games and charades, often inspired by Mrs Patrick Campbell, a frequent guest. A peculiar sort of hide-and-seek took place, too: blindfolded protagonists buffeted each other with rolled-up newspapers. There was an air of hilarity rather than of erudition.

But the great joy of Stanway was the talk. The youngest daughter, Bibs, uses the word 'exhilaration' to describe the conversation. Lady Elcho was the best of all hostesses at making her guests shine. Nobody was allowed to feel nervous or inadequate for a moment. If they were, the hostess (and her children, as they grew older) came to their rescue. Anyone who was temporarily left out of the conversation was thrown a 'lifeline' across the table to help them re-enter. Lady Elcho herself directed the talk, tossing ideas into the air so they might become infectious. Yet she was completely self-effacing; her aim, as her daughter Cynthia said, was to enable a player to make a boundary rather than to bowl them out. The tenor of the conversation was to talk of light things seriously and serious things lightly.

Her husband, Hugo Elcho, was educated at Harrow and Balliol, and became Conservative M.P. for Haddingtonshire in 1883, a seat traditionally occupied by a member of his family. In 1885 Lord Elcho lost his Parliamentary seat (to R. B. Haldane) but in the following year he was returned for Ipswich, which he represented for nearly ten years. He was already fifty-seven when he succeeded his father to the Earldom, and survived his eldest son, Ego, and his youngest son, Ivo, both killed in the Great War.

Lord and Lady Elcho in the garden at Stanway, c. 1886. Their eldest son, 'Ego', is sitting on the lap of the Duchess of Rutland

Lord Elcho, photographed in about 1890 in Ipswich when he was M.P. there. A man of great wit and totally lacking in self-consciousness, he was judged by Curzon to be the most amusing of the Souls

Like his great friend Godfrey Webb, Hugo Elcho had been a member of the Crabbet Club since the early eighties; but unlike Webb he did not attend the meetings regularly after the first one or two. His connection with the Souls was mainly as the host at Stanway. The unforgettable picture painted of her father by Lady Cynthia Asquith makes one thing about him abundantly plain; that his social appetites were conspicuously less than those of his wife, of whom her daughter said: 'No specimen of the human race seemed without interest to her.' Frequently he is to be seen in photographs, glaring uncompromisingly in the back row of an otherwise happy group of people staying in the house.

Lord Elcho's terror of being bored was as great as his wife's indifference to it. Lord Chandos, the son of Alfred Lyttelton, who became, in succession to Arthur Balfour, a reluctant trustee of the fund set up to rescue the family fortunes from the consequences of Lord Elcho's wild speculation on the Stock Exchange, wrote of him:

> He was one of the most amusing men to be found, and he would be on my short list of 'charmers I have known'. He was rather a scamp, made no bones about his indiscretions, one of which was a rather formidable mistress. I became much attached to him, at least between financial crises. We never had a hard word and seldom a dull one.

This opinion is succinctly endorsed by the verse in George Curzon's Crabbet Club poem of 1893, 'Sin':

> Elcho shall lend his humour
> To propagate the rumour
> That wickedness adorned with wit
>   is the cult to which we pander.

A sceptical politician, he made his mark only occasionally. The Parliamentary sessions forced his family to move reluctantly to their dreary town house at 62 Cadogan Square, bought for them by Lord Wemyss in 1886. These were regarded as no more than periods of unwelcome exile from their beloved Stanway. His Parliamentary career was marked by one memorable obsession: every year he delivered an impassioned speech recommending that the House should rise before Derby Day. His attitude to his Parliamentary duties was less the product of frivolity and lack of intelligence than of a keen sense of the ridiculous, which stood in the way of wholehearted commitment to a worthy cause. His wit was legendary, and his speech in 1892 on the subject of payment to Members of Parliament was described by no less a judge than Arthur Balfour as 'one of the most brilliantly amusing speeches I have ever heard in the House'.

Lord Elcho's life was constantly fraught with drama, usually concerning his finances. The wolf was often perilously near the door. Lady Cynthia Asquith remembers: 'Our horses, all of them definitely eccentric, were obviously "bargains".' In the management of the estate there is a preoccupation with insufficient resources which, in fact, was greatly to the advantage of Stanway itself. Only intermittently inhabited throughout the greater part of the nineteenth century, it thus escaped the thorough redecoration that mid-century taste might have dictated. In spite of this self-inflicted poverty and his flirtations Lord Elcho's regard for his wife and family was probably much greater than it might appear to an outsider, and when Lady Elcho (by then Lady Wemyss) died in 1937 he survived her by only a few months.

But he always made rather a shadowy consort for his vivacious wife. Such was Lady Elcho's passionate interest in people that her family would sometimes be embarrassed by the eager conversations she entered with total strangers, girls in shoe-shops, passers-by in hotels. Once when mother and daughters were on a train journey, other travellers in the compartment were amazed to see the very pretty woman opposite them putting her head on one side and endeavouring with swooping glances to read the names and addresses on their luggage-labels. Lack of self-consciousness was part of Lady Elcho's charm. She happily went to stay at Holyrood Palace taking with her a chow and one of the children's pet dormice. She was incurably unpunctual, like Queen Alexandra, and nobody applied the sensible Court method of advancing the clocks by half an hour. She took little notice of material things. When a frill of her hem was ripped by thorns she tore it completely off, and hung it on a rose bush. Her children were to deplore her haphazardness. Once, when her mother was staying with the superbly efficient Lady Desborough, Cynthia said: 'I hoped she would be able to discover the mysteries of Ettie's system and organisation of life, but I don't think she has gleaned much.' Lady Elcho would try to arrange the programme of her life by means of disarmingly discursive letters, written in exquisite calligraphy that one feels was wasted on the transcriptions of mere daily routine. Giving her guest, Professor Jacks, directions on how to reach Clouds (her parents' home) she wrote:

> I *expect* you'll find it best to go to London, but I do not dictate. If you come to London your best train will be the 3.30 from Waterloo arriving at Salisbury about five I think. You will change to Semley. However, we might motor from Salisbury, so I will look out for you there. If you prefer cross country you can get to Basingstoke from Reading I suppose.

She wrote as if she were talking aloud. In her perpetual thoughtfulness for others she tried to make everything easy for them, however confused they in fact became. Another letter to Jacks shows her peculiar brand of selflessness:

I don't quite know *when* I'll turn up but I hope it will be *before* seven. I wish only to say, that I was never thinking of bringing a maid – and please if any other friend of yours – or a son on leave suddenly turn up – you must let me go where I'll be perfectly happy – into any Oxford hotel. I have often done that, I'm a most independent gypsy sort of person and love wandering by myself. Of course it would be no inconvenience for me to sleep at any hotel – I am afraid I am bringing a fluffy chow – but she's very good, quite a lady, and never fights.

Her children remember her lying in bed in the morning, writing letters and detailed household lists, and keeping her diary in which she recorded all the family activities. They thought the complications of her life unnecessary; though to us it is completely understandable that someone with two large houses, a husband who was a Member of Parliament, and six children all of whom themselves were inviting weekend guests, should find life rather demanding. Indeed Mary Elcho did overtire herself and from time to time she took rest-cures, sometimes at Stanway, and once, surprisingly, at Taplow. She gave of herself constantly and unsparingly; and to her children she gave herself totally. They spent much more time with their mother than most Edwardian children, though she had chosen for them a nanny to whom they were devoted. They were brought up in an atmosphere of love and happiness. Cynthia wrote:

I know some people consider a very happy and sheltered childhood as harmful physical mollycoddling. They say it makes children morally delicate, so that when they have to leave home they shrivel up like greenhouse-reared plants too suddenly exposed to unconditioned air. I believe, on the contrary, that to be lapped in love throughout the first formative years is as harmlessly protective as the straw swathed round the roots of young trees; that to be given deeply imbued confidence is to be given strength; that to be cherished – made to feel valuable – quickens in all but the utterly graceless a sense of obligation: above all I believe that early happiness naturally taken for granted instils a kind of loyalty to life.

Her daughter Bibs recalls the joy the children felt in their mother's company. 'To be with her was like being on a picnic in an ideal climate.'

Although her solicitousness for them was very great, her educational methods were a trifle erratic. There was a whole series of governesses of different nationalities, the best a Russian girl. Cynthia was sent to boarding-school for a few months after, rather than before, her first London season. Bibs attended three different boarding-schools. Her mother kept a vigilant eye on her: when the little girl wrote home saying she was about to read *Jude the Obscure*, she instantly received a telegram urging her not to; Lady Elcho was distressed at the thought of her daughter reading so tragic a book.

She was an omnivorous reader of philosophy, poetry and history, and inspired her children with her own lifelong love of literature. There was reading aloud, there were walks on which Dickens, her favourite writer, was discussed and characters from his novels brought into the conversation as if they were alive. The passion for books which she instilled in her children was such that Lady Cynthia Asquith and her friends played a favourite quotation game called 'Gibbets' obsessively: they had special 'Gibbeting books', and even played the game in spare moments at dances.

When Lady Elcho's children were away from home, she sent them myriad affectionate letters. She had natural artistic gifts and her letters to her children were adorned for their delectation with scrolls of flowers and leaves like illuminated manuscripts. She teased them and laughed with them and loved them all dearly.

She also taught them exquisite manners, and insisted on the observance of every courtesy. Occasionally her prompting went a little far: as the grown-up Cynthia was about to shake hands with someone, Lady Elcho whispered into her ear: 'Right hand, Cyncie, right hand.' But, as a woman of the world, she understood how much the possession of perfect manners help the young and shy to find, in her own expression, their 'social wings'.

As Lady Elcho insisted on the outward graces, she bestowed her special virtues in her children. Completely open-minded in every way, she disdained gossip and thought it very harmful. She was utterly discreet and it is understandable that Arthur Balfour should have chosen her as his confidante. After he lost May Lyttelton, the only woman with whom he ever believed himself to have been genuinely in love, Lady Elcho's solicitude brought him comfort.

Margot Asquith said of her: 'She had the greatest feminine distinction among the Souls, and was as wise and just as she was truthful, tactful and generous.' She always looked for the best in everybody and in searching found it. As she said, 'I suppose I am not a good judge of character, because from my childhood I have always been taught to look for the good and not for the bad in people, and to look for the best in everybody.'

Lady Elcho's philosophy was optimistic, but not simple. She cherished the epigram of a housemaid: 'There ain't no happiness in life, so we've just got to be happy without it.' The merriment in her brown eyes concealed much sorrow. In the Great War, the death of her sons Ego, and the youngest, Ivo, who was aged only nineteen, caused her immense sadness. She was very brave, but she could not accept the philosophy then prevalent that to lose one's sons was to give a great gift to the country. Yet in her own grief, she held out a hand of consolation to Mrs Patrick Campbell, whose only son had died at the front: 'I wish I could save you from the suffering – the anguish; but alas! one can't, except just by deep loving sympathy, which does strengthen just a little.'

Lady Elcho is best known to posterity through Sargent's masterpiece, *The Wyndham Sisters*, showing her with her two sisters in the guise of professional beauties in their parents' Belgrave Square drawing-room. Her children found this grand portrait not at all representative of their mother's beauty of face and character. Lady Elcho had a soft brunette prettiness, with huge, beautiful and expressive eyes, sometimes looking far away, but most often with a lively and sparkling twinkle, 'darting everywhere like a swallow'. All her life she had the eyes of a young girl; Cynthia described them as having a 'dancing gaiety'. The lovely watercolour portrait by Poynter was pronounced too solemn by her family, and a similar impression is given by many of the photographs of the eighties. Early photographs of her are literally too 'Soulful', her features static, her large eyes uncharacteristically pensive. The Souls may have been influenced to adopt these typical poses by Julia Margaret Cameron, who had photographed previous generations of Charterises, and whose work was framed at Stanway. This artist was perhaps the originator of 'soulful' expressions, as she would lock up her unfortunate sitters by themselves in a room for an hour or so until the appropriate measure of gloom or distress was achieved. But the Souls were not so much 'soulful' as high-minded, and above all high-spirited. The family's

A watercolour portrait of Lady Elcho by Sir Edward Poynter, painted in 1886, and showing her in an uncharacteristic pensive mood

Lady Elcho with her son Colin, who died in 1892 at the age of three. This was her daughters' favourite photograph of their mother

Lady Elcho, drawn by Violet, Duchess of Rutland in 1886

favourite photograph is one which Mary Elcho pasted as a frontispiece into her daughter Bibs's copy of her book, *A Family Record*; it shows her with her son Colin, who died at the age of three. She is at her most true in unposed photographs when the camera does not impose a formal rigidity. The drawing she liked best of herself is the profile by Violet Rutland showing the extreme gentleness of character which was one – but only one – of the many aspects of her legendary charm.

It was Balfour who persuaded Lady Elcho to write a history of the Souls. She disliked the name and called it a 'fantastic appellation'; but she acknowledged that the coterie was a real one, and herself remained among its surviving members for nearly half a century. As late as the 1920s she, Balfour, Lady Desborough and Evan Charteris would spend Whitsun together, perhaps in a seaside hotel, and their enjoyment of each other's company was as keen as ever. They played cards (rather badly), they talked incessantly, and they found great comfort with each other after the tragedies which had scarred their lives. The Elchos' children married into Souls families: Ego married Letty Manners, the daughter of Violet Rutland; Cynthia married 'Beb' Asquith; Guy married Frances Tennant; and Bibs married the son of Lord Windsor and went to live at Hewell Grange.

It was the clannish connotation of the name 'Souls' which Mary Elcho, the most welcoming of people, found unattractive. She introduced into the circle various 'honorary Souls'. Henry James, who used to stay at Broadway, also visited Stanway; she loved his books. She was very fond of the American novelist Edith Wharton. The two children of Burne-Jones, Mrs Mackail and Philip Burne-Jones, were frequent guests. As a painter Philip was overshadowed by his father; he was a charming and gentle man much given to hypochondria. Once when he held an exhibition no visitors came for days; then one afternoon, when he felt he could take a lingering lunch at the Ritz, he found he had missed in the meantime three Queens: Queen Alexandra, Queen Mary, and the Queen of Portugal. He gave Mary Elcho an exquisite watercolour of Henry James's story *The Madonna of the Future*, indicating perhaps the feeling of futility he had about his own art. A family friend was Mrs Patrick Campbell, who came wearing gorgeous London clothes. She delighted Souls and Souls' children with her hilarious mimicry and imitations. Lady Elcho's 'honorary Souls' embodied the tastes of the group: good books, good art, a sense of fun, and yet a view of life essentially romantic.

Lord Wemyss had died in 1914. He was a remarkable and eccentric man of whom his contemporaries remember his excellence at all manner of sports, his wonderful good looks – Margot Asquith includes him in her list of the most handsome men she had known – and his enthusiasm as a collector of pictures and works of art. At one time a 'Botticelli' and a 'Mantegna' – the same one that was lent to Burne-Jones for some years – hung in the gallery above the marble hall at Gosford, the family seat at East Lothian; officious attempts on the part of experts, even the great Berenson, to discredit these attributions were ignored by Lord Wemyss. Later, Mary Elcho wrote in her *Family Journal*: 'Connoisseurs have often re-named them (and will again!) but I adopt the titles given to them by their purchaser.'

After his death the Elchos inherited palatial Gosford; there were, as there always are at such times, financial confusions and complications, and for a moment there was talk of letting Stanway. Cynthia recalls:

> I found Mamma sobbing in her room before dinner. Papa had said that she must live in London instead of Stanway this autumn and winter, so that she won't be able to have people staying with her.

But Lady Elcho continued to live much of the time at Stanway after she became Lady Wemyss – a title to which she never became quite accustomed. Family parties were given there, with charades in the barn and cricket matches. During the month of August, when the Wemysses were in Scotland, the house was let for several years in succession to J. M. Barrie. He employed Lady Cynthia Asquith as secretary-cum-advisor; indeed it was she who had made this happy and successful suggestion.

Barrie, like everyone else, fell under the spell of Stanway, and soon also under the spell of the family. He greatly admired the beauty of Lady Elcho's three daughters and, in a moment of munificence, offered to commission from Sargent a sequel to *The Wyndham Sisters*, portraying the Ladies Cynthia, Mary and Irene as the Three Graces. Alas, this wonderful idea was not to be, as 'Bibs' came rushing in half an hour late for the preliminary discussions, and so punctilious was Barrie's temperament that he cancelled the project. It would have been a historic souvenir of the happy time he spent in that enchanted house.

❦ EIGHT
St John Brodrick

From the Gosford preserves
Old St John deserves
Great praise for a bag such as Hilda;
True worth she esteemed,
Overpowering he deemed
The subtle enchantment that filled her.

George Curzon

St John Brodrick, who in 1907 succeeded his father as Viscount Midleton and in 1920 had his title elevated to an earldom, entered the Souls' circle less through the force of his own personality than by other means. He was a longstanding friend of Balfour; and his first wife, Lady Hilda Charteris, was Lord Elcho's sister. He married her in 1880 to general surprise: – she was a great catch for someone who was not at all suave or elegant; hence George Curzon's remark about his having 'bagged' her. She died in 1901. In 1903 he married Madeleine Stanley, one of the Stanleys of Alderley.

Brodrick's father was the owner of Peper Harrow in Surrey, a fine eighteenth-century house by Sir William Chambers; though after Brodrick himself inherited the property he made alterations and additions to the house which have somewhat destroyed the elegant unity of the original plan.

Brodrick was educated at Eton, where he had a brilliant career, and at Balliol. Although he was three years older than George Curzon, and already a member of the hallowed 'sixth' at Eton when Curzon arrived, their first meeting in 1874 was the start of a friendship 'which lasted without shadow for nearly thirty years'. He was elected to Parliament as Conservative M.P. for West Surrey in 1880, and in 1886 he became Financial Secretary to the War Office. In 1898 Curzon was appointed Viceroy of India and Brodrick succeeded him as Parliamentary Under-Secretary for Foreign Affairs, while George Wyndham succeeded Brodrick at the War Office. Political 'musical chairs' was a frequent occurrence among the Souls. In 1900 Brodrick became Secretary of State for War, and in 1903 Balfour transferred him to the India Office, in the hope that his friendship with the Viceroy would result in an inspired partnership. Unfortunately, however, although constitutionally the Secretary of State was supreme, the Viceroy considered that he himself should be; and inevitably their close and much-valued friendship foundered. Curzon wrote plaintively: 'In two years he succeeded in entirely destroying both my affection and my confidence.' All attempts to heal the breach were

Lady Hilda Brodrick (*née* Charteris), wife of St John Brodrick and the sister of Hugo Elcho

unsuccessful and their relationship became confined to the minimum of exchanges required in polite society.

In 1889 all this was far in the future. Curzon, before the fatal combination of ill health and disappointment had destroyed that genius for friendship which caused so many of his slights and cruel jokes to be forgiven, wrote the affectionate verse for the Bachelors' Club dinner quoted above.

Although loved by his friends for his unshakeable good nature, Brodrick was often the butt of the group at Souls' parties. He was celebrated for his gaffes, which he would sometimes compound by adding a further annihilating comment; but sometimes that comment was so appropriate that embarrassment was dispelled by hilarity and even by congratulation. Charty Ribblesdale wrote to Curzon of a party at which the guests had been required to define the words 'prejudice' and 'tact': 'The most tactless man in the room defined tact better than anybody, wasn't this remarkable?' Brodrick had astonished her by saying that tact is 'the tribute which intelligence pays to humbug', a witty adaptation of La Rochefoucauld's *'L'hypocrisie est un hommage que le vice rend à la vertu'*.

The schoolboyish side of Brodrick's humour is well illustrated by the menu-card which he devised for a dinner in 1900. The small folding card is the colour of a Government Blue Book and on the cover is printed:

ALIMENTARY PAPERS.	34, PORTLAND PLACE.
SUPPLY.	Dîner du 4 Juillet.
	*
CORRESPONDENCE	Consommé Confetti.
RESPECTING THE	Filets de Soles à la Régency.
DEPARTMENT OF THE INTERIOR.	Ris de Veau à la Nivernaise.
	Soufflé de Volaille en Kari.
Presented and Commended to both Houses of Parliament and their Sisters, and their Cousins, and their Aunts.	Selle d'Agneau Rôtis.
1900.	Jambon Froid, Salade de Fèves.
	Points Asperges à la Crème.
Laid on the Table Provisionally.	Omelettes Soufflés aux Abricots.
	Croûtes variées.
St. JOHN BRODRICK	
[A—No. 1.]	

The dinner took place at the Brodricks' London house, 34 Portland Place, on 4 July and consisted of the eight or nine courses usual at that date. Entertainment was not always confined to word games and witty exchanges: even Souls needed to be sustained.

As a boyhood friend of George Curzon and the husband of a Charteris, Brodrick's inclusion in the Souls' circle was inevitable, but it is impossible to escape the impression that he was in the circle without being entirely of it. Margot Asquith remembers Arthur Balfour saying 'laughingly . . . "St John pursues us with his malignant fidelity" '. She herself had known him since 1880 and was devoted to him, recording her opinion that he was unappreciated by his wife's family. She 'amazed' Lady Wemyss by asserting that he was better than all her Charteris brood put together. Her summing-up of people was often acute and her opinions unclouded by sentiment, and even she does not claim that Brodrick was the most scintillating member of the group. Brodrick had many solid virtues, for which he was much beloved, but he was neither witty nor romantic. He was high spirited, enterprising, and unswervingly loyal to his friends, qualities which made up for his inconvenient attachment to the literal truth – a virtue not much valued in the flattering exchanges of the social scene. Family connections were not enough to secure lifelong 'Soulhood'. Brodrick's long membership of the innermost circle may seem inexplicable; two factors which may have tipped the balance in his favour were Margot Asquith's liking for him and his own dogged insensitivity which allowed him to ignore rebuffs.

❦ NINE
The Windsors

'Lady Windsor is delightful and very beautiful, very slow and sad and a great contrast to all the Windsor Clives and Husseys.' So wrote Sybil Cust on a visit to the members of those families at Hewell Grange, their Worcestershire seat, in 1893. Curiously enough Gay Windsor's beauty was enhanced by her habitually sad and pensive expression. It is impossible to imagine what she would look like smiling; indeed, no image of her survives with a merry or laughing face. She was the daughter of Sir Augustus and Lady Paget and was christened Alberta, but had never since babyhood been known by that name. Her father was a diplomat, and at the time of his daughter's marriage he was *en poste* in Rome, later becoming British Ambassador in Vienna. Her mother, Walburga Paget, was a friend of the Princess Royal, Queen Victoria's eldest daughter Vicky, who became Empress of Germany; by virtue of this intimacy with the Royal Family Lady Paget was involved in the delicate negotiations surrounding the choice of bride for the Prince of Wales, later Edward VII.

Sybil Cust wrote, of her same visit in 1893: 'Sir Augustus and Lady Paget are here. Lady P. is very handsome, wears orange-coloured handkerchiefs arranged like a sort of turban on her head, and has no end of fads.' Lady Paget writes of having been distracted from her painting one morning by people coming to consult her about 'muzzling, anti-vivisectionists, doctors, magnetic cures and hospitals, dressmakers and artists'. Many of these crusading interests were kept up by her daughter, who in an unassertive way continued to practise – and preach – the benefits of a careful régime. She was a vegetarian, one of several habits that she inherited from her mother. Vegetarianism had an aesthetic purpose as it was reputed to be the most effective recipe for slimming. Not to be ethereally slender was regarded as a disaster in the Souls' circle.

In 1883 Gay married Lord Windsor, and, from having been a diplomat's daughter, embarked on a very different life as the wife of a wealthy country landowner. Robert Windsor Clive was born in 1857, and succeeded his grandmother, taking the title of Lord Windsor, when he was only twelve. In 1905 the lapsed Earldom of Plymouth was revived, and although Lord Windsor greeted this elevation with his usual reticence, his family were of the opinion that he was pleased. A man of wide cultural knowledge and great artistic taste, he had brought his appreciation of art and architecture to his Government appointment as First Commissioner of Works. He was also a Trustee of the National Gallery, and in 1908 he published a pioneering

Lady Windsor (Alberta 'Gay' Paget, and later Lady Plymouth).
This photograph was in the album presented to Lord Curzon

book on the painter John Constable, a biography which was to remain a standard reference work on the artist for many years. But a great part of his time – and, indeed, of his money – was to be devoted over the years to ambitious building operations, both on the Windsor estate at Hewell and in London, where a palatial house was built in Mount Street to the designs of Fairfax Wade.

Lord Windsor first met Gay Paget in Rome when he was just twenty-three. He was travelling with Dick Farrer, a great friend of George Curzon from Eton days. Although they would almost certainly have visited the Pagets in any case, the fact that Gay's brother Victor had been Farrer's fag at Eton made their welcome in that family absolutely assured. A man of exceptional brilliance, after a scintillatingly successful career at Balliol, Farrer had been elected to an All Souls Fellowship; but he was to die of tuberculosis at the age of only twenty-seven. In 1880 he and Lord Windsor were on their way to Greece to collect material for a book. Lord Windsor, a promising draughtsman, provided the illustrations for *A Tour of Greece* which appeared in 1882 as a handsomely bound volume which was priced at the then princely sum of three guineas. The drawings were neatly executed in the best tradition of the well-taught amateur, which so often marked the Etonian artist, but they may have suffered from the technique of reproduction, a process of wood-engraving which eliminates whatever individual personality they may have had. Farrer's text is so blatantly xenophobic that even Curzon, himself not conspicuously tolerant of other races, was moved to protest to the author: 'If I might make a criticism it would be that except in one or two notable cases (e.g. the chapter on Olympia) it scarcely rises in dignity to the level either of the subject matter or of the magnificent guise in which the book is presented to the public.'

In spite of the impression made by the monuments of classical Greece, Lord Windsor did not forget the serenely beautiful daughter of his hosts in Rome. Gay Paget was hardly out of the schoolroom, but she was already a beauty; tall and very slender with abundant copper-gold hair, she was described by Margot Asquith, who numbered Gay amongst the women whose looks she most admired, as 'an Italian Primitive'. She seemed shy and reticent, but was not without a precocious (and perhaps inherited) diplomatic instinct. Her mother related with satisfaction how the child Gay, on being asked to inscribe her name in Queen Victoria's birthday album, wrote without hesitation 'Victoria Alberta'. Sybil Cust's description of the 'very slow and sad' beauty conveys some flavour of her air of melancholy. This was caused, it was said, by a lost love, whose identity was only hinted at by Lady Paget, but whose ghostly presence was respected by her family for the rest of her life. Her habitual silence was to be noticeable in a world where a continuously ebullient 'talking all day' (to quote Henry James) life was the rule, but her distinguished fine-boned appearance and her highly developed aesthetic sensibilities allied to a considerable artistic talent – notably for sculpture – could not but appeal to Lord Windsor, whose own tastes were so similar.

Dick Farrer, who had returned with Lord Windsor from the tour of Greece, was already in the grip of his fatal illness, and he became deliriously obsessed with his friend's future happiness. It was hearing these feverish murmurings that first gave Lady Paget a hint of the seriousness of Lord Windsor's feelings for her daughter. They were married in 1883 at St Paul's, Knightsbridge, with the bride, ravishingly beautiful as all agreed, in a silver dress and veil which was unusual enough at the date to set a new fashion.

The year after their marriage the young couple began their great task of building Hewell

Grange, to replace a vast neo-classical mansion which had fallen into disrepair. The Windsors chose Thomas Garner from the architectural partnership of Bodley and Garner, who were renowned for their work in the 'Queen Anne' style, to design the new house. It was planned as a vast Renaissance palace modelled on Montacute House in Somerset. 'This is an astounding house,' wrote Sybil Cust in 1893: 'cost about a quarter of a million pounds, the hall is all green and white marbles, quite lovely; and there is an artist from Munich working all day on one of the ceilings.'

Though much of the interior is panelled in the Tudor or Jacobean style, some rooms are decorated in a later manner, with swags of flowers and fruit in delicate plasterwork, as in the small dining-room. Here the walls were hung with a flowered wallpaper like French chintz, which sets off the fine Louis Seize commode with panels inset with plaques of flower-painted Sèvres porcelain.

In keeping with the Italian taste of much of the decoration and furniture, one of the rooms has a ceiling copied from the d'Este apartments in the Corte Reale of the Gonzaga Palace in

The formal garden at Hewell Grange, with the house in the background, photographed by Bedford, Lemere in 1892. The design of the house was based on Montacute, the beautiful Jacobean mansion in Somerset, and the elaborate formal garden is in keeping with this style

Mantua, a maze of wood coffering painted with mottoes. Throughout the building of the house Lady Paget had interested herself in the smallest details of the planning. She remembered her first visit to Mantua in 1881, and, persuaded that she knew what her daughter would like, she took her son-in-law there in 1885 to see the d'Este apartments. There they sat all day making notes and drawings for use at Hewell. 'There is meaning and an idea in every leaf and flower,' she wrote. 'One room represents a golden maze upon an azure ground, with a motto and bay leaves running along the paths.'

All around the walls of Lady Windsor's dressing-room was a mural depicting scenes suggested by Beethoven's 'Pastoral Symphony', with the musical notation in a band beneath the pictures. This ambitious project was supposed by family tradition to be the work of Lady Paget who, as a young woman, had frequented the studio of an artist of the German 'Nazarene' school, where she would have been able to absorb the technique to undertake this task.

The dark blue bedroom at Hewell had a dado covered with blue and straw-coloured matting, which surely must have been Japanese in inspiration: an unusual departure in a Renaissance palace, but one much in tune with the taste of the period and of the Souls. Perhaps this was Sybil Cust's bedroom: 'My bedroom is so dazzling that I feel very grubby and dim in it,' she wrote, 'it is too splendid to be cosy.'

The 'Great Hall' at Hewell Grange, photographed by Bedford, Lemere, when it was still hung with family portraits. These were replaced with Cluny tapestries, giving an effect of even greater magnificence

By 1892 house and garden were deemed to be sufficiently advanced to be recorded by the celebrated firm of Bedford, Lemere, who specialized in the tricky job of photographing great houses and their interiors. The handsomely-bound volume of photographs which they supplied gives a comprehensive picture of the whole ensemble soon after its completion, before Lord and Lady Windsor's own first decorative intentions were obscured. The early pictures of the Great Hall show it lined with family portraits and marble busts, and with furniture including the famous Indian day-bed of fragile ivory which had belonged to Lord Windsor's distinguished ancestor, Clive of India. Later this strong emphasis on the family and their antecedents was to be lost when the portraits were replaced by Cluny tapestries.

When Queen Victoria was shown the album of photographs she was 'immensely interested', Lady Paget recorded. 'The Queen said to me in that naïve confidential way she has, "It must have cost very much building that house."

"Better than racing or gambling, your Majesty," I said.'

It is fascinating to compare Hewell with Clouds, the other 'great' house built by a family at the very centre of the Souls' circle. Lady Paget, writing at Hewell in 1895, says, 'I returned from white and blue Clouds, charming in its way, to this house blazing with gorgeous Italian colour.' She would not have disagreed with Doll Liddell, who wrote of Hewell: 'I think it is the best modern house I have seen.' Hewell was renowned as lavish and perfect, but the ornate Renaissance interior is the antithesis of the cool and reticent Arts and Crafts manner adhered to so faithfully at Clouds, which is now much more admired.

Hewell remained in use by the Windsor family for less than half a century: it was soon to be obsolete in a modern world where a great Renaissance palace had no function. Like Clouds, it too was given over to institutional use, and the carefully-preserved decorations, the murals, the carved panelling and the coffered ceilings are an incongruous reminder that it was once Sybil Cust's 'most astounding house'.

While all this activity was taking place at Hewell, Lady Windsor was occupied with another artistic venture, that of being painted full-length and life-size by Edward Burne-Jones. This was an act of greater significance than his patrons may have realized since it was Burne-Jones's only attempt to paint a 'society' portrait in the grand manner. It was notoriously difficult to persuade him to undertake portraiture, for he had no high opinion of his capacities in this respect; he once wrote ruefully to Frances Horner of a sight he remembered in Paris;

> Before the days of photography, the bane of art, there was an artist who had a booth just by the
> Madeleine – and outside his booth he wrote up a tariff of prices – as thus:

Ressemblance frappante	*2 francs*
Ressemblance ordinaire	*1.50 francs*
Air de famille	*50 centimes*

> I should never have an order for more than fifty centimes.

Lady Windsor's sittings began in 1891, and by the end of 1895 the picture was hanging on the staircase at Hewell. Lady Paget set down her reactions at length:

> This picture, one of the rare portraits he has ever painted, has been much abused by the critics. Gay is
> more beautiful, but the entire impression recalls her infinitely well to her best friends. The throat and

This painting of Lady Windsor is a rare attempt by Burne-Jones
to create a society portrait in the grand manner

hands are marvellously like, as is the gentle girlish appearance; but her eyelids are larger and her brows have a freer sweep, and the mouth and nose are more refined in their lines, and the contours of her cheeks are fuller and her complexion much brighter, and also the master has completely ignored the rich copper shades in her hair. What militates against the picture now are the huge sleeves worn at present which Burne-Jones entirely abominates. They give breadth and dignity to the figure, as in the old Venetian portraits, and make even a large head look small.

In the light of the esteem in which this picture is now held, this list of faults seems unduly critical; but these are the very details on which Sargent was to dwell so lovingly when he painted the Wyndham sisters in 1899, as can be seen from the letters written about him by Pamela Wyndham.

Burne-Jones has indeed taken considerable liberties, in particular with the dress which he has formalized into a timeless robe. Impossible to reconstruct from this penitential garb the flashing, glittering figure described by Lady Paget in her account of a ball at Hewell in 1893, dancing until three in the morning, 'in a grey and gold shot satin gown, a tiara of emeralds and diamonds with a matching necklace and another necklace of diamonds'.

As soon as the house was ready it became the scene of continuous entertaining. Lady Paget remembers:

> There was a great charm always about the parties here. Killing animals was not the chief feature. Music, art, literature, games of tennis on the fine court, and a general air of comfortable simplicity and *laissez aller* . . . Lady Granby [the Duchess of Rutland], a graceful shadow, sitting in flowery corners, always a little late for everything, floating about effectively in clinging garments; Lord · Granby, a lazy *bon enfant*, sometimes saying funny things. George Curzon in the most tearing spirits at his recent appointment as under-secretary at the F.O., talking nonsense in the most ornate and impressive English; Wallace [Lord Lamington], excellent and sentimental, but always happy when he can sit at the feet of a pretty woman and bow his curly pate before her in admiration.

But in spite of such glittering and lavish entertaining Lady Paget continually stresses her daughter's dislike of social life and her absorption with her beloved children; certainly, like Lord Windsor, she was immensely conscientious, almost seeming to welcome the grinding routine of official county work and the duties that came with being the wife of the Mayor of Cardiff. In 1885, Lady Paget remembers,

> There was a village concert at which Gay sang a Welsh song, to the intense delight of the natives. Mrs Lewis, of Greenmeadow recited and the rest was local talent of extraordinary varied quality and good calibre. They played the piano, the harp, and the violin; they sang in glees and parts, and seemed to have a wonderful musical understanding.

Such an evening could hardly be a greater contrast to the witty, fascinating talk of a Souls' party, where even the comparatively simple rules of a game like 'Letter Bags' (the predecessor of Scrabble) would be enlivened by the refinement of playing it in French! Lady Paget, anxious to present her daughter in the most favourable light to posterity has made her sound dull and stupid – attributes, as Lady Cowper makes plain, unheard of in Souls' circles.

> They shot, and ate, and drank, and flirted, and talked, and discussed and in fact were just the same as

others of their generation . . . the only unforgivable sin, it appears to me, was to be dull or stupid. That would exclude anyone; but nothing else did.

Lady Windsor's social life was also balanced by the duties of a country landowner and local magnate, and by artistic pastimes which were undertaken with enthusiasm. Her concern for the well-being of the tenants at Hewell took the practical form of providing classes in which useful country skills were taught. The traditional Welsh craft of quilting was revived; weaving tweed provided a prosperous sideline; and all manner of artistic crafts were encouraged and taught.

Meanwhile the embellishment of the house continued. A skilled cabinet-maker named Westover, imported from the East End of London, remained at Hewell for many years making furniture which was painted by the ladies of the family. The perfection of Hewell was a byword among almost all those who had seen it, but many people understandably preferred the beautiful, mellow and peaceful St Fagan's, the Plymouths' genuinely Elizabethan house near Cardiff: '. . . built within the *enceinte* of a Norman fortress, there is a pleasaunce and terraces and fishponds, and mazes of cut yews'. George Wyndham's description of 'this enchanted land of Arthurian romance', in a letter written to his cousin Wilfrid Blunt, constituted an irresistible temptation to that romantic man.

On one of his annual driving tours Wilfrid Blunt camped in the grounds of St Fagan's in his Arab tent, and was captivated by the silent, beautiful and mysteriously melancholy Lady Windsor. A week was spent in verbal fencing, with hints and half-made declarations, and his hopes were raised during the long summer evenings. In the autumn she was expected to lunch with him in London, and in deference to her eccentric eating habits he ordered a special vegetarian meal; but she did not turn up. The only result of this episode was that Blunt was persuaded to become a vegetarian like his hostess.

From St Fagan's Blunt journeyed on to Saighton Grange to stay with George Wyndham, where he found the house full of congenial friends, but '. . . nothing for a vegetarian to eat. I dined off two mushrooms and a raisin.' To have embarked wholeheartedly on vegetarianism on a long-term basis would have put Blunt to considerable inconvenience. Except in houses where this eccentric régime was specially catered for he would have had many experiences like the one at Saighton. The meals offered to guests in the nineteenth century were lavish to a fault, but few vegetables were served. During his vegetarian period Blunt could have satisfied his hunger only by scrounging a few morsels from the garnishes of the meat dishes, and by partaking of the salad and quantities of dessert. But he did not persist very long with this inconvenient and passion-inspired fad.

At this same time George Wyndham was also beginning to realize the strength of his feeling for Gay Windsor. He wrote movingly to Blunt: 'As a rule people do not know how to love; as an exception they love now here, now there, as a rarity almighty lovers find each other after both are married.' Unlike his romantic interlude with Lady Desborough, embarked upon with so little heart-searching some years before, this much more serious attraction was to be a test of the *savoir vivre* of all concerned. It was managed without scandal, largely through the loving and forgiving temperament of Sibell Grosvenor, who understood her husband's desperate need for companionship. She did not falter in her affection for Gay, the friend whom she had introduced into London society so many years before; and in this, as in so much else, she earned the gratitude of her husband. His last letter, written to her on 7 July 1913 from Paris, where he had gone with Gay (now Lady Plymouth) and her daughter to pay a visit to the Duke of Westminster, begins: 'I got a dear letter last night, quite entering into the spirit of my "outing"!' The next night he was dead.

Although Lady Plymouth was overcome with grief she had the satisfaction of knowing that she had made more tolerable his years of political disappointment and private melancholy; but it was a heavy blow, coming so soon after the death in India of her beloved eldest son, Other, in 1908. Her silences were now more prolonged, and her reserve a protection against life's intrusions. In her later years after her husband's death she left Hewell, with which her whole personality had been so completely identified, and lived very quietly in an old stone house in Painswick in Gloucestershire, which had been made habitable for her with great discretion and respect for its character by Detmar Blow. By this date the Souls' circle barely survived, and Gay Plymouth allowed her reclusive instincts full rein; but she had earlier made her mark in being portrayed by Burne-Jones as the very epitome of the female Soul.

Lady Windsor, photographed in about 1910 and still, in middle age, a figure of great elegance and grave beauty

TEN
Sir John and Lady Horner

If the Horners you add,
Then a man must be mad
Who complains that the Gang is the wrong sort.
George Curzon

Sir John Horner was a detached and benevolent observer of the Souls' circle: he attended their dinners, entertained them himself, and was on excellent terms with them all; but the real participant in the coterie was his wife Frances. To posterity, the most important aspect of her life was her long relationship with her beloved friend, Edward Burne-Jones, and even in old age she was still visited by people curious to see someone who had been one of that painter's models. Yet she had a powerful enough personality in her own right not to be engulfed by his encompassing and distinctive character. 'Lady Horner was a woman of great gifts, having the brains, energy, and high spirits which are essential for anyone if they are to hold a central position among a group of men and women,' recalls Violet Milner.

John Fortescue Horner had been educated at Eton and Balliol, and subsequently called to the Bar. In 1874, at the age of thirty-two, he succeeded to the estate at Mells Park in Somerset, which had been in the family since the Reformation; it was allegedly the 'plum' pulled out of the pie by little Jack Horner of nursery legend. (It is said that the title deeds of the manor were actually concealed in a pie – though the Horners dismissed the story.) In 1885 he became High Sheriff of Somerset, and ten years later Commissioner for Woods and Forests, a post for which he was well suited, for he was deeply versed in all the lore and language of the countryside, and had always been active in county matters.

John Horner was tall, fair and bearded. He possessed a considerable sense of humour, and was erudite on an astonishing range of subjects; but he was noticeably quiet and unassertive in manner. His high standard of moral discrimination was legendary. In *Time Remembered* Lady Horner tells a charming story illustrating this:

> Sir James Barrie was fond of telling how at a dinner at Birrell's with Duff and Diana Cooper and one or two others, in the course of conversation they were discussing what you would most mind being called – a bore or a cad.
>
> 'It depends who calls you that,' said one of the party.
>
> 'Suppose Sir John Horner called you a cad,' said another.
>
> 'Oh, my God! That *would* do you,' they all cried out.

With no aspirations to be a Soul himself, he was content to preside with suave but silent good humour over his wife's sparkling parties and dinners. These occasions brought unaccustomed life to the large rooms at Mells, many of which had been sparsely furnished or even empty before his marriage.

Maurice Baring's friend, Constantine Benckendorff, a frequent guest at Mells, was struck by this aspect of his host:

> In the background, Mr Horner, seldom visible out of his study, and then nearly always silent; until all of a sudden, reliable information would be in demand during one of the interminable discussions which, day and night, occupied the minds and tongues of all the inmates of Mells. He was then the person who in answer to a direct question would come out of his daydream, look up muttering 'Let me see', disappear for about ten minutes into his study and return to deliver a little lecture on any point under the sun, full of the most precise and relevant information.

Frances Graham, whom John Horner married in 1883, was the daughter of William Graham, Liberal M.P. for Glasgow and a well-to-do India merchant, who was a notable and indefatigable collector of pictures. Graham had a number of very fine early Italian pictures, but he is now best remembered as being one of the earliest patrons of Burne-Jones and a faithful patron of Rossetti. There are many glimpses of him in the role of collector and connoisseur in his daughter's book *Time Remembered*, which is one of the best accounts of life in the more intellectual and aesthetic circles of the society in which the Souls moved.

Frances Horner was a member of the Souls' circle from its earliest days, as can be seen from the mention of the Horners in Curzon's verses for the famous Bachelors' Club dinner of 1889. Oddly, there is no evidence that they actually attended the dinner, for by an uncharacteristic oversight they are not on the list of guests which was compiled by the host himself, and records both those present and those absent. Lady Paget called Frances Horner 'the High Priestess of the Souls', but that is not to say that Frances was a typical Soul, for although she had a fine sense of the ridiculous, she was too intellectual to be witty in the light-hearted but often heartless way that made up the flavour of the Souls' *badinage*. Lord Haldane, who became a friend of the Horners in 1893, and thereafter joined the select band of 'occasional Souls', said of Frances that she was 'one of the cleverest women I have seen, and as full of insight as she was clever'. Lady Horner remembers that it was at a dinner-party in London that they first met: Haldane, finding in his neighbour at the dinner-table an unusually well-informed knowledge of German literature, introduced her to the work of Schopenhauer. This she 'found most entertaining', though she reveals that the fantastic idea of unborn children trying to 'enter the world through the medium of lovers' meetings' as described in Schopenhauer's *World as Will and Idea* later reduced her and Charty Ribblesdale to helpless laughter as they read it aloud during the course of a party at Mells.

Haldane was invited to Mells for the first time at Christmas in 1893, and after 1895 the Christmas visits became an annual event. This generous hospitality was to be somewhat churlishly repaid many years later when he wrote his autobiography. On his first visit Haldane had been thrown into the company of some of the leading Souls: Harry Cust, Alfred Lyttelton, Charty Ribblesdale and the Harry Whites. His considered opinion of the group was not high:

'They sometimes took themselves much too seriously, and on the whole it is doubtful whether their influence was on balance good.' But he had the grace to admit: 'They cared for literature and art, and their social gifts were so high that people sought much to be admitted into their circle.' Haldane was at the time not displeased to be familiar with this charmed circle, and he was grateful enough for the opportunities which the Horners' hospitality afforded of meeting Arthur Balfour, a powerful political opponent.

Even as a young girl Frances was not pretty in the conventional sense. Seen full-face, her features were rather heavy, but her expression in profile was sensitive and serious; as an old woman her looks began to verge on the formidable. Nevertheless Doll Liddell, who was staying in Scotland with William Graham in 1882, chose his image well when he described her in a letter to Lady Wemyss (not Mary Elcho, but her mother-in-law):

> We had an excitement here yesterday, in the shape of a proposal. One Horner, who was at Balliol with us, securing the services of the 'Botticelli' as helpmate for life. It had been expected for some time and is very satisfactory. But somehow with true human perversity everyone who had been wishing it suddenly became plunged in gloom when it occurred and there has been a funereal atmosphere over the house ever since.

Frances Graham (later Lady Horner)
by Sir Edward Burne-Jones. A
photograph of the same date shows that
Burne-Jones has refined and
etherealized the features of his subject

The type evidently persisted, for just over twenty years later Raymond Asquith compared Frances' daughter, Katharine, to the 'Botticelli Madonna' in the National Gallery.

However 'funereal' the feelings of William Graham's guests in Scotland, they cannot have matched for despondency those of Burne-Jones, who was helplessly in love with Frances. Shortly after her marriage he wrote with sad resignation to Ruskin:

> . . . many a patient design went to adorning Frances' ways – Sirens for her girdle, Heavens and Paradises for her prayerbooks, Virtues and Vices for her necklace-boxes – ah! the folly of me from the beginning – and now in the classic words of Mr Swiveller 'she has gone and married a market gardener'. Well, I can't remember a tithe of the acts of folly there . . .

For Burne-Jones the relationship was one of the most important of the last twenty years of his life. It began when Frances was seventeen or eighteen years old and was to last until the artist's death in 1898. It inspired not only many drawings and designs but also a series of exquisitely fantastic letters from Burne-Jones, many of which are printed in *Time Remembered*. His passion invested Frances with an aura of romance which transcends the reality of mere prettiness. There is a magical excitement about attracting the love of an artist and acting as an inspiration to his work. This aura may partly explain the ease with which she was accepted into the Souls' circle, because, as she herself was at pains to explain, the Grahams were not 'in Society', an exclusion then still a very real social handicap.

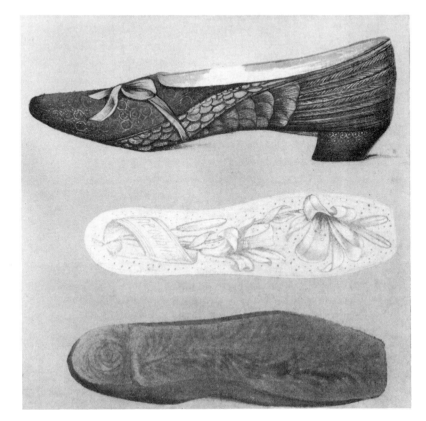

Burne-Jones's design for slippers for Frances Horner, to be embroidered by Agnes Jekyll (watercolour)

T.M. Rooke from Frances Horner July 1898

Like George and Mary Wyndham, Frances Graham had since girlhood been an *habituée* of the studios of the artists admired by her father. She was taken on Saturday afternoons in the seventies to visit Rossetti at Cheyne Walk, and heard him read the *House of Life* sonnets which he was then composing. The Grange at Fulham, Burne-Jones's house, seemed dull by comparison with Rossetti's, which boasted a garden with a menagerie in it. Burne-Jones had become a friend of his patron and dined with the family two or three times a week when they were in London. He seems to have begun to take particular notice of Frances in 1875. Mary Gladstone noted enviously on 14 February: 'Valentine's Day – Frances got such a beauty from Mr Burne-Jones – a big picture of Cupid dragging a maiden through all the meshes of love . . .' and the series of beautiful and delicate drawings of her in profile began about a year later. Her likeness also appears in the group of nymphs on the right-hand side of one of the Perseus panels destined for Arthur Balfour's music-room. Frances found conversation with Burne-Jones deeply enriching to her imagination, and this was to be of inestimable value in the social circle which she frequented as a married woman.

As a young girl she had regretted most keenly her parents' disapproval of balls and parties and of society in general. She was like the girl in the 1874 *Punch* drawing by George du Maurier, called 'A Pathetic Appeal':

> 'Mama, shall you let me go to the Wilkinsons' ball, if they give one, this winter?'
> 'No, darling.'
> '*You've* been to a great many balls, haven't you, Mamma?'
> 'Yes, darling – and I've seen the *folly* of them all.'
> 'Mightn't I just see the folly of one, Mamma?'

She wrote:

> I longed to go to balls, but we were never asked to any. . . I think all my later life I suffered from never having had the ordinary friendships and amusements and society of girls of my own age. A girl who has not been out, or danced, is like a boy who grows up without going to public school.

The desolate existence which this passage conjures up is somewhat exaggerated. The Lytteltons and Mary Gladstone were her friends, and through them Frances met many interesting people. In the country William Graham was a generous host, entertaining houseparties for shooting – an invitation that few sportsmen could resist – during the Season in Scotland. Margot Asquith, whose sister Laura was Frances Graham's most beloved friend, and who was able to make her own way into society by a mixture of determination and sheer effrontery, obviously did not see the Graham way of life as putting Frances at any great disadvantage: 'She was the leader in what was called the high-art, William Morris School and one of the few girls who ever had a salon in London.' She remembers her in the enviable position of having 'Burne-Jones at her feet and Ruskin at her elbow'. But the remembered sense of dissatisfaction with the social milieu of her girlhood must have been a spur to Frances when she faced the daunting task of turning Mells Park into a fit setting for the entertainment of her friends.

It is possible to detect, even through the buoyant anticipation of the bride-to-be, a lowering of the spirits as she first surveyed the neglected, empty rooms, the few rather poor family portraits, and the vast collection of stuffed animals and birds, minerals, seaweed, old scientific

Photograph by F. Hollyer of a drawing of Frances Graham by Burne-Jones, dated 1879.
This drawing, from the series of profile portraits of Frances, most resembles the image
of the nymph in the extreme right of the painting *The Arming of Perseus*, one of the
panels designed for Arthur Balfour's music room

instruments, and bound volumes of periodicals, all unrelieved by a single vase of flowers. But she was cheered by the ravishing view of the lake from a terrace in the park. Once married, she enthusiastically set about the task of transforming her new home. In spite of a chronic lack of funds Mells Park, and also the houses in the village, were gradually put in order. The former emerged as a spacious, light, and elegant eighteenth-century house of great charm, furnished with comfort but without pretension, and embellished with pictures from old Mr Graham's collection.

Doll Liddell visited Mells Park for the first time early in 1884. He recalls:

> . . . it was an old-fashioned house, like a lot of packing cases set down side by side and joined with doors. The park, an attractive one, just the right mixture of nature and culture. The Burne-Jones pictures looked a little strange in the comfortable rooms especially an immense cartoon for tapestry, representing Love with great red wings.

The furniture stored away in the unused rooms was rescued, and proved to be old-fashioned but comfortable: the large sofas were soon burdened with incessantly talking guests. As in the Wyndham household the food was delicious, in contrast to the establishment kept by the Rector of Mells, John Horner's brother and a distinguished Coptic scholar who, according to Frances, was 'celibate, vegetarian, teetotal, anti-sport, anti-smoking, anti-all amusements'.

Count Benckendorff was struck by the special quality of the hospitality:

> What mainly distinguished the atmosphere at Mells was the extraordinary nonchalance – Frances Horner had a wonderful capacity, while appearing herself a rather busy and slightly worried hostess, of inducing the rest of the household to take things as they came.

Much had changed since Frances had abandoned the high-minded régime established by the Horner sisters in the years before their brother's marriage. Simple excellence achieved with thoughtful care was now the theme throughout.

In 1900 the Horners moved from Mells Park to the Tudor manor house for reasons of economy. They much enjoyed the simpler life that could be led in these more modest surroundings, even though with family and friends the house was often very overcrowded. Earlier Burne-Jones had written to Frances Horner asking:

> Don't you a little bit wish you lived in a little house – and it was all sweet and tiny, and didn't take any thought or waste any time, and were rather poor – only with pocket-money for books and toys – and no visitors – all friends living in the same street, and the street long and narrow and ending in the city wall, and the wall opening with a gate on to cornfields in the south, and the wild wood on the north – and no railways anywhere – all friends and all one's world tied up in the little city – and no news to come – only rumours and gossips at the city gate telling things a month old and all wrong.

The Horners thought of themselves as 'rather poor', as did Lord and Lady Elcho – but surely neither would have welcomed the idea of 'no visitors'. Even Burne-Jones might have stopped short of imagining a house so tiny that no domestic help could be accommodated: being 'rather poor' never reached such a point of crisis that actual chores had to be undertaken by the family. Lady Elcho's youngest daughter remembers that tea-parties at Miss Eliza Wedgwood's house in Stanton, the beautiful village close to Stanway, were arranged deliberately to take place on the maid's afternoon off so that the children could be allowed the great treat of washing up. Percy

Wyndham too had begun to think himself 'overhoused' at Clouds towards the turn of the century. Mells Park never sheltered Horners again after 1900. It was burnt down in 1917, and rebuilt in a much altered form in 1922.

The village was cared for with the discretion that comparative poverty imposes. Burne-Jones loved the colour of the houses: '. . . when you go forth into the villages, will you love and praise them for their holy greyness?' Mells village survived the cleansing fervour of the nineteenth-century restorer, with whom Morris and Webb did valiant and ultimately effective battle through the efforts of the 'Anti-Scrape' Society, and has remained with all its 'holy greyness' intact.

The church reflects more obviously Frances Horner's artistic taste. Dominating one side is the large equestrian monument to her son Edward who was killed in the Great War. It was devised by Lutyens, whose handsome plinth supports a bronze horse and rider by Alfred Munnings. The figure stares with sightless eyes at St Francis with the birds and the fish in the memorial window to Sir John Horner, designed by William Nicholson; and both are watched over discreetly from the back of the church by an embroidered angel with great red wings, designed by Burne-Jones and executed with practised skill by Lady Horner herself. (It was the cartoon for this that Doll Liddell had seen hanging in the house.) Laura Lyttelton's monument, in the form of a great peacock, adds a note of exotic splendour, mockingly resplendent in contrast to the austere lettering of the Latin inscription on the opposite wall commemorating the death in action of the Horners' son-in-law Raymond Asquith. At one time his sword and steel helmet hung alongside the incised letters on the wall, a poignant reminder of the battlefield; while Edward Horner's gauntlets lay on the plinth beneath the mounted figure in bronze. Outside in the churchyard the visitor's eye may be struck by a group of gravestones whose restrained elegance is almost that of the eighteenth century. Family and friends are together as they were in the house during their lifetimes. Mrs Graham, who lived during her widowhood at the Park, is also buried here; her classical Grecian stele is conventional, unlike the polychrome mixed-metal memorial to William Graham in Glasgow, a masterpiece executed by Alfred Gilbert in the Japanese taste to honour a discerning patron of the arts.

Raymond Asquith's marriage in 1907 to Frances' second daughter, Katharine, united two more Souls' families. The tradition of hospitality established by Lady Horner at Mells in the heyday of the Souls was carried on into the second generation.

✿ ELEVEN

The Tennant Family

Here a trio we meet
Whom you never will beat
Tho' wide you may wander and far go;
From that wonderful art
Of that Gallant Old Bart.,
Sprang Charty and Lucy and Margot?

George Curzon

The 'Gallant Old Bart', Sir Charles Tennant, Liberal Member of Parliament and a wealthy and successful industrialist, was born in 1823. He lived to be eighty-three years old and was twice married, for the second time when he was seventy-five. Altogether he had sixteen children, of whom four daughters were to enliven the Souls' circle with their wit and irrepressible social high spirits. The most notable of them, the wittiest and the most socially intrepid, was Margot. But all the sisters were so gregarious that Doll Liddell described the Souls as 'a set of friends the nucleus of which had been brought together by the social arts of the Tennant family'.

The Tennants had been prominent Glaswegian businessmen since the end of the eighteenth century, when they founded the St Rollox chemical works. In 1842 the famous 'Tennant's Stalk' was built by John Tennant – a chimney towering three times as high as Nelson's Column, its height intended to prevent the noxious fumes from the chemical factory from polluting the Glasgow air. Sir Charles Tennant was the second son of John. He early showed an aptitude for business amounting to genius, and at the age of twenty he was made a partner in the family firm. Within a few years he had created a substantial fortune by speculation on the Stock Exchange. His business interests included railways in Britain and America (in the Midwest a town was named Tennant) and he was one of the partners in the construction of the Forth Bridge. The Mysore Gold Mining Company was perhaps his most brilliant and daring enterprise: he was immensely generous to all those who backed him, and in 1903 he paid a dividend of 165 per cent to the shareholders of the company. He practised his firm belief in the virtues of capitalism.

From 1880 Sir Charles diverted some of his formidable energy into the collecting of pictures and works of art, a taste for which he shared with his son-in-law Lord Ribblesdale. Margot, who had the rare faculty for taking an unprejudiced critical view even of members of her own family, wrote of her father:

He had a good eye . . . but he was no discoverer in art. Here I will add to make myself clear that I am thinking of men like Frances Horner's father, old Mr Graham, who discovered and promoted Burne-Jones and Frederick Walker. . . . My father's judgment was warped by constantly comparing his own things with other people's.

Sir Charles had compared his own things with William Graham's to good effect, and many of the contemporary works in his collection were by artists already favoured by Graham – for example, Walker, Clarkson Stanfield, Millais and Watts – but like many people who love the eighteenth century, which he preferred to any other, he could not admire Burne-Jones. In 1900 he lent pictures from his collection to Paris for the Centennial Exhibition, and in 1901 it was the subject of an admiring article by Max Roldit in the first issue of *The Connoisseur:*

> . . . ever since his first purchase, he has been guided by two fundamental principles to which he has firmly adhered: to buy works of the very highest standard, and to acquire these almost at any cost, whenever they came into his reach.

Discussing the collection seventy years later (also in *The Connoisseur*), Sir Charles's grandson demonstrated the wisdom of this policy by an analysis of the prices fetched by such of the works as had been disposed of to public and private collections. Sir Charles's youngest daughter was born in 1904, and he died two years later after a more than ordinarily full and satisfactory life.

The four famous Tennant daughters are best known under their married names: Lady Ribblesdale, Mrs Graham Smith, Laura Lyttelton and Margot Asquith. Lady Frances Balfour described them as 'a family highly gifted, of totally unconventional manners, with no code of behaviour except their own good hearts'. Their entry into London society was lively; indeed, in the instance of the youngest, Margot, a vivid assault. They were all renowned for a quality frequently praised by Margot, 'social courage'; and all were supported morally, socially and financially by their bountiful father, whose generous dowries in the American style made possible their marriages to eligible but impecunious husbands.

The family were brought up at The Glen, the Scottish baronial castle built by Sir Charles in Peebleshire, and they loved their home. 'I could never be unhappy in the most beautiful place in the broad earth,' wrote Laura.

During the seventies Sir Charles Tennant took his elder daughters to London for the season, staying in Thomas's Hotel in Berkeley Square. When in 1879 he was elected Liberal Member of Parliament for a Scottish seat, he bought a house in London, 40 (later re-numbered 55) Grosvenor Square, and from here the Tennant sisters were launched on their conquest of London.

Charlotte Tennant, nicknamed Charty, had married Lord Ribblesdale two year before. 'Dear Charty was already well known and beloved of all,' wrote Mary Elcho of the early eighties. Burne-Jones said that she had 'a beautiful presence'. According to D. D. Lyttelton, 'she was tall and fair, with rippling gold hair which seemed to express her eagerness and vitality'. She had the wit and Tennant vivacity tempered by 'sunny serenity' and gentleness. 'Heart and tongue of an angel to Charty,' praised George Curzon.

Her husband, Lord Ribblesdale, was known as one of the handsomest men of his day. 'For patrician good looks, expressing intelligence and sensibility, I have never seen his equal,' wrote Sir Leslie Jones, who stayed with him at his Yorkshire estate, Gisburne, in about 1910. Sargent begged to be allowed to paint him, and after much discussion he was portrayed in his hunting costume. When they went to view the picture at the Salon in Paris, Charty and Ribblesdale were pursued by an embarrassingly large crowd of people eager to draw attention to 'ce grand diable de Milord anglais'.

At the time of their marriage, the Lister family fortunes had all but vanished through the prodigality of his over-extravagant father. Sir Charles Tennant showed great generosity, paying off a large mortgage on the Ribblesdale estate at Gisburne, and buying the young couple a house in Mayfair, 57 Green Street. He also appointed Lord Ribblesdale to the board of several of his companies. Such generosity was much appreciated; 'Tommy is one of the few people in the world who has shown me gratitude,' his father-in-law wrote. Doubtless this benevolence enabled Lord Ribblesdale to accept appointments in the Royal Household, Lord in Waiting from 1880 to 1885 and, subsequently, Master of the Queen's Buckhounds. Oscar Wilde found the Ribblesdales ensconced in the Royal Box when he visited the Haymarket Theatre in 1894 to see Mrs Patrick Campbell in *John-a Dreams*; 'I felt it my duty to sit in the Royal Box with the Ribblesdales, the Harry Whites, and the Home Secretary [Asquith].'

Life was to deal the Ribblesdales heavy blows. Thomas Lister, their eldest son, serving in the 10th Hussars, was killed in Somaliland aged only twenty-six. In 1915 their second son Charles was killed in the Dardanelles campaign.

Lady Ribblesdale suffered from consumption, the dread ailment that also killed her two elder sisters, Posie and Janet. In 1911 she died after bravely fighting a three-year battle. During this time she barely saw her husband and her children as she was sent from one nursing home to another, to Davos, to Wales, and finally to Wimbledon. John Tennant wrote, 'Charty was most persevering; she would not let herself be beaten'. Lord Ribblesdale watched her decline sadly but stoically. According to his daughter, 'He bore these sorrows without flinching, reckoning that the span of life must be measured, not by its length, but by its excellence.'

After the death of his wife Lord Ribblesdale went to live under the benevolent sway of Mrs Rosa Lewis at the Cavendish Hotel, at that time still a haven of elegance and superior cooking. He eventually sold his London house and moved some of the furniture into the hotel to furnish his rooms. The 'goings-on' at the Cavendish provided a welcome and much needed distraction. Lord Ribblesdale's friendly and unaffected interest in other people, which had served him so well in his relations with the huntsman to the Buckhounds, allowed him to enjoy the daily round in this ramshackle establishment to the full. He took pleasure in the shrewd humour and calculated indiscretions of the proprietress. There was no echo here of the feline wit and discursive philosophizing of the Souls' parties.

Lord Ribblesdale looked upon his wife's involvement with the Souls and her hero-worship of George Curzon with tolerant amusement. In their turn, her friends were fascinated by the mixture of fastidiousness and urbanity which characterized 'the Ancestor', as he was widely known. His detached, stately manner and his immaculate attention to his dress were maintained even in the privacy of his family, while his impeccable manners made him punctilious in the service of the least of his children's friends.

Lady Ribblesdale, drawn by Violet, Duchess of Rutland.
Her brother Jack said that she had 'natural charm
allied to an armoury of beauty'

This portrait of Lord Ribblesdale by John Singer Sargent caused a sensation when it was
exhibited in Paris. It was seen as the embodiment of the ideal 'milord anglais'

Lucy Graham Smith, the next daughter, was invited by Curzon to the Souls' dinners, and complimented: 'To Lucy he gave the wiles which enslave.' She led a quiet and retiring life in the country, at Easton Grey in Wiltshire. She had married Thomas Graham Smith when she was very young, disregarding the wise advice of her parents. Although brave and dashing he proved to be of uncertain temper, and the marriage was not reputed to be happy. Mrs Graham Smith was regarded as the most talented of all the sisters and Doll Liddell said of her that she had 'a mild touch of genius'. She was a most gifted artist, and her parents wisely sent her to the Académie Jullian: her portraits in watercolour were especially skilful. She had a gentle wit: when a piece of coal was tossed on the fire, she suddenly cried, 'Oh, don't burn it now; it's lived so long.' Her brother and sisters all loved her for her sweetness of character. Sadly afflicted by arthritis, she suffered greatly and uncomplainingly for many years. At the Opening of Parliament in 1909 Lady Cust wrote: 'We all had to wait a long time on the stairs, and Margot came rushing down much fussed and asked thro' the glass door, "Won't Black Rod soften his heart for me, my sister is a cripple" – that was poor Lucy I think.'

Mrs Graham Smith, as photographed
for the Curzon album

The two youngest Tennant sisters, Laura and Margot, were brought up like twins: they shared a room, dressed alike, and had the same vivacious zest for life, carried to recklessness. All her life Margot was in the headlines: every exploit, every flirtation, every audacious *bon mot*, was pounced on by the Press. Laura foresaw the dangers of heady exuberance; she even wrote a prayer which was a plea against excessive high spirits. The reticence of behaviour practised by English society, the discretion which was an unwritten law, were joyfully flouted by the Tennant sisters. Writing in 1930, Mary Elcho recalled that the arrival of the Tennant sisters in London caused a tremendous commotion: 'They were quite unlike anyone that London had seen before . . . many were startled and most were delighted – the two girls[Laura and Margot] were astonishing.'

Laura Lyttelton – a posthumous drawing by Violet, Duchess of Rutland, made thirteen years after Laura's death

By the early eighties Laura and Margot already had many admirers and received numerous proposals. In 1884 they invited to The Glen such guests as George Curzon, Doll Liddell, Harry Cust, the Lytteltons and the Charterises. House parties at The Glen were organized entirely by Laura and Margot. Lady Tennant was quiet and retiring; as amazed by her daughters as everyone else, she was quite content for them to entertain in the way in which they wished. In Mary Gladstone's words:

> There was a kind of Star and Garter freedom and recklessness of manners and talk, there was no reserve, no restraint, no holy places kept sacred. All day it was one fury of fun and games and music and discussion, at meals you tore through subject after subject with the rapidity of lightning; retort, repartee, contradictions, capping, flew across the table with a constant accompaniment of shrieks and peals of laughter. Parting at bedtime only meant leaving the elders below. Here the pranks and fun and frolic grew faster and more furious, apple-pie beds, sponge fights, pillow games, nobody minding whose room was invaded.

On other evenings the two sisters, dressed decorously in bed-jackets, entertained both sexes in their bedroom, and the party would discuss art or literature or ideas until the small hours. The complete, transparent innocence of the girls disarmed scandal, but obviously encouraged gossip. When Gladstone's daughter, Mary, pointed this out to Laura, the latter explained, 'One gets so into the habit of saying "Dear me, if one does play the fool, what can it matter in ten years?" – and so "*laissez faire*" becomes one's motto.' However, she recognized the justice of Miss Gladstone's criticism. 'If it will make you believe in me – which I should like you to do – I will promise you never to ballyrag again.'

Laura Tennant was not a Soul, for she died in 1886 and the coterie coalesced a little later; Margot commented that in mourning for Laura they came closer together. However, as Mary Elcho wrote, Laura 'would have worn with better grace than any that fantastic label'. She was small, slender, large-eyed, highly vulnerable, with an air of delicacy about her that made many feel her life might not be long. Doll Liddell, who loved her, wrote

> O still, small face, like a white petal torn
> From a wild rose by autumn winds and flung
> On some dark stream . . .

Everyone felt protective towards Laura. She described herself as having a 'zig-zag' character, and in spite of her frailty had all the Tennant vivacity. In Lucy Lyttelton's words, 'She had the naughtiness, the grace and quickness and mischievousness of a kitten . . . nothing was safe in heaven or earth from the sallies of her wit . . . she could strike sparks out of dead wood.' Laura's charm became a legend. 'She is up one's sleeve and round one's neck and inside one's heart almost before one has even looked at her.'

In 1884 Laura and Alfred Lyttelton fell in love, and became engaged in December of that year. It was generally agreed to be the perfect partnership.

Alfred Lyttelton was the seventh of the eight sons of Lord Cobham. He was an ideal Englishman – an outstanding athlete at Eton, he is said to have played 'the champagne of cricket'. In his

Alfred Lyttelton, already a widower,
photographed by Lord Battersea at
Aston Clinton. Lord Curzon said that
everyone who had known Alfred
became a better person for it

subsequent career at the Bar, and later in politics, as Minister for the Colonies in Balfour's
Cabinet, he made only friends, and Curzon said of him that anyone who had the privilege of
knowing Alfred Lyttelton was a better person for it.

In January 1885 Laura wrote to Margot from Easton Grey: 'Alfred is here. I am so hap. I
think I will die of it. I don't see how it can last. It is so wonderful and mystic and sacramental.'
All Laura's images at this time come from nature: sun, mountains, fresh grass, bright spring
flowers. She described Alfred as '. . . a running stream with the sun on it. He is quite one of the
most dazzling bits of light God has put into the world.' Such ecstasy carries within it the shadow
of fatality. Laura and Alfred were married in May 1885, and in May the following year she died,
a few days after the birth of her son. (The son himself, devotedly cared for by the Ribblesdales,
died two years later.) The mourning was universal. But her death was considered elegiac rather
than tragic; it was accepted that those whom God loves so much he ennobles by death. Alfred
Lyttelton's reply to Gladstone's letter of condolence echoes this: 'Life does not begin in the
highest sense until Renunciation is learnt. The centre of her religion was her recognition of the
glory of sacrifice. Nothing could I believe teach me this, except the heart-breaking grief I now
suffer.'

Laura had had a premonition of her own death and had composed a romantic, rambling and discursive will. To all her friends there were praises and gifts. For Mary Elcho she left a child's cot, still at Stanway; to Arthur Balfour two books and an enamel brooch for his future wife, should he marry. To Frances Horner, who was Laura's greatest friend, she bequeathed a diamond and enamel bracelet, and some Burne-Jones 'spression' drawings, his small caricatures. Frances Horner had introduced Laura to Burne-Jones, and she now commissioned from him her memorial, depicting a peacock resting on a bier adorned with myrtle leaves. It was sculpted in relief in grey gesso, and placed in the church at Mells. The effect is somewhat mute for so vibrant a soul as Laura whereas the oil sketch, which Burne-Jones gave to Mary Elcho, is triumphant; the peacock in radiant colours recalls the brilliance of Laura, and her tomb is pure gold.

The memorial to Laura Lyttelton, by Sir Edward Burne-Jones. This is the oil sketch for the gesso memorial plaque commissioned by Lady Horner for the church at Mells

Margot was distraught at Laura's death. 'I can't help it, it may be selfish but it's true I *mind* Laura going, she's part of myself and I shall shriek at the empty bed now and work off what I've wanted to say by biting my pillow and burying my head,' she wrote to George Curzon. To her, Laura was 'the gilder of every pleasure, the soother of every sorrow', as Cassandra Austen wrote of her sister Jane. The loss was irreparable, and Margot's greatest consolation was to be in the company of her friends, who were now the Souls.

Margot possessed 'social courage' to the highest degree. It could mean daring, audacity, and sometimes even effrontery. She was often called 'the electric charge' of a party: however shocking she may have been, everyone always welcomes those who make them laugh. Margot was brilliantly and utterly spontaneously funny. The essence of her wit was to puncture the cliché, as when she said of Henry James that 'His brains have gone to his head', or of ghosts, 'Appearances are in their favour'. Such lightning repartee was relished with glee by the Souls; Curzon complimented her:

> To Margot the wit
> And the wielding of it,
> That make her the joy of a party

Margot Tennant with her terrier.
This was the photograph she gave for
the album presented to Curzon

Margot Tennant July 1890

When Margot was in her teens Mary Gladstone wrote that she was 'the most really pretty' of the Tennant sisters. She had pearly skin, pretty dark curly hair, and a slim elegant figure. A series of bad accidents in the hunting field, where she showed perhaps too much daring, spoiled her early looks; but her sisters said that as soon as Margot began to talk in her vivacious, witty way, her face was very attractive. The Marquis de Soveral said of her, as had been said of Sarah Bernhardt, '*Elle n'est pas jolie, elle est pire*', meaning that she had a charm more dangerous than that of mere prettiness. She held herself beautifully, her head high, her walk graceful, and she had the 'light of victory in her eyes'.

Margot was now a hostess on her own, an unheard-of position for an unmarried girl: *England* described her in November 1894 as 'practically mistress of her father's house in Grosvenor Square'. Autumn houseparties at The Glen became an annual event in the Souls' calendar.

Godfrey Webb, George Curzon, Harry Cust, George Wyndham, Arthur Balfour, all came to stay. Margot was described as 'probably the most active and indefatigable "Soul" of all'. Pillow fights gave way to pencil games, for which she was passionately enthusiastic. Some were simply fun, like 'Analogies'; others, such as 'Character Sketches', were too probing to be entirely amusing. 'Styles', in which contestants were given half an hour to compose an essay in the style of Carlyle or Meredith, reminds one uncomfortably of a home university course. (Margot, without extensive formal education, described herself as 'intellectually self-made'.) In 1886 Doll Liddell noted:

> . . . the disease of intellectual games such as 'Styles', 'Bouts rimés', 'Epitaphs', etc. of which symptoms have been appearing in our clique for the last year or so, was very pronounced. I must confess that I liked these diversions at first, but in after times many new games, some of them foolish or dull, were added to the list, and I think were overdone in the houses I mostly frequented, so that at the last I got heartily sick of the pastime.

Margot then thought of founding a magazine. The idea was good, as she had a brilliant list of contributors: Harry Cust was to write on gossip, George Wyndham on letters, Betty Ponsonby on conversation. She cajoled Oscar Wilde, John Addington Symonds, the actor Coquelin, Jowett of Balliol, and Ellen Terry to produce articles. Illustrations were to be by Burne-Jones and Lucy Graham Smith. Unfortunately the magazine, which was to be called *Tomorrow*, remained in a state of procrastination. But, as always with Margot, the Press pounced. Alternative names suggested had included *The Butterfly*, *Women's Wit and Humour* and *Causeries en peignoir*. Godfrey Webb's suggestion had been *Petticoats*, and this name was turned into a tease by the *News of the World*.

Her passion for dancing also attracted comment, as reported in *England* of 6 May 1893:

> Miss Margot Tennant has just got back from Paris, bringing her lovely Loie Fuller frocks, and is now quite an expert in the dance which everyone raves about here. It will amuse the 'Souls'.

There are other accounts of Margot and Lady Granby entertaining the Souls by 'fantastic dances'. 'Skirt dancing', as Margot called it, had been invented by Loie Fuller in Chicago in the late eighties. In 1893 she performed at the Folies Bergère, and overnight became the rage of Paris: she was drawn by Lautrec, sculpted by Larche as a sinuous electric lamp, and many said

that she inspired the curves of the buildings of the new Metro. Miss Fuller had many imitators, but no rivals. Her technique was brilliant. She wore a vast silk skirt, like a parachute; for some of her more ambitious dances the huge skirts contained over a hundred yards of fabric; this she supported by batons held in the hand, and whirled and twirled on a glass platform lit from below by multi-coloured electric lights. Obviously Margot's interpretation was limited to graceful manipulations of drapery, but her dancing was praised by many.

Margot, unlike most of her friends, wore fashionable and expensive clothes. She had true chic. She followed the Paris fashions, and doubtless a generous allowance permitted her to indulge her choice. In 1908 the new line of Poiret created as great a sensation as the New Look of 1947, though for opposite reasons; for whereas the New Look emphasized an hourglass figure, Poiret's dresses were high-waisted, uncorseted, free. Margot admired his clothes so much that she arranged to show his collection at 10 Downing Street. Naturally she was much attacked: Downing Street was dubbed 'Gowning Street'. For a season or two Margot had to content herself with English copies.

Such was the notoriety of Margot that in 1893 E. F. Benson wrote a novel based on her character, and entitled *Dodo*. It was a runaway bestseller, with eleven reprints. Dodo is Margot satirized; in her vivacity, her whims, her ambitions: 'I want to be the fashion.' The Souls are called 'the Apostles'. Just as *England* had said of Margot in 1892 that 'she has made and unmade more "Souls" than any other "Souls" in the coterie', so Dodo is the one who makes 'discoveries' of eligible additions to the circle. She rattles away in her own individual sort of nonsense, punning about the Apostles:

> I shall make a little golden hoop for him like the apostles in the Arundels, and another for you, and when nobody else is there, you can take them off, and play hoops with them. I expect the apostles did that when they went for a walk. You couldn't wear it round a hat, could you?

Dodo makes a grand marriage to consolidate her social position:

> Society constituted Dodo's world, hitherto her position had been precarious; she had felt that she was on trial. Her personality, her great attractiveness and talents, had secured for herself a certain footing on the dais of that room.

At the time of the book's publication, Herbert Henry Asquith was wooing Margot. When Lord Rosebery suggested to him: 'My dear Asquith, I advise you read *Dodo* . . . there is a great deal of truth in it', Asquith's response was to pursue his suit.

'Would Society stand it if she didn't happen to be herself?' E. F. Benson asked of Dodo. It was Margot's wit, 'social courage', and outrageous remarks that were her passport. Her sayings were known as 'Margots'. When her step-daughter, Violet Bonham Carter, inquired if she intended to wear a hat trimmed with ostrich feathers to Lord Kitchener's memorial service, she replied, 'How can you ask me? Dear Kitchener saw me in that hat twice!' She was quite unaware that others might be sensitive and wrote with surprise of Lucy Graham Smith that 'she had a fear of hurting the feelings of others so great that she did not tell people what she was thinking'. She thought Lady Desborough's diplomatic compliments were perhaps too profuse: 'Ettie tells so many white lies, she could ice a cake.' Margot regarded it as her duty to tell other people what she thought of them, and thereby created, as noted by her daughter-in-law, Lady Cynthia

Margot Asquith, drawn by John Singer Sargent in 1897.
Her husband, H. H. Asquith, was the Home Secretary

Charteris, 'a good many jars and jangles'. Just after Cynthia's wedding she told her that her
going-away dress was a 'failure' and, in Cynthia's words, 'denounced [it] with the scathing
eloquence of which she alone had command'. These candid comments were expected of her, and
were passed round like chocolates. It was to the great good credit of Lady Desborough that she
could laugh at herself, and in a letter to Julian she recalls with amusement an early epigram of
Margot's: 'Ettie is an ox, she will be turned into Bovril when she dies.' So familiar did Margot's
bon mot become that 'Bovril' became an adjective in the Souls' parlance. In 1894 Lady Ponsonby
wrote to her son:

> I rather agree with you about Margot. I saw the beginning of her mistake in living on her capital
> (mentally) three or four years ago, and it's beginning to tell by her talking more and more for effect,
> and playing the old set of tricks on young and old. Yet she has much more in her than the rest of the
> crew.

It does seem that Margot Asquith might have been a self-made caricature of Margot Tennant;
but this was perhaps because she thought that her histrionic talent was expected by her
audience.

Margot was the first of the Souls to publish an account of the group in her autobiography of
1920. It was not then the custom to write discourteously about the living, and Margot's book is
charmingly complimentary about the female Souls. To Curzon and Balfour she is not so kind;
married herself to a Liberal Prime Minister, she felt herself alienated from them politically. She
published the verses Curzon wrote for the first Souls' dinner without asking his permission, and
he was naturally offended.

In her memoirs Margot says that the Souls existed only for a decade. It is true that after her
marriage to H. H. Asquith in May 1894 she ceased to be an active Soul. Mr Asquith was a most
serious and un-Soul like man; Margot's marriage to him seemed an unlikely match, but it was a
very happy one. It caused surprisingly little stir, for as Lady Frances Balfour said: 'It was an
event for which society was prepared, as one partner in the happy event had taken all and sundry
into her confidence.' Only from Windsor was there a private voice of disapproval; Queen
Victoria wrote to Sir Henry Ponsonby that she considered '[Margot] most unfit for a Cabinet
Minister's wife'. Margot now devoted herself to her family of two children and five
step-children, and to her husband's career. H. H. Asquith was Home Secretary at the time of his
marriage, Chancellor of the Exchequer from 1905, and Prime Minister from 1908 to 1916. Her
wit, hilarious and increasingly tactless, was as piercing as ever, but Margot now developed an
inordinate passion for bridge, which she had once despised, playing for long hours and tiny
stakes. Guests at the Asquiths' country house, The Wharf at Sutton Courtenay, near Oxford,
were all expected to join the card table. 'I spent my time trying to make her just talk, for her
conversation, unexpected and wholly spontaneous, was unique,' said Christabel Aberconway of
Margot in the 1920s. At dinner, Margot would rap on the table and demand 'General
Conversation', for, as she said to her step-daughter, Violet, she deplored the modern habit of
'dreary muttering away in whispering couples'. She also told her how inadequate, dull and
unspirited she and her friends were in comparison with the Souls; perhaps her nostalgia was
increased when two of her stepsons married into the circle, for Raymond Asquith became the
husband of Katharine Horner, and Herbert ('Beb') married the lovely Lady Cynthia Charteris.

✣ TWELVE

The Indispensable Bachelors

Any hostess knows that the key to successful entertaining is a supply of amusing, possibly flirtatious, and essentially unencumbered men. Such people will have a varied and relentless social life, dining out every night of the week, hurrying off to weekend parties, and choosing fastidiously which villa on the Continent should be visited in the summer, and which shooting-party in Scotland should be honoured in the autumn. The Souls' circle was conspicuously well supplied with delightful bachelors; inevitably a number of them succumbed to the temptation of marriage as the years passed, but this did not necessarily interfere with their bachelor habits.

In the very centre of the circle was the most eligible bachelor of them all, Arthur Balfour, of whom it might be said that he had everything to recommend him – wit, charm, good looks and great abilities – except the wish to commit himself. Balfour was, of course, far more to the Souls than that: without him they would not have existed, and it was partly because he was at their head that they became an object of fascination, and relentless comment, to their contemporaries and one of interest and curiosity ever since. Nor is it surprising that Godfrey Webb, or Evan Charteris or the young Maurice Baring, were welcomed into the group. Webb was over forty years older than Baring, but they shared that sparkling sense of humour, the product of preternaturally quick wits, which was the hallmark of the amusing 'Soul'. It is harder to imagine what special qualities recommended the taciturn Doll Liddell, the austere Spencer Lyttelton, and Maurice Baring's elder brother, the shy, self-conscious Lord Revelstoke. But these were certainly private affections, the product of long involvement from childhood with the Souls' families.

While the bachelor enjoys the absence of dragging family and financial responsibilities, usually he misses one great pleasure: that of playing host in a spacious and elegantly organized family establishment. Balfour, however, had managed to create just such by proxy for himself by keeping perpetual open house for his relations at Whittingehame.

Doll Liddell remembered one visit to his own family home at Ravensworth with particular gratitude because he had, momentarily, enjoyed this very pleasure:

> . . . I was thoroughly happy at returning to my old haunts with such congenial hosts, the more so because my cousin being not in the best of health, I had the management of the shooting, and so tasted for the only time in my life the joy of being a landed proprietor.

Most bachelors were condemned for life to the dreaded 'bachelors' wings' of the country houses they frequented. These were grim, Spartan rooms in the best tradition of the English public school, and often shared by two or three people. Nonetheless their occupants enjoyed the fullest possible social round, and one cannot but envy them.

In her diaries Mary Gladstone recalls the following dinner-table discussion:

> One evening at dinner we were discussing the respective merits of people, for social purposes, and our host wondered how far the company would differ as to whom they would choose for the ideal small dinner party. I think there were twelve of us and we were each asked to select the nine ideal people for a dinner party of ten. I quite forget who chose which. I can only recall at once remembering whom I had found ideal company. Everybody else chose five men and five women, and all were green with envy of my dinner party, which consisted of nine men and one woman – eight Lyttelton brothers, A. J. Balfour, and M. G. [herself].

> No, if humour we count,
> The original fount
> Must to Hugo be ceded in freehold,
> Tho' of equal supplies
> In more subtle disguise
> Old Godfrey has far from a wee hold!
> *George Curzon*

Godfrey Webb was described by Lady Paget as 'a mysterious man holding some appointment in the House of Lords, and devoted to spiritualism and the Black Art'. In fact he was a Clerk in the House. A regular attender at Crabbet Club meetings since the days of its association with the Wagger Club in the early eighties, Webb had for many years been an *habitué* of the circle from which the Souls were drawn. He was older than most of the rest of the group, and in many cases had known their parents.

Webb was as indispensable to the Souls as was Balfour; Margot Asquith called him 'the *doyen* of the Souls'. Others called him their 'court jester'. A celebrated raconteur and wit, he was the best at the intellectual games which were such an important part of Souls' entertainments. He had an inexhaustible fund of inspiration for extempore verse which he could summon immediately whenever the occasion demanded it. One memorable offering was prompted by reading an absurd item in the newspaper in the dining-room at The Glen. Seeing that a Mr Pickering Phipps had broken his leg as he rose from his knees after family prayers he immediately improvised the following:

> On bended knees with fervent lips,
> Wrestled with Satan Pickering Phipps
> But when for aid he ceased to beg,
> The wily devil broke his leg!

Curzon places Webb slightly below Hugo Elcho as the wittiest of the Souls, but it is possible that Elcho could afford to be more outrageous because he had less to lose in forfeiting a social position which he did not value. Curzon himself was a bad judge of the permissible limits to which wit can go before becoming offensive, and had himself been known to overstep the mark, indulging in unkind practical jokes.

Webb must have had an unusually forgiving nature, at least towards Curzon, since he seems to have borne without rancour a good deal of Crabbet Club ribaldry. When Curzon married in 1895, Webb was among the subscribers for the handsome silver table-centre presented to him by a number of his Souls friends.

Both Webb and his exact contemporary Sir Algernon West, who was Gladstone's secretary, fell victim to the attractions of Laura Tennant. After her death they both spent many holidays at The Glen with Margot, reliving old memories. Enslavement to Laura was such an inevitable, and often life-long, affliction for all men who met her that their marital suitability was rarely assessed by her family. Neither Webb nor West, both over fifty at that time, was in the slightest danger of finding himself married to her. West had in any case been married for twenty-five years. Horace Hutchinson, the editor of his diaries, remembers:

> Augustine Birrell said to me once, 'What keeps dear old Algy so young is that he's always been in love with somebody.' It was quite true. It was all *en tout bien et tout honneur*. Never in any instance was there a ghost of a question as to that. He had a genius, in fact, for platonic affection, and the ladies realized it, and took it at its worth.

Godfrey Webb, on the other hand, was a classic example of the confirmed bachelor – a now almost extinct species – conforming to the popular image even to the extent of tolerating the tyranny of an eccentric valet, a Basque named Saubaud. Saubaud was pressed into service as a loader for his master at shooting-parties, and when Webb missed a shot he would say consolingly: '*Ah! Monsieur, vous l'avez bien blessé.*' In the Souls' circles his interest in spiritualism and what Lady Paget spoke of rather sinisterly as 'the Black Art' was no eccentricity, being shared by many of them, notably Balfour. This fascination with séances and apparitions strikes an unexpected note, for the whole subject is nowadays discredited, at least among people of their intellectual level. However, it was greatly in vogue at the time and investigations into psychic phenomena were conducted with the utmost seriousness.

Webb was one of the most faithful members of the Crabbet Club, contributing more memorably to the poetry contest than to the games of tennis, at which he was notoriously inept. At the last meeting in 1894 he won the coveted laureateship with a poem on the subject of 'Civilization'. On that occasion the guests remained at the table from eight in the evening till three in the morning.

Webb died in 1901. Margot Asquith wrote sorrowfully of his loss: 'He was a man in a million, the last of the wits, and I miss him every day of my life.'

Here is Doll who has taught
Us that 'words conceal thought'
In his case is a fallacy silly.
                              George Curzon

A. G. C. Liddell was always known as 'Doll', short for Adolphus. He was a grandson of Lord Ravensworth, and many of his childhood summers and school holidays from Eton were spent in the large castellated family seat, Ravensworth, near Newcastle. On later summer vacations from Balliol he was accustomed to go on a walking tour in the Isle of Wight, ending up at Freshwater where he stayed with Julia Margaret Cameron and became a victim of her camera, posed incongruously in Robin Hood costume but looking more deranged than intrepid, probably from embarrassment. At this period he became friends with Franco (Frank) Charteris, the older brother of Hugo Elcho, who died in 1870; and with Rutherford Graham, the older brother of Frances Horner, who died in 1874. Through these two friends he became, and remained, an habitué of the set from which the Souls' circle was to grow. He was always a welcome guest at

A. G. C. (Doll) Liddell
photographed as a young man by
Julia Margaret Cameron, wearing
fancy dress – much to his
embarrassment

Stanway and at Mells, as well as at the houses of the older generation, Gosford, Panshanger, Escrick, Ashridge, Wilton and Clouds. After coming down from Balliol he decided to follow his father's footsteps into the law, and was called to the Bar in 1871. He practised for ten years, without any great success, and was then offered the chief clerkship in the Crown Office which he accepted with relief, for he had no real taste for the legal profession.

If Godfrey Webb was the most indispensable of the Souls, Liddell was the most incomprehensible. He was tall, fair and good-looking, and had a lugubrious resignation in the face of difficulties which Frances Horner found hilariously funny; but he was unusually silent, only occasionally breaking into abrupt speech, often in order to deliver himself of a woundingly caustic or disconcerting comment.

Liddell had to endure, not once but twice, the misfortune of courting a woman who immediately afterwards became engaged to Alfred Lyttelton. He was one of the innumerable aspirants for the hand of Laura Tennant, and, with what many people might consider good reason, believed that he might win her consent to marriage. His account in *Notes From the Life of an Ordinary Mortal* of the Tennants' life at The Glen is the result of careful observation, and the picture of Laura that he draws gives some idea of the mysterious fascination which she exercised over every person with whom she came into contact. The Tennant daughters were allowed unusual freedom in speech and social encounters; the suggestion that the entertainment of young men in their bedroom in the evenings might be open to misconstruction was treated with derision, and their letters abounded in intimacies and expressions of affection that seemed to encourage the romantic aspirations of their correspondents. Liddell must eventually have come to suspect that the liberties that Laura permitted him meant little. He faced formidable competition, for Arthur Balfour was an admirer as well as Godfrey Webb and Algernon West; but it is doubtful whether he would have stood a better chance even if he had been more voluble and ebullient, since Laura had set her heart on Alfred Lyttelton.

Although cast down by this failure, after Laura's death Liddell ventured again to pay cautious advances to Edith Balfour (no relation of Arthur Balfour), who was known always as 'D. D.' This venture too was doomed, D. D. preferring to accept Alfred Lyttelton's proposal, just as Laura had done before. The situation is the more ironical in that Liddell so much wanted to marry, and that Alfred Lyttelton was losing on both occasions a carefully-constructed and much-valued freedom from emotional encumbrances.

There is no record of witty repartee or spontaneous versifying on Liddell's part but, fortunately for us, his powers of observation – which may have been sharpened by his reticence in company – leave nothing to be desired. His book, partly written in the form of a diary, is full of telling vignettes. The following is an illuminating glimpse of Oscar Wilde in 1891 which shows him holding the centre of the stage in the way that was most deplored in the Souls' circle:

> Wrest. Mr Wilde came. He was a great talker and *raconteur*, and occasionally said good things. The only one which I remember is, that he said there ought to be 'a Form of Prayer used for a Baronet'. In the afternoon he sat on the lawn, surrounded by a large audience of ladies, to whom he told stories. His signing of the visitor's book was characteristic. It was a huge tome, with large, thick creamy sheets. He did not sign on the same sheet as the rest of the party, but took a fresh sheet, on which he wrote his name towards the top, and then executed an immense flourish, so that no other name could be written on the same page.

Spencer, too, would show what
He can do, were it not
For that cursed laryngeal nemesis.
                        George Curzon

The Hon. Spencer Lyttelton was a shadowy and eccentric figure who hovered for many years on the fringes of the Souls' circle. However, the mysterious lines addressed to him by George Curzon at the first Bachelors' Club dinner seen to signify no more than that he was a noted singer but had a sore throat. Elder brother of Alfred Lyttelton, he was an early and very close friend of Arthur Balfour, whose musical interests he shared.

'He was a superbly handsome and vigorous man . . . a Victorian old bachelor but not at all spinsterish,' recalled his nephew George Lyttelton in 1958. A recent visit to the Literary Society had reminded him of the story of a former occasion '. . . when Spencer Lyttelton and Lord Curzon were the only attendants. Very embarrassing for old Uncle S., who hated a *tête-à-tête*.' Spencer, with a superb singing voice, was willing to perform at the amateur concerts at which entire Handel oratorios were given to the accompaniment of the 'Infernals' (as they termed concertinas) which were so much enjoyed by Arthur Balfour.

Mary Gladstone spent much time and energy in trying to persuade her reluctant cousin to take up a career and to marry, neither of which appealed to him. An uncompromising description of him is given by E. F. Benson:

Spencer was grim and blunt and bearded and rich: he lived alone in a house in Hill Street, into which no friend ever penetrated. He was a bachelor, he sang in the Bach Choir, and on being asked if he had ever in his life kissed a woman he replied: 'Once. On the brow.'

A more intimate acquaintance with Spencer Lyttelton led John Bailey to paint a more sympathetic portrait of his stepbrother-in-law – though perhaps some considerations of family piety may have coloured his judgement, for it was produced at the time of Spencer's death. Nevertheless, this happier face is surely the one which his Souls friends saw:

. . . though he seemed to do so little for people of the ordinary kind of things people do for each other, yet his affection was so obvious and his interest and sympathy with what one was doing or suffering – so quick and visible that he won far more love from his friends than people who would appear to do much more for them.

A banker in the family firm, Baring Brothers, John Baring became Lord Revelstoke in 1897, when he succeeded his father as second Baron. He also succeeded him as senior partner in the bank, at a time when the firm was still recovering from a catastrophic crash which had almost ruined the family and the business. By prodigies of hard work on his part the firm was successfully re-established as one of the leading London bankers.

John was a lifelong admirer of Lady Desborough, whom he first met in 1891; almost at once he embarked on the correspondence in which he was to express his passionate devotion to her, and which he kept up faithfully for nearly forty years. He shared Ettie Desborough's affections, not only with her husband who always claimed her first loyalty, but also with other admirers in a

Lord Revelstoke (John Baring),
a photograph from one of the
Taplow Court Visitor's Books

similar position, like Evan Charteris, similarly faithful, and, briefly, George Wyndham. Only once did he defect from the ranks of her admirers, in 1904 when he fell in love with a beautiful American visitor whom he had met on the hunting field. He pursued Nancy Shaw, as she then was, with eager determination, and his feelings seemed to be returned; but disaster overtook his promising suit when she found out about the long years of devotion to Lady Desborough. Later she wrote: 'He had been having an affair that had been going on for years, with a married woman many years older than he was' – and that was that for his hopes. In 1906 Mrs Shaw became Mrs Waldorf Astor, and embarked on a life of politics and public achievement.

It is almost impossible to recognize the enchantingly attractive 'Mrs Ettie' of John Revelstoke's letters in 'the married woman many years older than he was'. His junior by four years, and at thirty-seven still at the height of her beauty, she was then at the centre of a crowd of new young admirers, among them Maurice Baring, Lord Revelstoke's brother; but to Nancy she was no more than an exigent old gorgon, kept up with through habit rather than inclination.

Lord Revelstoke was not forgiven his disloyalty for some time; but persistence won in the end and in later years Lady Desborough was happy to resume the old relationship. His faithful care for her happiness and comfort supported her in the terrible sorrows that were to come; he never married and his emotional life was fulfilled in his devotion to her.

Dear Evan was there,
The first choice of the fair
To all but himself very gentle!
        George Curzon

Evan Charteris was later Sir Evan Charteris K.C., acquiring these distinctions considerably after the heyday of the Souls during a long and distinguished career in which he was a barrister at the Parliamentary Bar. He married Lady Edward Grosvenor, daughter of the fifth Earl of Kenmare, in 1930. He was also notable as the author of a life of the artist John Singer Sargent, and of *The Life and Letters of Edmund Gosse*.

Evan Charteris, younger brother of Lord Elcho and Lady Hilda Brodrick. Another photograph from a Taplow Court Visitor's Book

Evan Charteris was a faithful and lifelong admirer of Lady Desborough, with the sympathy of his wife who loved her too. His inclusion in the Souls' circle, through his family connections, his Eton education, and his friendship with George Curzon and the Tennants, was a foregone conclusion; but his urbane good looks and his long bachelorhood were added attractions. He had to a consummate degree those qualities, so much prized by the Souls, of wit allied to that quickness of perception which made their companions seem as witty and perceptive as themselves. His 'lightness of touch' concealed the labour behind his considerable achievements in his career at the Bar and in his literary work. It was an attribute held in the greatest esteem by his friends, and indeed in Lady Desborough's view it constituted the special 'Soul' quality. His elegance and urbanity were deceptive: behind the scholar and the aesthete there hid a man who was a notable sportsman, a crack shot and an intrepid bicyclist. In 1895 he went on a cycling tour to Normandy with Ettie Desborough and Alfred Milner, and they braved rain and thunderstorms, doggedly covering thirty miles a day on rough and hazardous roads.

As Chairman of the Trustees of the Tate Gallery, his combination of aesthetic sensibility with shrewd legal knowledge enabled him to fulfil a doubly useful role. His knowledge of art and artists went far beyond mere dilettante appreciation of beauty: for example, the long passage in his book on Sargent describing the painting of the famous picture *Carnation, Lily, Lily, Rose* must be one of the best accounts ever written of the intellectual and physical labour involved in creating a work of art. Lord Clark recalls Evan Charteris in his seventies when he was on the National Gallery's board as well as the Tate's:

> . . . the most elegant figure of his time, who for years had been at the summit of the literary *beau monde*. Having practised at the Bar he could present a case very persuasively. He was a consummate liar, but always gave one warning when he was going to tell a lie by delicately patting his moustache with a handkerchief.

Clark also remembers the unshakeable urbanity that was proof even against the chore of more than once having to go bail for the inebriated Director of the Tate Gallery, J. B. Manson, in the middle of the night. Dressed in his customary old-fashioned, dandified style, he would make his way to the police station and persuade the officers of the law to release their victim.

Maurice Baring, fourth son of the first Baron Revelstoke and younger brother of John, was in the diplomatic service from 1898 to 1904, but is now remembered as a successful novelist. One work, *C*, is a *roman-à-clef* about members of the Souls' circle. Maurice Baring had been familiar with the Souls and their world since boyhood through his brother John, and like so many of the Souls had been educated at Eton. His brilliant wit and fantastic imagination ensured him a place in the social life of the group as soon as he was of an age to enter society. Like so many others he immediately became a passionate admirer of Lady Desborough. H. H. Asquith stated, on being asked whom he considered to be a man of genius in his generation: 'For genius in the sense of spontaneous, dynamic intelligence, I have no doubt that I would say Maurice Baring.' The early chapters of Maurice Baring's autobiography, *The Puppet Show of Memory*, conjure up an unforgettable picture of this lost world, both at the Baring family home, Membland Hall in Devon, and at the other country houses where the Souls gathered. Of the year 1896, he wrote:

I stayed at Panshanger; and at Wrest, at the end of the summer, where a constellation of beauty moved in muslin and straw hats and yellow roses on the lawns of the gardens designed by Lenôtre, delicious with ripe peaches on old brick walls, with the smell of verbena and sweet geranium; and stately with large avenues, artificial lakes and white temples; and we bicycled in the warm night past ghostly cornfields by the light of the large full moon.

In the Great War Maurice Baring served in the Flying Corps. A collection of his letters from this period has recently been published, and the freshness and humour and the keenness of the observation still gives a thrill of pleasure. His conversation was full of wit and interest, and even as an old man suffering from a painful and crippling illness he kept up his curiosity in all manner of subjects. He spent the last years of his life at Beauly Castle, the home of Lord and Lady Lovat in Scotland. Lady Lovat, the daughter of Lord and Lady Ribblesdale and the Laura Lister of Sargent's most successful child portrait, was one of his many friends from the younger generation. He happily spanned the gap that separated that 'Corrupt Coterie' from the parent Souls, for he had a soulless side to his character that appealed to a generation in flight from what they saw as the languid affectations of their elders. He revelled in heartless practical jokes: 'Maurice passed away peacefully this afternoon,' he once telegraphed to Edmund Gosse, causing utter consternation. The attitude of those at the receiving end of such pranks can be guessed from Maurice's rueful but essentially unrepentant justification: 'It's *fun* to throw a tortoise up in the air.' This incident is recounted in *A Number of People* by Edward Marsh, Winston Churchill's private secretary and a noted patron of the arts. Marsh's view of the Souls' generation is somewhat reminiscent of a man using a telescope the wrong way round – he sees them small, but very sharply defined. He loved them, and even more he loved the 'golden boys' of the younger generation, but he knew and secretly deplored their defects of exclusiveness and arrogance.

Maurice Baring, taken from
the 1896 Taplow Court
Visitor's Book

✿ THIRTEEN
Americans in the Souls' Circle

It was a society into which you had to take the precaution to be born. If you were not born into it you never found your way in. There was no effort to keep people outside of it. None was required. The people who were outside did not dream of forcing themselves in. There was no reason why this little clique should be on the defence. The Climbers did not exist, as an aggressive body, or as a force of any kind.

So wrote George Smalley of English Society in his *Anglo American Memoirs* published in 1911. How delightful then to come across a section of this impenetrable world where inclusion by wit, beauty, charm and intelligence was not only possible but necessary. It is a measure of how greatly evident were these qualities in such American Souls as Daisy White, Amélie Chanler and, on the fringes, Lady Randolph Churchill, Edith Wharton and Consuelo Vanderbilt, that Margot Asquith, whose part in forming and defining the Souls' circle was pre-eminent, and who disliked women, and American women in particular, was prepared to welcome their inclusion.

In the nineties the 'American invasion' reached greater proportions than ever before. Some members of the aristocracy gave the impression of being prepared to barter a title and social position for such necessary but expensive items as a leak-proof roof, or new-fangled luxuries such as central heating. Blenheim, for example, had benefited in this respect in two generations, but neither of the American Duchesses was happily married to either of the two Dukes of Marlborough, and their own valuation of their part of the bargain was not so high as to prevent them from leaving the grandeur of ducal life for the luxury of privacy and personal happiness.

Expatriate Americans were often criticized for being over-forceful in their pursuit of social success in London, in spite of many rebuffs. Indeed, George Smalley, London correspondent of the *New York Tribune*, recalls that a considerable amount of bad feeling was always generated among visiting Americans each season when the very small number of presentations at Court allocated to the American Ambassador were quickly used up. Accustomed to the more informal arrangements at the White House they found the impenetrable royal circle frustrating and mystifying. E. S. Nadal, a fellow-American and friend of Henry James over many years, disapproved of these social aspirations, but James disagreed with him, remarking: 'I think a position in society is a legitimate object of ambition.' James had established for himself a social

159

round of almost awe-inspiring dimensions. In 1882 when he was visited by Edmund Gosse he received him stretched on a sofa; his explanation was that 'a muscular weakness of his spine obliged him to assume the horizontal posture during some hours of every day in order to bear the almost unbroken routine of evening engagements'.

Henry James was the 'occasional Soul' whom every hostess delighted to entice to her house. He loved their company, he revelled in observing the flash of wit, the merriment and the rare profound reflection, but he remained determinedly an observer, not a participator. He was like Oscar Wilde, one of the few whom the Souls pursued but failed to ensnare – he preserved the cherished detachment of the creative artist.

The Souls welcomed a select few of the expatriate Americans into their innermost circle. Present at many of their gatherings, notably Curzon's dinners at the Bachelors' Club, were Mr and Mrs Henry White.

The Whites were drawn indirectly into the circle of the Souls partly through their friendship with Edith Wharton, the American novelist and friend of Henry James, who spent much of her time in Europe – mainly in France. Margaret White, known as Daisy, was a Rutherford by birth, and the Rutherfords were neighbours of Edith Wharton's family at Newport. The two women established a firm friendship shortly before Margaret's marriage in 1879 to the diplomat, Harry White, who was then attached to the American Embassy in Paris. The Whites went immediately to live in France; as a result Margaret's friendship with Edith Wharton could be kept up, and they continued to meet at intervals for the rest of their lives. In 1884 the Whites came to London where he had been appointed First Secretary at the American Legation. In the same year there appeared at the Royal Academy the magnificent portrait of Mrs White by Sargent, who was exhibiting for the first time in London. On seeing it Henry James wrote in a letter:

> His [Sargent's] big portrait of Mrs Henry White, at the Academy here (she belongs to our Legation), is splendid and delightful. She is at full length (a very big canvas) in white satin and white lace, with a vague, pinkish, pearly background. It is a masterpiece (*selon moi*) of style and tone, and has had, among the artists, an immense success.

(A later passage in the same letter records the opinion of his friend George Howard, later Earl of Carlisle, that it could only be patriotism that would make James care for such a work.) Sargent had been encouraged to come to England by James, who foresaw a brilliant career for him painting the beautiful women of the English aristocracy. In the event Sargent did become what might be described as 'portrait-painter by appointment' to the Souls. Some of his finest portraits are of members of the circle, notably Lord Ribblesdale and the Wyndham sisters.

The Whites were very popular in London and were entertained everywhere. James, always interested in the fate of expatriate Americans, wrote to Grace Norton in 1888:

> *The* happy American here, beyond all others, is Mrs Henry White, wife of the First Secretary of the American Legation – who is very handsome, young, rich, splendid, admired and successful, to a degree which leaves all competitors behind. A lady said to me the other day (a certain queer Lady Lothian), 'She is very high up, isn't she.'
> 'Very high up?'

Mrs Henry White by John Singer Sargent, 1883. This portrait was exhibited at the Royal Academy in London in the same year that Sargent arrived in England

'I mean tremendously well-read; all the new books and that sort of thing.'
She has never read a book in her life; but she is 'high up' all the same.

In the attitude of even the best-mannered members of the English upper classes towards Americans living in England, there is often a slight air of condescension, and even a tinge of surprise at their acceptable appearance and delightful manners. When Consuelo Vanderbilt came to England as the young bride of the Duke of Marlborough she remembers being deeply hurt on finding that her new compatriots believed it the highest form of compliment to say that she did not seem in the least like an American! In this respect the Whites had a considerable advantage for he, at least, had lived in Europe for most of his life, and since 1870 had made his home in England whenever his career allowed it. In the event, they were to be in London for just over twenty years, but in 1905 Harry White was made Ambassador to Spain, and in 1907 he returned as Ambassador to Paris. He was recalled when Taft was elected as President of the United States, an action which was widely deplored as he was very popular in Paris.

Mrs J. A. Chanler was also a fully-fledged Soul, introduced by Curzon, rather than one of the 'occasional' variety. Both her interests and her artistic associations made her a natural Soul. Americans were naturally drawn to the intellectual and aesthetic diversions of the Souls' circle as their expectations of life, particularly among the women, had often been raised by being much more widely travelled and better educated than their counterparts in England. Consuelo Vanderbilt was shocked and bored by the invincible lack of culture and knowledge of affairs that she found in the social circle in which she moved as the Duchess of Marlborough, and the fact that such ignorance was frequently worn with pride and satisfaction. Her contacts with the Souls' circle, which gave her the greatest pleasure and amusement, came after she had separated from the Duke and was living in London. 'Brilliant men are not insensible to a beautiful woman,' she remarked, 'even when her beauty surpasses her wit, and in England they are free to indulge in more serious conversation with other men once the ladies have left the table.' It is possible that Margot Asquith and Ettie Desborough would have been startled by this view of their function in the charmed circle, but their beauty was a weapon to be deployed with discreet skill.

George Smalley remarked sapiently: 'The English like an American to be an American. If he is a writer they like his writings to be American.' This was not a counsel which many had the strength of mind to follow, and Consuelo Vanderbilt said: 'Looking back on the little circle I knew of American women married to Englishmen, there are, I realise, very few who remained definitely American.' Many were, of course, intimidated into becoming counterfeit Englishwomen and this did not appeal in a circle where self-confident insouciance was admired and encouraged. Mary Curzon seems to have had little wish to penetrate the innermost heart of the Souls' group. It would not have been in her character to have been conspicuous in company or to have taken her public position lightly, thus her ability to shine in Souls' society was hampered by a sense of duty. Lady Randolph Churchill, on the other hand, was not afraid to shock and disconcert the other members of her husband's social circle, once giving a notorious 'Dinner of Enemies' for long-time opponents who had sworn never to exchange another word with each other.

The Souls' tolerance of eccentricity and encouragement of social behaviour that often verged on the outrageous fascinated Henry James and Edith Wharton, though both were content to view Souls' activities from a safe distance. To enjoy the amusing talk without becoming emotionally involved was an ideal way of tasting Souls' delights in tranquillity. James himself was not unaware of the social cachet attached to this group and would have had no false shame at responding to their overtures. He was frequently entertained at Souls' houseparties and became a valued member of the circle, but only on the fringes, from which vantage point he could feed his novelist's imagination through the minute observation of the complex type of character which most interested him.

To do James justice, however, he would have been drawn towards the members of the Souls' circle whatever their antecedents for the sake of their aesthetic tastes. He was deeply interested in art and artists, in patronage and collecting, and these interests were entirely shared by the Wyndhams, Frances Horner, Lord Ribblesdale and Arthur Balfour. No fewer than twenty-five of Henry James' first thirty stories are concerned with art or collecting, and some of the most successful of his critical writings are about painting and sculpture. It was not usual in society circles to find such like-minded companions.

There is no doubt that these Transatlantic importations added an important extra dimension to the Souls' circle. The danger with a small, closed society of the kind which still existed in London in the nineties is that it can become very parochial. The exchange of tired anecdotes and well-worn gossip makes for weary evenings. This company of friends came to dread the *longueurs* of 'Soulless' evenings, seeking each other's company as a respite from the terrors of boredom, and the Americans saw Souls' parties as a welcome relaxation from the pitfalls of conventional society entertaining.

Henry James, the American novelist, on the occasion
of a visit to Aston Clinton, *c*. 1890

❧ FOURTEEN
The Fringes of the Circle

The older generation of the Souls' circle contributed greatly to that picture of privileged and unclouded enjoyment which was the envy of the rest of the world. The Countess Brownlow, the Countess of Pembroke and the Countess Cowper – the 'Aunts', as they were irreverently known – were persons of legendary magnificence and beauty. Lady Cowper was the one of the 'Aunts' most closely involved with the Souls, but Lady Brownlow and Lady Pembroke, with their sister Lady Lothian, added a spice of eccentricity to the dignified gatherings of the older generation. Margot Asquith described Lady Brownlow as 'a Roman coin'; as early as 1865 Mary Gladstone had remarked on her 'classic loveliness'; nearly thirty years later, in 1893, Lady Paget describes a visit to her:

> The most beautiful of three sisters, every one of them the salt of the earth. She was seated between Lady Lothian and Lady Pembroke, the former in trailing black and the latter in trailing white draperies. Lady Brownlow was in sober grey of the same make, and they looked like the Three Fates. They all asked questions in high-pitched voices.

Each of these three daughters of the Earl of Shrewsbury had married a man who matched her looks. Lord Pembroke and Lord Brownlow were very tall, well over six foot and very handsome, as was Lord Lothian, though he was crippled by creeping paralysis at an early age; he died young. In the church at Blickling is his recumbent effigy sculpted by G. F. Watts, a rare and dazzling venture into this field, which depicts the noble countenance complemented by frail draperies in the manner of Nicholas Stone. The families in and around the Souls' circle had a notable liking for recumbent effigies, then unusual. Lady Lothian lived during her widowhood at Blickling, the enchanted – and haunted – Tudor house in Norfolk, a still beautiful, noble, but stern figure, always in black.

Disdaining the dictates of fashion, they dressed to suit their own taste. Unconventional style in dress, which itself became almost a convention among the female Souls, was a tradition which had begun with the older generation and was to persist with the younger. The great couturier Worth was rarely called upon. Most of the dresses were devised by their wearers, often with the benefit of advice from artist friends, and were confected from pieces of priceless old lace yellowed by time to the colour of ivory; from softest smoky-toned cashmere shawls from India, many of them given by their friend Lady Wenlock, souvenirs of her years as the Governor's wife in Madras; and from old Italian silk velvets. Lady Brownlow was painted by Leighton in a creamy-white dress edged with gold, which resembled classical draperies. Mary Gladstone, writing in 1875, describes her wearing it: '. . . at teatime today in white embroidered with gold regular toga sort of thing, and tonight with the red beads, white handkerchief on head. Oh lovely!'

Ashridge, the Brownlow seat in Surrey, was very beautiful. Two great architects, the Wyatts, father and son, had been involved in the designing of the great romantic Gothic palace, rising impressively in the park where there still remained fragments of former monastic buildings. Constance Sitwell, a Talbot cousin, remembers staying there as a child:

> . . . when we had finished our lessons it was to the garden that we went; I don't remember ever reaching the end of it – it stretched so far; the 'pleasure grounds', as they were called, and walks and thickets, and grottos; the round enclosed rose-garden, the monks' garden, where the Elizabethan cloisters had been in the part, the Italian garden, with its great stone vases and formal beds; the ponds surrounded by square yew hedges; the lavender-garden with its sundial and herbs. It all seemed a little overwhelming . . .

Part of the pleasure of staying at great country houses was provided by the extent and beauty of the gardens. At Ashridge no fewer than thirty-six gardeners were needed to keep up the huge pleasaunce. The 'Italian' garden at Wrest Park, the Cowpers' house in Bedfordshire, with its statuary and great urns filled with flowering plants amid geometrical patterns of clipped box, had been designed by Lord Cowper's maternal grandfather to match the layout of the early eighteenth-century formal arrangement of the rest of the park, traditionally but incorrectly ascribed to Le Nôtre himself. The gardens at Wilton were described by Mary Gladstone as a 'paradise, like the Garden of Eden with its three rivers'.

In the nineties, when the Plymouths' vast house at Hewell was completed, an ambitious and elaborate formal garden was created in the same taste with parterres and clipped hedges of yew and box. The taste for a very different type of lay-out, the 'wild garden' devised by William Robinson and Gertrude Jekyll, had by this date become widespread; but the publication in 1892 of Reginald Blomfield's beautiful little illustrated handbook, *The Formal Garden in England*, may have inspired the traditional design of the Hewell garden. The gardens of Wilton and Wrest are both illustrated, as is the garden and terrace at Montacute in Somerset, the house on which the design of Hewell was based.

These houses and their gardens were protected by large private parks from the outside world, and in them was unbroken quiet. It is difficult now to imagine the contrast between the noisy bustle of the London season and the deep peace of the countryside. Part of the joy of a country visit was the arrival by train at a wayside station, often at dusk, to be greeted as the sound of the engine faded into the distance by a profound silence, hardly disturbed by the sound of the carriage sent to meet the visitor.

Equally unfamiliar now would be the sense of endless leisure. Social duties were few and did not obtrude, for there were often no near neighbours; the days passed in reading and talk, music and sewing, drawing and painting, while the men engaged in whatever sporting activities were appropriate to the season. Invitations to the Brownlows at Ashridge or Belton, to the

Cowpers at Panshanger or Wrest, to the Pembrokes at Wilton, or to the Wenlocks at Escrick were much coveted. While the style of life in these houses was still very much in the grand manner, conducted with a considerable degree of formality and with all the conventional amusements in the form of shooting and hunting, visits were also enriched by intellectual and artistic diversions. Guests and hosts indulged in talk ranging from political gossip to philosophical speculation and literary and poetical discussion.

One diversion was reading aloud; Constance Sitwell remembers how she once took a message to Ashridge and was directed by the butler into the garden, to find the company thus happily engaged. After traversing the beautiful rooms scented with flowers and great bowls of *pot-pourri* and filled with pictures, the blinds drawn against the bright sunlight, she came upon the ladies reading poetry. Tennyson, Matthew Arnold and Browning were the favourites:

> I stood looking at them before going out, half shy of disturbing the group. They sat in long chairs under the old yew trees, which were there when the place was a monastery . . . I listened to the voice for a little unperceived; –
>> Ah, sure within him and without
>> Could his dark wisdom find it out
>> There must be answer to his doubt –
> and then as the reader paused, stepped out into the sunlight . . . Cousin Guity [Pembroke] looked up, saying in her rather querulous, haughty voice, 'Well, little girl, and what are you doing here?'

At one Easter party at Belton both Browning and Carlyle were present, and sometimes musicians such as Joachim, the great violinist for whom Brahms wrote his violin concerto, or Mme Norma Neruda would be invited and could be persuaded to play in the evening. Failing this, there were usually enough musicians in the party, for music was an essential accomplishment of a well-brought-up young lady. The Souls' talents in this respect were far above the average, though George Lyttelton was to remark many years later to Rupert Hart-Davis: 'The Pastoral Symphony, now playing on a long record, is better than my Aunt Sybil's piano-playing!'

Such an idyllic mode of existence depended much on the brilliance of the company. Without such as the Souls, a country house weekend could be a grim affair. No greater contrast can be imagined to the tranquil poetry reading life at Ashridge than the disastrous weekend party at Tranby Croft, scene of the notorious 'Baccarat scandal' when Sir William Gordon-Cumming was accused of cheating at cards, and had to leave the country. Nowadays, when untroubled and leisurely social life seems an unattainable dream, it is hard to imagine the boredom of a 'Soulless' country house visit in the autumn for anyone unwilling to shoot or hunt. 'For men, visiting means sport, but for women it is most deteriorating,' grimly wrote Lady Paget. For a woman of her dietary affectations, nothing could be more deteriorating than a shooting lunch. Gabriel Tschumi, who spent most of his career as a chef with the Royal Family, remembers these occasions at Sandringham and Balmoral; in October 1906, for instance, the menu included Scotch broth and mulligatawny soup, hashed venison, stewed mutton, game pies, Irish stew, and finished with plum pudding and apple pudding. Not a vegetable in sight. In addition the ladies were met with the spectacle of the day's 'bag', laid out in rows by the picnic spot.

Above. The Monk's Garden at Ashridge being tended by four gardeners from the team of thirty required to keep the magnificent gardens in order
Below. The Terrace at Wrest Park, a garden famous for its formal beauty, which was designed in the style of Le Nôtre in the early years of the nineteenth century

Lady Wenlock (*née* Constance Lascelles). She chose this photograph for the album presented to Curzon

The day's activities followed one another in predictable succession; in the morning, after the early departure of the sportsmen, sewing to the accompaniment of talk about children and servants, then the shooting lunch, taken often in damp and uncomfortable conditions wherever was most convenient for the guns; in the afternoon, more sewing, more servants' misdeeds, more children's ailments; then the return of the men and tea, for which a special costume, the tea-gown, was prescribed; then, after another change of dress, dinner at which the ladies listened to the exploits of the sportsmen. In all too short a time the ladies retired to the drawing-room and yet further sewing; the men might be seen no more for they often stayed in the dining-room until making their unsteady way up to bed, overcome by fatigue and drink. For the men, the alternative to remaining in the dining-room was, of course, to repair to the smoking-room. The house-steward of Panshanger had a special recipe for a drink which he prepared for the sessions in the smoking-room. It was christened 'Archangel' and consisted of equal quantities of cream and honey liberally laced with whisky: 'A very popular night-cap, I can assure you,' he remarked. This 'deteriorating' routine would be followed for five days at a stretch. Many of the wives rebelled, preferring to remain at home rather than endure the effort of making conversation when every conceivable subject had been exhausted.

Very different was the hospitality of Lord and Lady Wenlock at Escrick in Yorkshire. Constance Lascelles had seized the earliest opportunity of escaping the hated sporting world of Harewood House in order to concentrate on her own interests, poetry and painting. In 1872 she married Beilby Lawley, third Baron Wenlock, and in the freedom of her own establishment she was able to give rein to the originality of mind that made her such a valued member of the Souls' circle. Her personality was distinguished by a disarming eccentricity in all her everyday arrangements. When she was absorbed in painting, meal-times would pass unnoticed. She was rather deaf, which imparted to her conversation a particularly inconsequent and inscrutable flavour. Doll Liddell described her '. . . elfin grace and originality – a far-away look in her face as if she belonged to another world'. Her clothes, of delicate muslin draped with Indian shawls in grey and pink, were so unlike those of her fashionable contemporaries that her young nieces felt an unworthy desire to dissociate themselves from her in public. She was a voracious reader: when she was in India with her husband, who had been appointed Governor of Madras, she persuaded George Leveson Gower regularly to send quantities of books out to her.

Autumn shooting-parties at Escrick took place in an atmosphere of welcome and unaccustomed *laissez-aller* on very much the same lines as at Hewell. Lady Wenlock's niece, Lady Sybil Lubbock, noted:

> . . . two or three, Harry Cust, Evan Charteris, Doll Liddell, I clearly remember, seemed to prefer the society of the ladies and stayed at home on stormy or doubtful days, reading aloud to my aunt and her friends while they painted or modelled – or sometimes just talking, whimsically, wittily (as I know now, if I didn't then), the whole day long. In our small hearts we rather despised these men, rashly assuming them to be poor things, afraid of a drop of rain. Later we learned that Mr Charteris was a renowned shot, and that no inclemency prevented Harry Cust from doing whatever he wished. But at that time of course we knew nothing of the versatility and brilliance of the 'Souls', as this little society came to be called and we gave our admiration to our uncle's manly and tweed-coated friends.

Her child's-eye view of the Souls is full of fascinating details, for many people drop their affectations in front of children, forgetting the chief characteristic of 'little pitchers'. Lady

Sybil's account of this group shows many of its members *en déshabille*, not trying to exert their social charm; but her shrewd observation rounds out their personalities into a convincingly realistic picture.

Many people have described the pleasure of being among the guests – sometimes as many as thirty or forty in number – of Lord and Lady Cowper at Panshanger in Hertfordshire, historic as a centre of the Palmerston circle, or at Wrest Park. 'Lord Cowper was ineffably distinguished. He was the only peer at King Edward's Coronation able to carry off a coronet: such wear even became him,' wrote Lady Edward Cecil, later Viscountess Milner. At the time of Lord Cowper's death in 1905 Edmund Gosse devoted a long passage in his diary to a description of his taste in literature and art; his love of the eighteenth century, of Racine and of French poetry, and of his picture-collecting in which he continued to take a passionate interest until the very end of his life. Of his manner Gosse wrote: 'He was not witty, but graceful, calculated and just in conversation.' In the atmosphere of cultivated and dignified life the Souls' ethos flourished.

Doll Liddell thought that Wrest was 'the *beau-idéal* of a *grand seigneur's* villa', a rather belittling description of the house built in the 1830s in the style of a Louis XV château. In 1883 he wrote:

> I paid my first visit to the Cowpers at Wrest in the beginning of August this year. It was the first of many delightful sojourns at Wrest and Panshanger, where in later years I generally met the same lot of friends who frequented Wilton and The Glen, though the parties were not consciously confined to this set. These gatherings were the origins of the 'Souls', who a few years later were talked of in society as if they were a definitely organised association.

In her privately printed *Memoir* of her husband Lady Cowper claimed that she had devised that most civilized of country house entertainments, the Saturday-to-Monday visit, of which Henry James wrote admiringly when he first established himself in England:

> . . . the combination of the spacious, lounging, talking-all-day life, the beautiful place, the dinner-party each night, the walk to church across such ideal meadow paths . . . all this was excellent of its kind.

Entertaining over a long weekend had been made possible by the development of the railway system, which by the end of the nineteenth century had formed a dense network over the greater part of the country. Even by 1858 the railway was so widespread that Lord Stanley of Alderley could write to his wife from Rushmore in Dorset: 'This is, I believe, the only place in England 18 miles from a railway station.' Doll Liddell, staying at Wilton, was easily able to visit the Wyndhams at Clouds by travelling on the little railway which wound its way through the Nadder valley the eighteen miles to Semley, the nearest station to East Knoyle. Apparently he returned on foot. Such of the Souls' houses as were within easy reach of London by train were the scene of constant parties. Although a visit to the depths of Somerset for only one night might be considered less than convenient, Lady Horner recalls that Asquith and Haldane, both at that time busy lawyers, were only too happy to arrive at Mells on a Saturday afternoon and to leave again at ten on Sunday evening, driving the thirteen miles to Bath to catch the night train which got them to London in time for the Courts on Monday morning.

By the turn of the century much of this enchanted social life had come to an end. Lord

Pembroke had died in 1895, and Lord Cowper followed in 1905. However, in some houses the foundations had been so well laid that the younger generation were well able to take over, and to add their own special flavour to the parties at Stanway and Taplow Court. With nostalgia Constance Sitwell wrote:

> . . . in earlier days we never imagined that the existing order of things could be shaken: untroubled by world problems we passed the happy summers: and when I look back, like a large Veronese picture I see them in my mind, bathed in that ample evening light, standing and talking to each other on the top of stone steps; the stone urns filled with striped and velvety petunias: the graceful dog, the rich 'gowns' of the women, and hats with curling feathers, the proud bearded heads of Lord Brownlow and Alfred Talbot [Lord Pembroke's brother], all making a noble picture. They would look rather grandiose, perhaps, to our modern eyes, and graver than is the fashion now, but impressive they were, and would be still, with their idealism and public spirit and taste.

Lady Cowper (*née* Katie Compton) by Sir E. J. Poynter. Being without personal vanity, she did not see herself as a worthy subject for portrayal

It is startling to reflect that Wilfrid Blunt was a contemporary of the 'grave and grandiose' Lord Cowper, for it is hardly possible to imagine two more different social settings than the serene dignity of Ashridge and Blunt's Crabbet Park in Sussex, scene of the ebullient, night-long revelry of the Crabbet Club. Blunt was not in any sense a 'Soul'; his connection with the group was a tenuous one, based on family ties with the Wyndhams and on the fact that many Crabbet members were also Souls. The Crabbet Club was evolved in imitation of Lord Pembroke's club at his own house, Wilton, the 'Wagger' (for 'Wilton Bagger') Club. It was in essence for men only, though Lady Anne Blunt and her daughter Judith were included in the yearly gatherings. One of the most loyal of Crabbet Club members was Godfrey Webb, the Souls' 'court jester' who was adept in the poetry contests. The meetings in the nineties were enlivened by the uninhibited high spirits of Harry Cust, George Curzon and George Wyndham who, in the intervals of composing poetry and talking and arguing about politics, indulged in great bouts of swimming and tennis, once played, rather uncomfortably it might seem, in the nude. The equilibrium of the Crabbet Club was intermittently threatened by the violence of Blunt's radical political opinions, particularly on the subject of Irish Home Rule, and the meetings were given up by tacit consent after 1894, when their host's habit of using them as a forum for diatribes of a highly controversial nature became unendurable for the guests.

A carte-de-visite photograph taken of
Wilfrid Blunt when he was a young man

By his own account Blunt was a compulsive philanderer. His *Diaries* are filled with tantalizingly oblique references to tales untold, but a detailed account of his 'Pilgrimage of Passion' has recently been extracted by Lady Longford from his private papers. From this a fuller picture emerges of his encounters with the Souls, with whom he shared many literary and artistic tastes. On his return from the East in 1891, he recalls:

> I turned with redoubled zest to my social pleasures of the year before, and at this time saw much of that group of clever men and pretty women known as the 'Souls', than whom no section of London Society was better worth frequenting, including as it did all that there was most intellectually amusing and least conventional. It was a group of men and women bent on pleasure of a superior kind, eschewing the vulgarities of racing and card-playing indulged in by the majority of the rich and noble, and looking for their excitement in romance and sentiment.

Nothing could be more attractive to a man of Blunt's temperament than the excitement of 'romance and sentiment' mixed with literature, art and politics. It was precisely the kind of excitement that he was most conspicuously well equipped to provide. Adventurous traveller, poet, artist and political activist, he was blessed with spectacular good looks which contributed to the irresistible quality of his personality. Inevitably he was drawn to make advances to a number of the beautiful women who frequented the Souls' parties – indeed one particular situation was rendered the more piquant by his belief that his rival for Lady Windsor's affections was his young and handsome cousin, George Wyndham. However, he was doomed to discover the truth of Harry Chaplin's witticism about them: that the Souls' creed was: 'Each woman shall have her man, but no man shall have his woman.' Blunt recorded this remark ruefully in his private diary. Among the Souls, for the most part, the tradition of courtly love was carried on, with intensely romantic sentiments exchanged in letters and in poetry; only rarely were their carefully ordered lives seriously disrupted.

The fringes of a circle exist only in relation to the centre. Arthur Balfour and Margot Asquith are usually described as the leaders; but a distinction can be drawn between them: she might be called the 'animator' of the group, and he the 'pivot'. It was not in his nature to be a social leader, a position that implied a ruthlessness which he reserved – well concealed behind the well-known languid charm – for his political life. Lady Paget's observations were often sharp, and on this matter are worthy of note. George Wyndham, who knew her well, considered her very entertaining, and she was certainly often uncharitable and indiscreet. She called Frances Horner 'the High Priestess' of the Souls, but allocated the leading role to George Curzon:

> He is the Captain of the Souls, though he does not take them so much *à sérieux* [sic] as the lesser members take themselves. I praise them to the skies as a bulwark against *mauvais genre*, for though the soulish manners are not immaculate, they try to be as good as they can and some of them make feeble efforts to elevate the moral tone. They have odd habits too. The young women call the young men by their Christian names, and, failing that, call everyone 'Dear Man'. There is a want of grace and stateliness which belongs to good society in such things.

The Wyndham and Charteris families were both well represented at the very heart of the 'Gang', but Curzon's lists of guests at the Bachelors' Club dinners include the names of many friends who feature little, if at all, in accounts of the Souls' gatherings. They were 'occasional Souls', to quote the expression invented by Burne-Jones to define his own position. Edgar Vincent (Lord D'Abernon), who was invited to each of Curzon's three dinners, described these guests as 'neither within the circle nor without' – here speaks the insider, confident of his own membership – and went on to say:

> After sixty years' experience in half the countries of Europe, I recall no social group equal in charm, interest and variety to the Souls of 1890. Intellectual without being highbrow or pretentious; critical without envy; unprejudiced but not unprincipled; emancipated but not aggressive; literary but athletic, free from the narrowness of clique, yet bound together in reciprocal appreciation and affection. No association of society had less ostentation or pretence; none was more free from false standards, dull conventions and antiquated prejudices.

In the nineties, when the activities of the Souls were arousing general interest, there were those who believed themselves qualified for admission to the 'inner circle', but after they found themselves tacitly excluded became hostile critics. Mrs Humphry Ward's intelligent and magnanimous awareness of her own limitations was unusual:

> I was never a Soul nor could have been. I came from too different a world. But there were a certain number of persons – of whom I was one – who were their 'harbourers' and spectators. I found delight in watching them. They were quite a new experience to me; and I saw them dramatically, like a scene in a play, full of fresh implications and suggestions.

Among the 'occasional souls' there were a number who belonged by right of family connections. Balfours and Lytteltons could of course exercise their birthright in this matter if they chose. In women, beauty was itself a qualification; but it was even more welcome when allied to wit and spirit, the qualities so conspicuously displayed by Miss 'D. D.' Balfour, for instance, or Mrs Edward Bourke or Miss Julia Peel. Lady Katie Thynne, Miss Betty Ponsonby (later Mrs Montgomery), an intimate girlhood friend of Lady Desborough, and Mollie Sneyd are in the same category. Mrs Ralph Sneyd was the daughter of Major-General Sir Arthur Ellis, Comptroller to the Lord Chamberlain's Department from the time of Edward VII's accession, a man of wit and taste with considerable knowledge of art. Lady Paget knew Arthur Ellis from his days as Equerry to the then Prince of Wales, a position he occupied for over twenty years, and she entertained the newly married Sneyds in Vienna in 1887:

> . . . a little couple who both look about sixteen; he rather good looking and belonging to the self-sufficient school of young England; she, a little flaxen-haired, brown-eyed, pink-and-white delicate thing, full of giggles at the nonsense every man feels himself obliged to talk to her, but sharper than they think.

One of Alma-Tadema's few portraits was of Mollie Sneyd, exhibited at the Royal Academy in 1890. A portrait of Balfour by the same artist was exhibited in the following year, and it is possible that Mrs Sneyd persuaded him to sit – because he disliked having his portrait painted.

Schomberg ('Pom') McDonnell was Principal Private Secretary to Lord Salisbury, so his presence among the friends of Curzon and Balfour needs no explanation. It was something of a triumph for McDonnell that his friendship with Curzon continued through the Viceroy's years in India, maintained by sympathetic and tactful letters, for during this period, when Curzon's nerves were stretched to breaking-point, he broke with many of his friends. McDonnell was killed in the trenches in Flanders in 1915, at the age of fifty-five.

Both Major-General Lawrence Drummond, Military Secretary to Lord Minto, the Governor-General of Canada, and Lord Lamington, Governor of Queensland and later of Bombay, were Eton friends of Curzon's; Lord Lamington was best man at his wedding. Their wit was of the light-hearted type that characterized suitable candidates for Soulhood; education at Eton was not, in itself, enough, nor was it essential; but it was never a disadvantage.

On the other hand, the presence at these parties of the worldly and cynical Harry Chaplin is surprising. It is difficult to know what he made of this rarified company, so unlike his own circle of racing and gambling friends in the Prince of Wales's set. The appearance of the name of Ferdinand Rothschild always raises an unworthy suspicion that he was being repaid for financing something for somebody. Even had this been so, he was in fact much liked in the Souls' set; they enjoyed entertaining him in return for many visits to the luxurious Rothschild houses, remembered by the more sybaritic Souls with regret when enduring the rigours of chillier and more austere hospitality. Princess Wagram was also a member of the Rothschild family. Her splendidly eccentric husband, a grandson of the Napoleonic Maréchal Berthier, once treated Wilfrid Blunt to an account of one of his more discreditable exploits. He revealed that he and two of his gamekeepers had shot and buried three poachers and informed no one of the summary execution. The story was well calculated to appeal to the lawless side of Blunt, but even he seems to have been shocked. Blunt was the victim of Berthe Wagram's insatiable desire to meddle in other people's romantic business; but in such matters he preferred to make his own arrangements. So too did Mary Leiter, whom the Princess propelled unwillingly – and unsuccessfully – towards a well-connected but dissolute French nobleman. She was later to marry George Curzon, having resisted many offers during the years of patient waiting.

Two families of famous sisters were, to a greater or lesser degree, Souls proper or peripheral. The Earl of Feversham had four daughters: the eldest, Lady Hermione Duncombe, married the Duke of Leinster. She was considered by many to be the greatest beauty in England and Lady Desborough considered her to be the most beautiful woman she had ever seen. The Duchess barely enters the Souls story, save as a legend of loveliness; most of the time she lived in her huge Irish house, Carton, where she was isolated in an incompatible marriage. She died of consumption in 1895, aged thirty; her husband had died a year before. Her younger sister, Lady Helen Vincent, had helped to reconcile husband and wife in the last months of their marriage by tactful suggestions of compromise.

Lady Helen Vincent was a beauty of international repute. She was described in her obituary in *The Times* as 'being at home in most European capitals', and her photograph appears in *Les Modes* – the 1900 Parisian equivalent of today's *Vogue*. It is easy to see why she was particularly admired in France: she had the looks of a painting by Fragonard, huge blue eyes with a gaze both provocative and haughty, a *retroussé* nose, and a tiny perfectly formed Cupid's-bow mouth. Meeting her in 1910, the French art dealer, René Gimpel, wrote in his diary that she 'must be the prettiest woman in England'.

In 1890 she had married Sir Edgar Vincent, a baronet of long line, and, like Lord Curzon, the son of a clergyman. Before his marriage he had attended both Bachelors' Club dinners, and with foresight was thus described:

And Edgar in bower
In statecraft and power
The favourite first in the betting.

In his thirties he had made a fortune as Governor of the Ottoman Bank. He retired in 1897, and returned to England. One of his recreations was to write a handbook on modern Greek, in his leisure hours, which remains a standard work.

He and Lady Helen lived at Esher Place, and it was there that they entertained the Souls for many weekend parties. There were established Souls, and there were also initiates, who, Consuelo Marlborough noted, 'often disappeared'. It was through the Vincents that the Duchess of Marlborough entered the Souls' circle for a brief time, and it is apparent that she considered them a defined clique, in 'their intellectual tastes, their aesthetic manner, and their exclusive aura'.

In the Great War both Sir Edgar and Lady Helen distinguished themselves. He was appointed Chairman of the Central Control Board, in which he showed great ability. He also, at this time, became a Trustee of the National Gallery. Lady Helen trained as an anaesthetist, and worked for the Red Cross; she was proud of the fact that all thirteen hundred of her patients survived her ministrations.

The marriage was one of singular happiness. Sir Edgar was known as a man of great geniality and good humour. He was also known for his aphorisms. When Billy Grenfell was in Paris in 1912, studying French and French history, he found the Vincents spending Christmas at the Ritz; *'les amis passent, les hôtels restent'*, remarked Sir Edgar laconically.

In 1920 Lord and Lady D'Abernon (the peerage was an acknowledgement of his wartime work) were appointed, on the advice of Lord Curzon, to the Embassy in Berlin. Their mission, in times of obvious difficulty, was highly successful. Lady D'Abernon quickly learnt to speak German, and her organization of Embassy life was highly praised by Lady Curzon. Lord D'Abernon died in 1945. His wife lived until 1954, retaining her great loveliness to the end of her life. George Moore had once inscribed in her album:

Porquoi vous plaignez vous des ans, belle marquise:
Une rose d'automne est plus qu'une autre exquise.

In the photograph of the dinner of 1898 given for Lord Curzon, and seated at the same table as the future Viceroy, is the glamorous Lady Warwick, adorned with twin diamond bows worn as brooch and tiara. She was one of the second family of sisters and stepsisters, daughters of Blanche Fitzroy by her first marriage to Charles Maynard and her second to the Earl of Rosslyn, who appear in all books on Edwardian Society, and who were intermittent Souls. Lady Warwick was a luminary of the Marlborough House Set, but she appreciated the intellectualism of the Souls, and their love of books and art. She had a particular admiration for Lord Curzon, and writes of him with sympathy and perception in her memoirs.

Her younger sister, Lady Millicent St Clair Erskine, became the Duchess of Sutherland. She was engaged to the Marquess of Stafford (the heir to the title) at the age of fifteen, and was married on her seventeenth birthday. Very early in life this young girl had to assume huge social burdens: at the vast receptions at Stafford House she would sometimes have to stand for four

Lady Helen Vincent, a charcoal portrait by John Singer Sargent.
'The prettiest woman in England' declared René Gimpel
when he met her in 1910

This is the photograph that Millicent, Duchess of Sutherland presented for the Curzon album. In 1889 the Duchess (then Lady Stafford) was twenty-one, and had just published her first book, *How I Spent My Twentieth Year*

long hours ('like a pillar of salt'), holding a bouqet of lilies so that her hands would not be bruised by constant greetings. On Friday nights she would give smaller parties in her London palace, when she entertained the Souls, and members of the literary and artistic worlds. She attended both Bachelors' Club dinners, where she was hailed:

There was much envied Strath
With the lady who hath
Taught us all what may life be at twenty;
Of pleasure a taste,
Of duty no waste,
Of gentle philosophy plenty.

The young Duchess was brave and enterprising, and took life very seriously. She was not at all content to enjoy the pleasures of Society, which she adorned – 'beautiful as a Scottish ballad' said Margot Asquith. She was an aspiring social reformer: one of the Sutherland palaces, Trentham Park, was near the Five Towns of the Potteries, and the Duchess was much concerned by the conditions she found there. She campaigned against the use of lead in the manufacture of pottery, and she founded 'The Cripples Guild' to help the local disabled. Arnold Bennett unkindly satirized her under the pseudonym of the Countess of Chells, and Consuelo Marlborough teasingly nicknamed her 'The Democratic Duchess'.

She had literary aspirations, and wrote several highly readable novels in the genre of the day. One of her short stories is hard to forget; called 'The Visit', it recounts the tale of Mrs Leonid, who wishes to rent a London house for the season; she views what she thinks is the perfect house, when she is shown a dead girl of great beauty laid out in a bedroom. This macabre story is coolly told, and was much praised. In 1905 she wrote a play in blank verse, entitled *The Conqueror*, which was put on by Forbes-Robertson at the Scala, but only had a brief run.

After the death of the Duke in 1913 her life was fragmented. Her novels show her to be a romantic in search of ideal love, and she married again twice, and was twice divorced. She lived most of the rest of her life in France. One wonders if she ever knew the history which was jotted down by Henry James in his notebook in 1884 – that Lord Stafford, like many others, had fallen hopeless victim to the charms of Sibell Grosvenor – that just after his engagement to herself, Sibell was widowed, and he was faced with one of those dilemmas which James so liked to dissect. The short story in which Henry James describes this is named 'The Path of Duty', which was the path taken.

The Duchess's sister, Sibyl, who was four yers younger, was married to the Earl of Westmorland. She was at one time rumoured to have been courted by George Curzon, and he invited her to both Bachelors' Club dinner parties. Her loveliness was unforgettable, and, like Lady Helen Vincent, she had no qualms about enhancing her natural looks with cosmetics. Consuelo Marlborough remembers her as being the outstanding beauty at the Devonshire House Ball. 'She had perhaps the most perfect face. I can see her now in a Greek peplum impersonating Hebe. The grey feathers of a life-like stuffed eagle perched on her shoulder, set off the glorious sheen of her red-gold hair.' Such was her temperament that Lady Westmorland found life very sad, and she died at the age of thirty-nine.

The youngest of the Rosslyn sisters, Lady Angela Forbes, was a totally different character, living life with great gusto and loving horses, her independence and her admirers in that order. She makes a brief appearance in the Souls' world during the Great War because she was a friend of Lord Ribblesdale's and Lord Elcho's. When the canteen which she ran for the soldiers in France was closed down because of a breach of footnote regulations, questions were asked in the House of Lords, and Lord Elcho (having sought Lady Desborough's advice) spoke in her defence.

Although there is general agreement about the most important Souls, it is more difficult – perhaps impossible – to draw up a definitive list of all those people who were regarded as Souls; it is doubtful whether even the innermost members of the circle could have done so. Margot Asquith described them as: 'an unconscious and accidental grouping of brilliant, sincere and loyal friends'. Curzon always had the main say in the matter because the members of the 'Gang' themselves recognized the methodical chronicler in their friend; but even his view is open to question and modification. A list of the people for whom Soulhood was claimed by their friends or relatives would include many more names. None the less, with all these reservations, it does seem possible to pick out the most central and most influential of the Souls; this, then, is their anthology.

Lady Westmorland attended both Curzon's dinners, the first at the age of eighteen. The belle of the Devonshire House Ball in 1897, her impersonation of Hebe is based on a painting by Sir Joshua Reynolds

✣ DRAMATIS PERSONAE

Changes of name among the Souls were frequent through accession to titles or marriage. To avoid confusion, here follows a list of the principal Souls, their families and intermarriages and the houses where they met.

Asquith, Margot. *See* Tennant.

Balfour, Arthur James, 1848-1930. Created Earl of Balfour, 1922. Statesman, politician and philosopher. Entered Parliament as Conservative member for East Manchester, 1874. His successful political career culminated in his becoming Prime Minister, 1902-1906. Known as 'King Arthur' among his friends, he was the most important member of the Souls' circle; his charm and intellectual distinction gave the group an aura which transcended social considerations. Whittingehame, East Lothian and 4 Carlton Gardens, London.

Baring, The Hon. John, 1863-1929. Eldest son of the first Baron Revelstoke, he succeeded to the title, 1897. A banker in the family firm, Baring Brothers, he also succeeded his father as senior partner. Membland Hall, Devonshire.

Baring, The Hon. Maurice, 1874-1945. Fourth son of the first Baron Revelstoke, and younger brother of John Baring, he was in the Diplomatic Service, 1898-1904. He wrote several successful novels and a volume of autobiography, *Puppet Show of Memory*. His letters were noted for their wit.

Blunt, Wilfrid Scawen, 1840-1922. Traveller and politician. Founder of the Crabbet Club to which many of the Souls' men belonged. His diaries contain many references to members of the Souls' circle, for he was also related to the Wyndhams. His wife, Lady Anne, was the granddaughter of Lord Byron. Crabbet Park, Sussex.

Brodrick, The Hon. William St John Fremantle, 1856-1942. Succeeded his father as ninth Viscount Midleton, 1907. Created first Earl of Midleton, 1920. Member of Parliament for West Surrey, 1880-1907. Married Lady Hilda Charteris, third daughter of the tenth Earl of Wemyss and March, 1880; she died 1901. Married for the second time to Madelene, eldest daughter of the Hon. J. C. Stanley, 1903. Peper Harrow, Godalming, Surrey and 34 Portland Place, London.

Brownlow, Earl and Countess. Adelbert, third Earl Brownlow, 1844-1921, married Lady Adelaide Talbot, youngest daughter of the eighteenth Earl of Shrewsbury, 1868. She died a fortnight after her husband's cousin and heir, Harry Cust, 1917. Belton House, Lincolnshire and Ashridge Park, Surrey.

Charteris, The Hon. Evan, 1864-1940. Sixth son of the tenth Earl of Wemyss and March, and younger brother of Hugo Elcho and Lady Hilda Brodrick. A barrister at the Parliamentary Bar, he took silk 1919, and was knighted 1932. Married Lady Edward Grosvenor, daughter of the fifth Earl of Kenmare, 1930.

Charteris, Hilda. *See* Brodrick.

Charteris, Hugo. *See* Elcho.

Cowper, Earl and Countess. Francis Thomas de Grey Cowper, 1834-1906, succeeded his father as seventh Earl Cowper, 1856. Married Katrine Compton, daughter of the fourth Marquess of Northampton, 1870. Panshanger, Hertfordshire, Wrest Park, Bedfordshire and 4 St James's Square, London.

Curzon of Kedleston, Marquess, 1859-1925. Traveller, writer, politician, statesman and

181

Viceroy of India. Eldest son of Viscount Scarsdale of Kedleston in Derbyshire; educated at Eton and Balliol; became a Fellow of All Souls, 1883; Member of Parliament for Southport, 1886; the high points of his career were the viceroyalty, 1898-1905; membership of the wartime Coalition Cabinet from 1916; Foreign Secretary, 1918-1924; Lord Privy Seal, 1924. One of the foremost Souls, in his bachelor days he repaid their hospitality by giving the famous dinners at the Bachelors' Club. Married Mary Leiter of Chicago, 1895, and had three daughters, one of whom was to marry Sir Oswald Mosley. After his first wife's death, 1906, he married Mrs Alfred Duggan, 1917. Hackwood Park, Basingstoke, 1 Carlton House Terrace, London and Kedleston House, Derbyshire.

Cust, Henry John Cockayne ('Harry'), 1861-1917. Great-grandson of the first Baron Brownlow, Harry Cust was heir to his cousin, Adelbert Cust, Lord Brownlow, but predeceased him. Entered Parliament as Unionist Member for the Stamford Division of Lincolnshire, 1890, but did not stand at the General Election of 1895. Returned to Parliament as Member for Bermondsey, 1900-1906. One of the most intellectually brilliant of the Souls, he showed his gifts as editor of the *Pall Mall Gazette*, a London evening paper owned by Waldorf Astor, 1892-1896. Delahaye Street, London.

Cust, Mrs Henry, 1867-1955. Born Emmeline Welby-Gregory, daughter of Sir Glyn Welby-Gregory of Denton, Lincolnshire, she was always known as 'Nina'. Married Harry Cust, 1893. A talented writer and sculptress.

D'Abernon. *See* Vincent.

Desborough, Lady, 1867-1952. Born Ethel Fane, daughter of Julian and Adine Fane, she was usually called 'Ettie'. Her mother, a sister of Lord Cowper, died when she was very young, and she was brought up by the Cowpers at Panshanger, the house she was to inherit in 1913 when Lady Cowper died. Married, 1887, William Grenfell, 1855-1945, the celebrated athlete, who was later created Baron Desborough, 1905. Lady Desborough was one of the great hostesses of her era, presiding at the Grenfell house, Taplow, and the Cowpers' London house, over the most memorable of the Souls' parties. Of the Desboroughs' three sons the two elder, Julian and Billy, were killed in the

Great War; Ivo died in 1926 and the title is now extinct. Her two daughters, Monica and Imogen, married Sir John Salmond and Viscount Gage. Taplow Court, Buckinghamshire, Panshanger, Hertfordshire and 4 St James's Square, London.

Elcho, Lord, 1857-1937. Hugo Charteris, fourth son of the tenth Earl of Wemyss and March, succeeded his father as eleventh Earl, 1914, his three elder brothers having all predeceased their father. Entered Parliament as Conservative Member for Haddingtonshire, 1883; lost this seat, 1885; but the following year was elected for Ipswich, which he held for nearly ten years. Married Mary Wyndham, 1883. Two of their three sons who survived infancy, Hugo ('Ego') Charteris (who became Lord Elcho when his father succeeded as Lord Wemyss) and Ivo, were killed in the Great War. 'Ego' had married Lady Violet ('Letty') Manners, daughter of the Duke and Duchess of Rutland, 1911. The surviving son, Guy, married Frances Tennant, a granddaughter of Sir Charles Tennant. Two of the three Elcho daughters also married into Souls' families: Cynthia to Herbert Asquith, 1910; and Irene ('Bibs') to Ivor Windsor Clive, later Lord Plymouth, 1921. Stanway House, Gloucestershire and 62 Cadogan Square, London; at his father's death Hugo inherited Gosford, East Lothian.

Elcho, Lady, 1861-1937. Born Mary Constance Wyndham, eldest daughter of The Hon. Percy and Mrs Wyndham, she married Hugo Charteris, Lord Elcho, 1883, and went to live at Stanway where she presided over its famous house-parties.

Grosvenor, Sibell. *See* Wyndham.

Horner, Sir John and Lady. John Fortescue Horner, 1842-1927, educated at Eton and Balliol, was called to the Bar in 1868. In 1874 he succeeded to the family estate of Mells Park. Married, 1883, Frances Graham, 1858-1940, daughter of William Graham, Liberal Member of Parliament for Glasgow, a wealthy India merchant, who is remembered as an indefatigable collector and patron of the arts. The Horners' son, Edward, was killed in the Great War, 1916. Their younger daughter, Katharine, married Raymond Asquith, son of Herbert Asquith and stepson of Margot. Mells Park, Somerset.

Liddell, A.G.C., 1846-1930. Adolphus Liddell, always known as 'Doll', was a grandson of Baron Ravensworth; many of his childhood summer holidays were spent at the family seat, Ravensworth, near Newcastle. Educated at Eton and Balliol, he was called to the Bar in 1871. His autobiography, *Notes from the Life of an Ordinary Mortal*, is a fascinating account of the Souls' world.

Lindsay, Violet. *See* Rutland.

Lumley, Sibell. *See* Wyndham.

Lyttleton, Alfred, 1857-1913. Younger son of the fourth Baron Lyttelton. Married Laura Tennant, 1885; she died 1886. Married secondly Edith Sophy Balfour (known as 'D.D.'), daughter of Archibald Balfour (no relation of Arthur Balfour).

Lyttelton, Spencer, 1847-1913. Elder brother of Alfred, a friend from youth of Arthur Balfour.

Pembroke, Earl and Countess of. George Robert Charles, thirteenth Earl, 1850-1895, married, 1874, Lady Gertrude Frances Talbot, daughter of the Earl of Shrewsbury; she died 1906. Lord Pembroke's 'Wagger' or 'Wilton Bagger' Club was the model for Wilfrid Blunt's Crabbet Club. Wilton House, Salisbury, Wiltshire.

Plymouth, Earl of. *See* Windsor.

Revelstoke, Baron. *See* Baring.

Ribblesdale, Baron, 1854-1926. Thomas Lister lived in France for much of his childhood from 1858, was educated at Harrow and went into the Rifle Brigade, 1874. Succeeded his father as fourth Baron, 1876. Married, 1877, Charlotte Monkton ('Charty') Tennant; she died 1911. Married secondly, 1919, Ava Willings, widow of Jacob Astor. His two sons were both killed, Thomas in Somaliland, 1904, and Charles in the Great War, 1916. He had three daughters, all his children being of his first marriage: Barbara; Laura, who married Lord Lovat and provided a home for Maurice Baring in the last years of his life; and Diana, who married Percy, only son of George Wyndham and Sibell Grosvenor and later Lord Westmorland. Gisburne Park, Yorkshire and 57 Green Street, London.

Rutland, Duchess of, 1856-1937. Born Violet Lindsay, daughter of The Hon. Charles Lindsay. Renowned equally for her artistic gifts and her great beauty, she was already an exhibitor at the Grosvenor Gallery before her marriage, 1882, to Henry Manners, 1852-1925, who became Marquess of Granby, 1888, and Duke of Rutland, 1906. Henry Manners was principal private secretary to the Prime Minister, Lord Salisbury, 1885. Their first son, Lord Haddon, born the same year, died aged nine, 1895, and the younger brother John became heir: he married Kathleen, a granddaughter of Sir Charles Tennant. The Rutlands had three daughters: Marjorie, who married the Marquess of Anglesey; Violet ('Letty') who married the Elchos' eldest son Hugo ('Ego') and Diana, a beauty as celebrated as her mother, who married Duff Cooper. Belvoir Castle, Leicestershire and 16 Arlington Street, London.

Sutherland, Duchess of, 1867-1955. Lady Millicent St Clair Erskine, eldest daughter of the Earl of Rosslyn, married the Duke of Sutherland, 1852-1913, on her seventeenth birthday. She was an ardent social reformer, nicknamed 'the Democratic Duchess', and aspired to being a novelist. Beautiful and charming, she was an ornament more than a participating member of the Souls. Her sister was Countess of Westmorland. Dunrobin Castle, Sutherland and Stafford House, London.

Tennant, Sir Charles, Bt, 1823-1906. A rich and successful industrialist, he became Liberal Member of Parliament for the Partick division of Glasgow, 1879, and was made a baronet, 1885. Married twice, for the second time at the age of seventy-five, he had sixteen children. The Glen (or simply 'Glen'), Peebleshire and 35 Grosvenor Square, London.

Tennant, 'Charty' (Charlotte Monkton), 1858-1911. Third daughter of Sir Charles Tennant. Married Lord Ribblesdale, 1877.

Tennant, Laura (Octavia Laura Mary), 1862-1886. Fifth daughter and appropriately named eighth surviving child of Sir Charles Tennant. Married Alfred Lyttelton, 1885, but died the following year after the birth of a son.

Tennant, Lucy (Katherine Lucy), 1860-1942. Fourth daughter of Sir Charles Tennant. Married Thomas Graham Smith, 1879, and went to live at Easton Grey in Wiltshire, the scene of much Souls' entertaining.

Tennant, 'Margot' (Emma Alice Margaret), 1864-1945. Sixth daughter of Sir Charles Tennant. The most vital and enthusiastic Soul in the early years of the group. Married, 1894, Herbert Asquith (1852-1928), who was to be

Prime Minister, 1908-1916. Thus she became stepmother of Raymond, who married Katharine Horner; Herbert, who married Lady Cynthia Charteris; and Violet, who married Maurice Bonham-Carter.

Vincent, Sir Edgar and Lady Helen. Sir Edgar Vincent, 1857-1894, was made a Baron, 1914, taking the title of Baron D'Abernon, and a Viscount, 1926. He married, 1890, Lady Helen Duncombe, second daughter of the Earl of Feversham and generally considered the prettiest woman in England. The Vincents were leading hosts to the Souls. Lord D'Abernon was appointed Ambassador to Berlin, 1920. Esher Place, Surrey and Stoke D'Abernon, Surrey.

Webb, Godfrey, 1832-1901. He was always known as 'Webber'. A noted wit, called by Margot Asquith 'the doyen of the Souls', he was a Clerk in the House of Lords.

Wemyss and March, Earl of. *See* Elcho.

Wenlock, Lord and Lady. The Hon. Beilby Lawley, third Baron Wenlock married Lady Constance Lascelles (d. 1932), eldest daughter of the fourth Earl of Harewood, 1872. He became Governor of Madras; she painted numerous scenes of India. Escrick, Yorkshire.

Westmorland, Countess of, 1871-1910. Lady Sybil St Clair Erskine was daughter of Lord Rosslyn and younger sister of the Duchess of Sutherland. Her striking beauty was much admired by George Curzon, who invited her to both Bachelors' Club dinners. Married the Earl of Westmorland, 1892.

White, Mr and Mrs Henry. Harry White, 1850-1927, American diplomat, married, 1879, Margaret ('Daisy') Stuyvesant Rutherford, daughter of Lewis Rutherford, Professor of Astronomy, Columbia University. They started married life in Paris. Harry White was appointed First Secretary at the American Legation in London, 1884. They returned to Paris 1907; Mrs White died 1916.

Windsor, Lord and Lady. Robert George Windsor Clive, 1857-1923, succeeded his grandmother as fourteenth Baron Windsor, 1869. Married, 1883, Alberta ('Gay') Paget, daughter of Sir Augustus Paget, British Ambassador in Rome where Windsor had first met her, 1880. The earldom of Plymouth was revived by Edward VII, 1905. Their eldest son, Other, died in India 1908; the second son, Ivor, married Irene ('Bibs') Charteris, daughter of Lord and Lady Elcho, 1921. Hewell Grange, Worcestershire, St Fagan's, near Cardiff and 36 Mount Street, London.

Wyndham, The Rt Hon. George, 1863-1913. Educated at Eton and Sandhurst, he went into the Coldstream Guards 1883. Elected to Parliament 1889, he became Chief Secretary to Ireland 1900. Married, 1887, Sibell, Lady Grosvenor, 1855-1929, widow of Lord Grosvenor, born Sibell Lumley, youngest daughter of the Earl of Scarbrough. Their son Percy, born 1888, married Diana Lister, daughter of Lord Ribblesdale, 1912, but was killed in the Great War, 1914. Saighton Grange, Cheshire.

Wyndham, The Hon. Percy Scawen Wyndham, 1835-1911, second son of the first Lord Leconfield, married, 1860, Madeline Campbell, 1835-1920, daughter of Sir Guy and Lady Campbell. They had three daughters: Mary, later Lady Elcho; Madeline, who married Charles Adeane of Babraham, Cambridgeshire, 1888, and died in 1941; and Pamela, 1871-1928, who married Edward Tennant, first Baron Glenconner, 1859-1920, and secondly the first Viscount Grey of Fallodon. Clouds, Wiltshire and 44 Belgrave Square, London.

THE SOULS' CIRCLE

= married
♥ proposed
✝ killed in the Great War

❧ BIBLIOGRAPHY

Antrim, Louisa, Countess of, *Recollections*, privately printed, 1937

Arts Council, *Burne-Jones* (exhibition catalogue), 1975

Askwith, Betty, *The Lytteltons*, Chatto and Windus, 1975

Asquith, Lady Cynthia, *Haply I May Remember*, James Barrie, 1950
Remember and be Glad, James Barrie, 1952
Diaries, Hutchinson, 1968

Asquith, Herbert, *Moments of Memory*, Hutchinson, 1938

Asquith, Margot, *Autobiography*, vols I and II, Thornton Butterworth, 1920 and 1922

Bailey, John (ed.), *Diary of Lady Frederick Cavendish*, 2 vols, John Murray, 1927

Balfour, A. J., *Chapters of Autobiography*, Cassell, 1930

Balfour, Lady Frances, *Ne Obliviscaris*, 2 vols, Hodder and Stoughton, 1930

Balsan, Consuelo Vanderbilt, *The Glitter and the Gold*, Heinemann, 1953

Baring, Maurice, *Puppet Show of Memory*, Heinemann, 1922
Dear Animated Bust, Michael Russell, 1981

Battersea, Constance, *Reminiscences*, Macmillan, 1922

Beerbohm, Max, *Seven Men*, Heinemann, 1919

Benckendorff, Count Constantine, *Half a Life, Reminiscences of a Russian Gentleman*, Richards Press, 1954

Benson, A. C., *Memories and Friends*, John Murray, 1924

Benson, E. F., *Dodo*, Methuen, 1893
As We Were, Longman's Green, 1932

Blunt, W. Scawen, *My Diaries*, 2 vols, Martin Secker, 1919 and 1920

Bonham Carter, Lady Violet, 'The Souls', *The Listener*, October 1947

Burne-Jones, Georgiana, *Memorials of Edward Burne-Jones*, Macmillan, 1904

Buchan, Susan (Lady Tweedsmuir), *An Edwardian Lady*, Duckworth, 1966

Chandos, Viscount, *From Peace to War*, Bodley Head, 1967

Channon, Sir Henry (Chips), *Diaries*, Weidenfeld and Nicolson, 1967

Charteris, Evan, *John Sargent*, Heinemann, 1927
Life and Letters of Edmund Gosse, Heinemann, 1931

Christie's, *The William Graham Collection* (sale catalogue) Ap 1, 1886
The Cowper Collection, Panshanger (sale catalogue), 1953

Churchill, W. S. C., *Great Contemporaries*, Thornton Butterworth, 1937

Comyns Carr, Mrs J., *Reminiscences*, Hutchinson, 1925

Cooper, Lady Diana, *The Rainbow Comes and Goes*, Rupert Hart-Davis, 1958

Cowper, Lady, *Memoir of Lord Cowper*, (*Earl Cowper KG*), privately printed, 1913

Crathorne, Nancy, *Tennants' Stalk*, Macmillan, 1973

Curzon of Kedleston, Marchioness, *Reminiscences*, Hutchinson, 1955

Cust, Sir Lionel, *King Edward VII and his Court*, John Murray, 1930

Cust, Nina, *Gentlemen Errant*, John Murray, 1909
The Wanderers, Jonathan Cape, 1928
A Tub of Goldfishes, James Bain, 1950

Cust, Sybil, *Letters*, The Women's Printing Society, 1930s(?)

D'Abernon, Viscount, *Portraits and Appreciations*, Hodder and Stoughton, 1931

Desborough, Lady, *Pages from a Family Journal*, privately printed, 1916

Dugdale, Blanche, *Balfour*, 2 vols, Hutchinson, 1936
  Family Homespun, John Murray, 1940
Dugdale, James, 'Sir Charles Tennant, the Story of a Victorian Collector', *Connoisseur*, September 1971
Edel, Leon (ed.), *Henry James, The Conquest of London, 1870-1883*, Rupert Hart-Davis, 1962
  The Letters of Henry James, vol. III, Rupert Hart-Davis, 1980
Egremont, Max, *The Cousins*, Collins, 1977
  Balfour, A Life of Arthur James Balfour, Collins, 1980
Ellenberger, Nancy (Carpenter), 'The Souls and London Society', *Victorian Studies*, Indianapolis, Winter 1982
Esher, Lord, *Cloud Capp'd Towers*, John Murray, 1927
Estorick, Michael, *Heirs and Graces*, Weidenfeld and Nicolson, 1981
Fitzgerald, Penelope, *Edward Burne-Jones*, Michael Joseph, 1975
Fitzroy, Sir Almeric, *Memoirs*, 2 vols, Hutchinson, 1925
Forbes, Lady Angela (St Clair Erskine), *Memories and Base Details*, Hutchinson, 1922
Franklin, Jill, *The Gentleman's Country House and its Plan, 1835-1914*, Routledge and Kegan Paul, 1981
Gatty, Charles, *George Wyndham: Recognita*, John Murray, 1917
Girouard, Mark, *The Victorian Country House*, 2nd ed., Yale University Press, 1979
  The Return to Camelot, Chivalry and the English Gentleman, Yale University Press, 1981
Glenconner, P., *The White Wallet*, T. Fisher Unwin, 1912
  Edward Wyndham Tennant, John Lane, 1919
Glyn, Elinor, *A Romantic Adventure*, Ivor Nicholson and Watson, 1936
Hallé, Charles, *Notes from a Painter's Life*, John Murray, 1909
Hartcup, Adeline, *Below Stairs in the Great Country Houses*, Sidgwick and Jackson, 1980
Hart-Davis, Sir Rupert, *The Caricatures of Max Beerbohm, a Catalogue*, Macmillan, 1972
  Lyttelton-Hart-Davis Letters, 5 vols, John Murray, 1978, 1979, 1981, 1982 and 1983
Horner, Frances, *Time Remembered*, Heinemann, 1933

Hutchinson, Horace, *Portraits of the Eighties*, T. Fisher Unwin, 1920
  Algernon West, John Murray, 1922
James, John, *The Memoirs of a House Steward*, Bury, Holt & Co., 1949
Jolliffe, John, *Raymond Asquith, Life and Letters*, Collins, 1980
Jones, L. E., *An Edwardian Youth*, Macmillan, 1955
Lethaby, W. R., *Philip Webb and his Work*, Oxford University Press, 1935
Leveson Gower, Sir George, *Years of Content*, John Murray, 1940
  Years of Endeavour, John Murray, 1942
  Mixed Grill, Frederick Muller, 1947
Liddell, A. G. C., *Notes from the Life of an Ordinary Mortal*, John Murray, 1911
Leicester Warren, Margaret, *Diaries and Letters*, 2 vols, privately printed
Leslie, Anita, *Jennie, the Life of Lady Randolph Churchill*, Hutchinson, 1969
  Edwardians in Love, Hutchinson, 1972
Longford, Elizabeth, *Pilgrimage of Passion, the Life of Wilfrid Scawen Blunt*, Weidenfeld and Nicolson, 1979
Lovat, Laura, *Maurice Baring, a Postscript*, Hollis & Carter, 1947
Lubbock, Lady Sybil, *The Child in the Crystal*, Jonathan Cape, 1939
Lutyens, Lady Emily, *A Blessed Girl*, Rupert Hart-Davis, 1953
Lyttelton, Edith, *Alfred Lyttelton*, Longmans, 1917
Lytton, Earl of, *Wilfrid Scawen Blunt*, Macdonald, 1961
Mackail, J., *The Life of William Morris*, Longman, 1899
Mackail, J., and Wyndham, G. (eds), *The Life and Letters of George Wyndham*, 2 vols, Hutchinson, 1925
Mallet, Victor (ed.), *Life with Queen Victoria, Marie Mallet's Letters from Court 1887-1901*, John Murray, 1968
Marsh, Edward, *A Number of People*, Heinemann, 1939
Masterman, Lucy (ed.), *Mary Gladstone: Her Diaries and Letters*, Methuen, 1930
Midleton, Earl of, *Records and Reactions 1856-1939*, John Murray, 1939
Milner, Viscountess, *My Picture Gallery*, John Murray, 1951

Mosley, Nicholas, *Julian Grenfell*, Weidenfeld and Nicolson, 1976

Nevill, Lady Dorothy, *Reminiscences*, Edward Arnold, 1906

Nicolson, Harold, *Curzon: The Last Phase 1919-1925*, Constable, 1934

Nicolson, Nigel, *Mary Curzon*, Weidenfeld and Nicolson, 1977

Olivier, Edith, *Four Victorian Ladies of Wiltshire*, Faber and Faber, 1935

Ormond, Leonée, *George du Maurier*, Routledge and Kegan Paul, 1969

Oxford and Asquith, Earl of, *Memories and Reflections 1852-1927*, 2 vols, Cassell, 1928

Paget, Walburga, Lady, *Embassies of Other Days*, Hutchinson, 1923

In My Tower, Hutchinson, 1924

Linings of Life, Hurst and Blackett, 1928

Portland, Duke of, *Men, Women and Things*, Faber and Faber, 1937

Ribblesdale, Lord, *The Queen's Hounds*, Longman's & Co., 1897

Charles Lister, T. Fisher Unwin, 1917

Impressions and Memories, Cassell, 1927

Riddell, Lord, 'Arthur Balfour', *Country Life*, March 1930

Robertson Scott, J. W., *The Life and Death of a Newspaper*, Methuen, 1953

Rose, Kenneth, *Superior Person, A Portrait of Curzon and His Circle*, Weidenfeld and Nicolson, 1969

Salmond, Monica, *Bright Armour*, Faber and Faber, 1935

Smalley, G. W., *Anglo-American Memories*, Duckworth, 1911/12

Sitwell, Constance, *Bright Morning*, Jonathan Cape, 1942

Storrs, Ronald, *Orientations*, Ivor Nicholson and Watson, 1937

Stuart, Denis, *Dear Duchess: Millicent Duchess of Sutherland*, Gollancz, 1982

Sutherland Gower, Ronald, *Reminiscences*, John Murray, 1903

Ward, Mrs Humphrey, *A Writer's Recollections*, Collins, 1918

Warwick, Lady, *Life's Ebb and Flow*, Hutchinson, 1929

Wemyss, Countess of, *A Family Record*, privately printed, 1932

Wharton, Edith, *A Backward Glance*, Appleton Century, 1934

Young, Kenneth, *Balfour*, Bell, 1963

Webb, Beatrice, (Norman and Jeanne Mackenzie, eds), *The Diary of Beatrice Webb*, vol. I, 1873-1892, Virago Press, 1982

Wells, H. G., *The New Machiavelli*, Bodley Head, 1911

Experiment in Autobiography, 2 vols, Gollancz, 1934

Ziegler, Philip, *Lady Diana Cooper*, Hamish Hamilton, 1981

✿ INDEX